I Can Be Any- thing

THIRD
EDITION

A Career Book for Women

Joyce Slayton Mitchell

NEW YORK
COLLEGE ENTRANCE EXAMINATION BOARD

Copies of this book may be ordered from:
  College Board Publication Orders
  Box 886
  New York, NY 10101
The price is $9.95.

Editorial inquiries concerning this book should be directed to:
  Editorial Office
  The College Board
  888 Seventh Avenue
  New York, NY 10106

Photos on pages 35, 55, 62, 195, 260, 263
Copyright © by Betty Medsger

Library of Congress Catalog Number: 82–72390

Printed in the United States of America

9 8 7 6 5 4 3 2 1

I CAN BE ANYTHING

Other Books by Joyce Slayton Mitchell

CONTENTS

BUSINESS: COMPUTER OPERATIONS

BUSINESS: MONEY MANAGEMENT

BUSINESS: SALES

COMMUNICATIONS

EDUCATION

GOVERNMENT

HEALTH

SCIENCE AND TECHNOLOGY

SOURCES AND ACKNOWLEDGMENTS

The primary sources of information for **I Can Be Anything** are working women in every part of the country and the 1982–83 edition of the *Occupational Outlook Handbook,* published by the United States Department of Labor. In addition to hundreds of personal and written interviews with working women, other examples of models were cited, with credit, from *Savvy, The Wall Street Journal,* and *Working Woman.*

It is a pleasure to thank the many contributors to this book: working women who told what work is like in their careers; Sandra MacGowan, Editor, The College Board, who worked so conscientiously on the manuscript; Sue Wetzel Gardner, Director of Publishing, and Jean Yoder, Managing Editor, The College Board, for getting this third edition in progress; and Linda Magoon, typist and neighbor.

Wolcott, Vermont
August 1982

WARNING!

Job Opportunities Keep Changing!
A Good Paying Job is Hard to Get!
Minorities Are Still in the Back of the Bus!
Career Readings May Be Racist and Sexist!
Unearned Income Counts, Too!

JOB OPPORTUNITIES KEEP CHANGING

Not even the United States Department of Labor can make foolproof predictions about what the future demand will be for jobs in any field. Predictions that the Department of Labor makes have to be based on particular economic and social assumptions, and these assumptions are always changing. For the past several years, the job future for college graduates has been poor and unemployment rates have been high. Besides unemployment, underemployment is at an all-time high in the 1980s. College graduates are underemployed when they wait on table, tend bar, pack groceries, or hold word-processing jobs that do not require a degree but provide ways to earn money until they find jobs related to their degrees and qualifications. When you realize that thousands of teachers and psychologists are still being prepared in spite of the scarcity of job openings, you will want to think about how you will find work if you are considering a teaching or counseling career.

As you read the career sections in this book, remember that predictions about the job futures in particular careers are based on the fact that the U.S. economy in the 1980s, so far, has been in a recession.

For the present, the good news about your job future is that some fields, such as accounting, nursing, engineering, and computer science, *are* continuing to grow, and that the chances for your future employment in these fields are excellent.

A GOOD PAYING JOB IS HARD TO GET

That is, for women. With all the talk about women's rights and women's liberation, many people think that women are better off financially than they used to be. The truth is that they are worse off. The earning gap between men and women is *widening.* In 1982, women earned 59 cents on the white male dollar. Quite a difference. Just one fact will tell you where women stand in earning ability: *Women with college degrees earn, on the average, less pay than men who finish the eighth grade.* That's right! The average income for female college graduates is $12,347. Their brothers who never entered one semester of high school have an average income of $12,965. And one more fact. In 1982, average full-time salaries for male college graduates started at $12,500 compared to $9,700 for female college graduates. This lower average salary is for white women. Minority women earn less. *Equal work* is the issue here, not equal pay for equal work. When more women go after and get jobs as airline pilots, engineers, architects, stockbrokers, or senior corporate executives, the earning gap will begin to close.

▶ MINORITIES ARE STILL IN THE BACK OF THE BUS

Racism and sexism, both in education and in employment, are against the law. But in a society where white males are considered "normal" and everyone else must adapt as best they can, racism and sexism are practiced both at school and at work. Getting a job, getting equal pay for equal work, getting promoted, and getting laid off are easy ways to measure how discrimination works. In all cases, minority women are at the lowest end of the scale, with unemployment figures being the highest for minority teenage girls.

In 1982, the Alabama State Department of Education paid two-thirds of the white women and three-fourths of the black women $10,400 or less per year. As salaries increased, the proportion of black women decreased.

Laws governing employment and education are now on the side of minorities and women. But, in order to test the law or to push for compliance of the law, women and minorities must aspire to and go after careers traditionally followed by white men, such as actuary, engineer, systems analyst, agricultural economist, and geologist. If that's where your interests lie, be prepared to stand alone, and also be prepared to bring your friends with you into these well-paid fields, where everyone has a right to be.

The network newsletter for Black Women's Educational

Policy and Research was developed to create a network of women interested in black women's equity issues and to encourage research on the education of black women. If you are interested in receiving this free network newsletter, write to: BWEPRN, Wellesley College Center for Research on Women, Wellesley, MA 02181.

▶ CAREER READINGS MAY BE RACIST AND SEXIST

As you read and look at career information, be aware that, like most books and materials, they are stereotyped by sex and race. That is, the pictures are mostly of white boys and men, the pronouns used are "he" and "him," and unless the career is nurse, secretary, or teacher, the content of the article or book is written as if it will be read only by white males. Therefore, get the information you need, but if you are interested in becoming a dentist, a senator, an FBI special agent, an astronaut, or an accountant, don't expect these readings to encourage you, a woman, to pursue such careers.

▶ UNEARNED INCOME COUNTS, TOO

During the 1970s, some women have achieved equal pay for equal work, but few women have realized the potential of putting their earned money to work for them through investments.

The goal of *I Can Be Anything* is to help women aspire to and achieve economic independence. An important part of achieving economic independence is to understand what is meant by *invested income,* sometimes called *unearned income.* Unearned income means the interest you earn on your money.

Ask yourself these questions: Is your money working as hard for you as you are? Is your money invested at the best interest rate available? Or do you keep some money in a noninterest checking account and other money in a 5.5% savings account, as inflation eats it up with a double-digit bite? Is your money invested in ways that shelter income from taxes so that you are keeping the largest amount of dollars that you earn? You don't have to earn a huge salary before you learn to manage your money well. It's just as important to make your money work for you at $10,000 a year as it is at $50,000 a year.

Have you invested in an Individual Retirement Account (IRA)? Only since January 1, 1982, has *everyone* who earns $2,000 become eligible to contribute $2,000 tax-free each year to an IRA account. Saving $2,000 tax-free each year while it gathers tax-free interest is about the best investment deal most people ever get. Here is how it can work for you. If you start at 25 years old, you will retire at 65 with over *one and a half million dollars* ($1,718,284.21), based on a 12% annual assumed rate of return. If you are 35 years old and start your $2,000-a-year IRA plan now, at 65 you will have one-half million dollars ($540,585.21). And even if you are in the group of us who will start our IRA at 50 years old, you can retire in fifteen years with $83,309.56.

There are all kinds of ways to invest your money. One more way is a new salary-reduction plan that permits saving up to 10% of your pretax income a year to accumulate tax-free earnings until age 59½. But, whatever your age, unearned income is worth thinking about as you plan your career and finances. Don't let investment language frighten you away. There are many good books about investment and money management, several of them especially for women. Two good ones to get you started are *The Joy of Money*, by Paula Nelson (Bantam, 1980), and *The Women's Money Book*, by Gene Mackevich (Bantam, 1981). When you get some sense of the possibilities, talk with an accountant. Be a woman who knows that good money management is crucial to economic independence.

I CAN BE ANYTHING!

When children are asked, "What are you going to be when you grow up?" little girls answer, "married"; little boys answer, "a cowboy," "a fireman," "an astronaut," or "a something." All through school, boys are expected to work toward the "something" they are going to be; girls are expected to *say* they are going to be "something," but everybody knows that if all goes well — according to fairy tales, television, parents and friends, and educators — they will be married and "live happily ever after." Pictures of marriage dance through their heads, but seldom is a career credited for the "happily ever after" part — and it should be.

No one talks about it — you don't either — but, if somewhere in your mind is the idea that someone else will be financially responsible for you, then you probably think you don't have to make a serious career decision. The whole world assumes that young men will support themselves plus their families. Because of this, men can live where they want, have their domestic work done for them, and can decide how much time, energy, and space they need to move and grow with a career. The world assumes that young women will be taken care of, and because they will be, their time, energy, and space will be decided about by someone else.

When you think about it, do you wonder why it is that you don't feel as committed to choosing a career or making money as are boys and men you know? Probably it has something to do with your idea of your future. Girls have been systematically taught that *if* they succeed in their career they can support themselves, but they won't need to support others and they will never succeed in love. Boys are taught just the opposite, that if they succeed in their career they will be rewarded with money *and* love.

It's not marriage and being supported that makes women choose their careers differently — both women and men plan to get married — it's the *kind* of marriage where men have control that limits women. A marriage where the husband makes the money and the decisions doesn't give a wife much freedom to choose the kind of work she wants to do.

No one should have to choose between love and making money! But you *can* choose between one kind of marriage that permits meaningful work to both husband and wife and another kind that doesn't. The kind of marriage where both people have some control over having children, where they live, where they move, and how much money the family needs is called an equal partnership marriage. It is the kind of marriage that assumes that what is best for each person is best for the family. A marriage like this, where each person has some control over and participates in making family decisions, is the only way a woman can be free to make educational and career choices.

What will your life be like five years from now? Ten years from now? Fifteen years from now? Will you be married? Will you have children? Will you be working? If you are like most women, you will be doing all of these things at some time in your life. Years ago, most mothers of school-age children were not employed outside their homes. Today things are different. Everyone, especially young women, should know that in the United States, more than one in every three mothers with *preschool* children (41 percent) is employed full-time outside her home. That's with children under six years old! The rate is even higher for mothers with school-age children under eighteen, where more than one in every two mothers (58 percent) is employed.

Women are working because, like men, they need money to support themselves and their children. Helping you aspire to and plan for a career that earns you money is a goal of this book. How does a young woman go about choosing a career? After all, you probably don't know the answers yet to where you want to live, what the work opportunities will be, what your income will be, whether or not you will marry, what your husband will be doing, whether or not you want to have children, or how many you will want to have.

Something good happens to you right now if you realize that you aren't choosing the one and only right career for you — *or* the wrong career. Something good happens to you when you can use everything you experience to build what you eventually become. In other words, if you are a student right now, your school work is your career. Your part-time work and summer work, whether volunteer or paid, are your career. A career starts in early childhood education and extends through retirement. There isn't any work you do that does not count as part of your career. Caring for babies and children, managing a home, fund raising, working as an engineer, or working part-time in sales are all part of your career development. It's all work, even though some is paid and some unpaid, some part-time and some full-time or overtime.

Work requires skills, to be learned and managed. A skill is a developed aptitude or ability that relates to a specific job or occupation. Many skills are transferable from one job to the next within your lifetime career. Some transferable skills that you may learn at work are speaking, listening, letter writing, leadership, decision making, persuasion, and time-management. By this definition, transferable career skills can be learned anywhere and they are learned *everywhere* – including in the family. Family work counts toward your career development as definitely as work in the military counts, or work in apprenticeship, or in college, or the first five years in a paid job.

With the attitude that everything counts – even motherhood – and that choosing your career is a long process, it may be easier for you to see how your school or family work or present job and interests fit into this process. The subjects you study, sports you play, music you listen to, summer jobs you work, children you raise, friends you have, and test scores you get all add up to your career development. All of the decisions you make now *are* career decisions.

 ## COLLEGE: A CAREER DECISION

At any age, deciding to go to college ~~or back to college~~ is a career decision. For teenagers, choosing a college can be your first move away from home, and this move makes it different from career decisions you have made before this time. But, whether you live away from home or at home, choosing a college changes your life more than selecting Spanish IV or mathematics IV in high school.

Which College Should You Choose?

Does it make a difference where you go to college? Is it true that graduates of some colleges get all the good bank and corporation training opportunities while others never have a chance? Does a photographer or an actress have to go to college? Each career description in *I Can Be Anything* cites the necessary education needed for that career. You will read that business executives often come from a liberal arts background, pilots from military training, commercial artists from two-year professional art schools, psychologists from Ph.D. programs.

Deciding where to go to college is difficult because, like the job market, the college situation is changing too. Costs are soaring. Community colleges have mushroomed everywhere, and students continue to transfer, dropout, stopout, take college courses by examination or in the corporate world, and further their education in lifelong learning programs that educators and your parents never dreamed possible just a few years ago.

There are lots of ways to select a college. One way is to choose the college closest to your home, where you may know the most number of students. Another way is to choose a college that is recruiting the hardest for students. Many students select a college by a particular program offered, or because they have decided upon a particular career. Still another way to select a college is to make a systematic survey of all the universities and colleges available to you and to choose a few that have the most meaning for you. *When you get as much information about a college as the college gets about you, then you will have the basis for a good decision.*

Important factors to consider are a college's admission requirements, where the college is located, and how much it costs. It is also essential to understand in some detail what a college is like, and if it is a setting in which you are likely to achieve success. You must ask more than, "Can I get in?" You should also ask, "What will it be like *after* I get in?" Only then can you begin to ask yourself these questions:

▶ "What are the implications for me of one type of college life over another type?"

▶ "Will I be different if I go to a collegiate college, or an experimental college, or a technical college?"

▶ "What effect will one campus atmosphere have on my selection of friends, or possibly of spouse, and on my political, religious, and career values?"

A student choosing a college has much the same job as a college admission officer in selecting a student. From your record, the officer can look at your height, weight, age, college admission scores, and high school grades. However, until the admission officer meets you personally and reviews personality reports from your high school, he or she doesn't have a precise idea of who you really are. Likewise, from information about the college, you can look at cost, location, programs offered, and requirements for admission to the college. But, until you see the college, or at least talk to students who have gone there, you will not have a total picture of the kind of education you are likely to get at that college.

Should You Choose According to Majors Offered?

What about selecting a college by a curriculum it offers? If you select a college for a particular field, look at offerings in several related programs rather than at a specific program. For example, if you are interested in chemistry now, you may end up in one of the physical sciences but not necessarily in chemistry. If you are like most students, you aren't quite sure yet what you want to be, or which major is best for you. Many courses that colleges offer will be completely new to you.

Students change. They change majors and they change colleges. Over 75 percent of all first-year college students leave the college they choose. That means that three out of four first-year students change the decision they made about their college choice. And the more specialized the school (engineering, business, architecture), the higher the rate of transfers and dropouts. In fact, 50 percent of all graduating *seniors* don't even go into work that is related to their major! With statistics such as these, you can easily see that selecting a college for its program may not be as good a reason to decide as it appears. If you are planning a four-year college program, the most helpful direction you can take right now is one of general exploration — not specialization — for the first year. After all, there are many majors and courses in college you haven't tried and maybe haven't even heard about, so it is difficult for you to know which ones you should choose before you go there.

For more information about college majors, read *What's Where: The Official Guide to College Majors* (J. S. Mitchell, New York: Avon, 1979) and the annual *Index of Majors* (New York: The College Board).

Consider the Transferable Skills You Can Learn

In choosing your college according to the programs it offers, remember one important fact: the world of work is *not* divided into college majors. Learning the transferable skills that people use over and over in many careers is the goal of the college student, whatever the major. Some examples of transferable skills learned in college are how to understand fundamental principles, weigh evidence, listen and speak intelligently, argue persuasively, write clearly, learn new techniques and approaches, and adjust to new circumstances. These skills can be learned in any college major, from philosophy to physical education, from computer science to liberal arts. And keep in mind that half of all college students go into careers completely unrelated to their college major. This means that transferable skills are really what they are getting out of college. As you choose between a technical and a liberal arts program, think about what transferable skills you could learn in each program that you can use to your advantage in many work environments.

If you choose a liberal arts, or general, education, nothing will be more important than the transferable skills you will learn in that program. According to the President of Princeton University, Dr. William G. Bowen, "Some sensitivity to other people and their feelings, and a reasonable broad perspective on the world and its inhabitants, are of enormous value in many callings." President Bowen continues, "I am continually getting letters from representatives of leading business firms in New York who say, 'For the individuals we hire with a view to moving up into management, we feel that the liberal arts degree is the most desirable fundamental preparation.' "

A Matter of Money

Money usually is a factor to consider when you choose a college. With a shrinking economy, severe cutbacks in government-funded student loans, and skyrocketing college costs, paying for a college education is more difficult to do than ever before. As you consider which colleges to apply to, read as much information as you can to get a realistic picture of what colleges cost today and ways that might be available to help you finance that cost.

Each year, The College Board publishes a step-by-step

guide to financing a college education, called *The College Cost Book* (New York: The College Board). This book lists expenses at 3,200 schools and colleges and gives you directions for computing how much money a college might expect your parents or you to pay toward your educational expenses. It also provides information about financial aid programs and tells you exactly how and where to apply for them.

Another useful booklet with some creative ideas about how to pay for college costs is *The College Financial Aid Emergency Kit: The Best-ever Pocket Guide to Scholarships, Loans, and Other Remedies for Skinned-up, Broken-down, Wiped-out Budgets* (Sun Features, Inc., Box 368J, Cardiff, CA 92007).

After you find out how much each college you are applying to costs, and how much your family and you can afford to pay for your education, you will want to check further with the financial officer of each college. The college financial officer has the most up-to-date information about grants, aids, loans, and work programs. The financial officer also will be able to tell you about military and private industry tuition plans for college students. Once you are accepted in a college (and financial need is increasingly a factor in your acceptance), the college is usually very eager to find a way for you to pay.

Many students with financial need are led to believe that they must qualify for loans, grants, or scholarships by having top grades or the highest rank in class. As you think about your college choice, it is crucial for you to know that most government grants and loans and many from colleges are based on financial need, not on academic merit. If you have the academic standards to get into a college, then you have enough merit for the college to award help with your finances. If you are an older college applicant who has worked for a few years, whether for the work experience or because you needed to earn money, your age cannot influence whether or not you receive financial aid either. In other words, if you need the money, regardless of your test scores, or rank in class, or age, or sex, or race, *ask* about financial aid!

Today, many students are trying to keep their college expenses down by enrolling in less expensive community college programs where they can live at home at a much lower cost, rather than choosing a residential public or private college that can cost as much as $10,000 a year. If you are headed for an advanced degree or a professional school after four years of college, such as medicine, law, business, or education, you may want to save money by going to a community college nearby your home for your basic liberal arts training.

Consider the Saleable Skills You Can Learn

Because of the tremendous cost of colleges and the changing college employment market, you may decide not to make the capital investment in a four-year college. If you aren't enthusiastic about studying and learning academic subjects, chances are that four years in college may not be worth it for you financially, especially in terms of the few available jobs when you graduate. Instead, you may choose to go to a community college for a two-year program in a technical or business field that will teach you the saleable skills for a specific job with good employment possibilities, such as computer science, technical engineering, or technical health care.

With a little planning ahead, you can learn saleable skills in a four-year liberal arts college, too. Planning can save you the trouble and expense of having to learn these skills after graduation. Even if you select a major in Japanese religion or Russian literature because of your interest, it can be developed toward a paying career. If you add a few courses to your Japanese religion and Russian literature curriculums that help you acquire saleable skills, such as word processing, accounting, or basic computer programming, it may mean the difference between getting a job that requires a college degree when you graduate or not getting such a job. Or you may see the tie-in between business and Russian or Japanese studies in a broader sense, and then use your original academic interest in a practical way in your career.

Women who have not been aware of their need to make money, and have not planned ahead toward employment while they are still in college, often have to go back to school at added expense and time to learn a saleable skill. A Kansas State University graduate with a degree in psychology couldn't find a job related to her major. She then took a one-week word processing course that cost $300.00 in order to get a $6.00 an hour part-time job that she could live on while she went to graduate school — which still did not guarantee her a job in psychology when she graduated! The word processing job that begins at $6.00 an hour will turn into a $10.00 an hour job after a few months' experience. Almost every bank, law firm, and insurance company has word processing jobs, many at night and on weekends.

Another woman, with a Ph.D. in education, was laid off from her teaching job in Boston. With no educational opportunities in sight, and hundreds of other laid-off educators competing for jobs, she took a two-month business career course offered by a university to learn to market her analytical skills to become a loan officer trainee in a Boston bank.

No matter what your subject interest, think about ways you can learn one or more saleable skills before you graduate. Consider how these practical skills can be combined with your subject interest to make it more marketable in the career world. This will give you that competitive edge in the job market over other applicants.

Should You Choose According to Campus Life?

The college guides suggested on page 15 will give you an idea of how one college is different from another. When you compare the rules of various colleges, you will learn about their attitudes toward student responsibilities and college authority. You will get an idea of campus character and personality. Remember, however, that the kind of campus life a college offers does not indicate its academic standards for admission. You can't tell how difficult it is to get into a college by the number of hours the library is open. You don't have to be a superior student to find a college with an intellectual atmosphere where much of the academic responsibility is given to the student. And the reverse is true. Many colleges that accept only above-average and superior students provide a social and sports-oriented atmosphere rather than an intellectual one, with little academic responsibility given to the students.

Whatever the quality of a college campus, you must relate it to your own expectations of what college life will be like. Look for the type of campus environment you think will be most successful and most productive for you. Find a setting that gives you a chance to try out your interests and abilities, one that gives you the kind of support and encouragement you need. For example, if you don't have a brother, and have very few male friends, you may find that co-ed living makes you too uptight to cope academically. Or you may decide that learning to live and work among men is a top personal priority for you right now. You must relate your findings about differences in college life to yourself. These findings have no meaning for anyone else. As you look around at your friends, you can see that some of them will want a very different type of campus life than you want. Ask yourself these questions:

▶ "To what degree can I accept academic and social responsibility?"

▶ "How much responsibility do I take *now* for my life?"

▶ "How strict are my parents' rules compared to the college's rules?"

▶ "In what kinds of classroom climate do I work the hardest?"

▶ "How do the colleges I'm looking at relate to what I know about myself and the degree of responsibility I accept?"

Try to answer these questions about yourself as you find out what campus life is like at various colleges.

What about Prestige?

Many students do not think about the prestige of a college until they are already attending the college. Then they begin to hear about their college's prestige – or lack of it.

What does *prestige* mean, anyway? It means having a well-known reputation for being one of the best. Sometimes prestige is misleading. A college can have a great reputation in its own state, or even in its own region, but not be nationally well-known. For example, Denison University in Ohio is a prestigious liberal arts college in the Midwest. But few students on the East or West coasts would consider it equal to Oberlin, also in Ohio but better known nationally. A university can get its prestige from its medical school or its graduate school in business, and yet its undergraduate school, where you will be heading, may be very ordinary and have classes taught by graduate students rather than by fully qualified professors. Ohio State and other "Big Ten" colleges get their prestige from their football teams, but the quality of the football team has little to do with a university's academic standards.

Hundreds of colleges may have the academic program, the campus environment, and other advantages you are looking for. Prestige may or may not add to fulfilling your requirements for a college. The point to be made here is that it's helpful for you to know about the prestige of a college (determined by a great variety of factors), but the most prestigious college may not necessarily be the best college for you.

If you are choosing among Wellesley, Swarthmore, University of Chicago, and the local state college—and you have the money and grades for all four—go to the private college with the prestige. College can be where you begin to build your network of friends who will keep you tuned in to new career opportunities as you advance. If money or your academic record or geography keep you out, and you long for a degree from prestigious Smith, MIT, Harvard, or Stanford, then you can always apply later as a transfer or graduate student. Other than medicine and law, many graduate schools are easier to get into than their undergraduate colleges.

College Guides to Choosing

There are many kinds of college guides, and your high school guidance officer will certainly have the basic ones. Read the college descriptions in the guides to find out about the options available to you in higher education. In them you can learn about student enrollment, the size of the community where the college is located, the programs offered, the cost, the level of competition for admission, the social clubs on campus, the quality of student life. Two basic and complete college guides are *The College Handbook* (New York: The College Board) and *Comparative Guide to American Colleges* (J. Cass and M. Birnbaum, New York: Harper & Row). An important guide to colleges designed especially for women is *Everywoman's Guide to Colleges and Universities* (The Feminist Press, Box 334, Old Westbury, NY 11568).

THE FOCUS IS ON YOU

Choosing a college, a major field of study, and a career are not easy decisions for anyone to make. One way to help decide what you are going to do is to focus your attention away from the outside pressures and back onto yourself. You don't have to concentrate immediately on a school's expectation of you, your career education, the world of work, possible prejudices and sex-role stereotypes, the inflated economy, and the changing labor market. All of these things will be factors in your eventual decision, but what you need right now is to explore your career possibilities, no matter what conditions exist or what changes might take place.

You've Got Loads of Career Possibilities

There are hundreds of jobs in every field for you to investigate. You can work full-time. Or you may wish to share a job and use the rest of your time to write, make furniture, or raise a child. You may want to work part-time, or volunteer some of your time. Or you may want to create your own job.

Some women choose their career by the opportunity it gives them to be with their children—even though this means some of their work interests cannot be met. Judy Daloz, a visiting nurse in northern Vermont, works three days a week because she wants to be with her two preschool children most of the time. For now, she would rather take on less than a full-time work commitment in order to focus on her family at home. But she experiences certain drawbacks: "The problem with part-time work," says Daloz, "is that too often the job is routine and I can't get into the challenging, innovative work that nursing promises until my children are in school all day."

Other women choose careers that become extremely important to them—that become their very lives. They love every part of their work, and every spare moment goes into it. Their work is their hobby, and they are seldom off-duty. Everything they do fits in, in some way, to learning even more about their work. A bookstore owner spends her vacation in other bookstores, a writer sees how a given experience will fit into a future story, a car salesperson notices who is driving what car, and a businesswoman puts in eighty-hour weeks to plan every detail the way she wants it. Judi Hofer, for instance, got carried away with making money, setting goals, and reaching for the top when she earned her first money picking strawberries at the age of seven. At fifteen Hofer worked as a stock girl during the summer, at sixteen she moved to salesclerk, and at twenty-one she became the youngest buyer in a department-store chain in Portland, Oregon, called Meier & Frank. She left at twenty-five to test her skills with other retail experiences, and then came back to the department-store chain fifteen years later as President. According to *Savvy,* a magazine for women, Hofer fits her leisure into weekends and around the edges of business trips. A single woman, Hofer explains that entertainment revolves around couples. "I've tried to let people know that I'm perfectly happy to come to a dinner or other occasion by myself, but our society seems to be a long way from being comfortable with that." Her social life is *not* uppermost on her mind. She is turned on by the challenge of motivating and rewarding employees to sell more goods. Hofer has moved ahead fast, and it's easy to see that her work is her life.

These examples are extremes. Most of you will develop your career in ways that bring a balance to your life that suits your own personality and values. This balance will include your job, your family and friends, your volunteer work, your sports and hobbies. And the balance will *change.* Babies, promotions, and midlife changes will add transition and off-balance that always must be managed.

Today, people have more options for career choices and lifestyles than at any time in this country's history. You can choose to earn the money you need on your own, or to let a partner take the major responsibility for making money while you do something else—or any career arrangement in between. Focus first on *you* and the kind of life you want, and next on jobs, as you make your choices and changes to develop your career.

Female Expectations

The main reason women do not have career goals is because they are not expected to have them. A young woman who is interested in choosing a career is in a very different position from a young man. She is expected to be financially supported by someone else when she grows up. He is expected to financially support himself plus others when he grows up. She has been programmed to count most according to the money her husband makes. He has been programmed to measure himself as a person who counts most according to the money he makes. She is expected to find self-esteem through her family. He is expected to find his worth through his career. She has been programmed as a "sex object." He has been programmed as a "success object." The more you understand how you as a woman are systematically set up for certain choices, the more you will see a chance to vary the system.

Given that women are brought up differently and treated differently than men are, in both school and at work, you have to accept these differences—and the anxiety that goes with them—before you can seriously plan your strategy for a career. You may always be in conflict over achieving success in your career *and* being a successful mother. You may always be worried about personal criticism of your work in ways that don't bother your husband or male competition. You may always find it difficult to be assertive and initiate your business plans compared to the ease with which your brother performs the same business behavior. In other words, women have to learn to manage by accepting the traditional conflicts of successful women. A woman must be able to say with confidence that she wants a career and that she is willing to confront the problems that she will have *because* she is a woman. This advice is not only for women planning to go into business and management, it is also for women intending to go into law, politics, theology, engineering, medicine, mathematics, science, health administration, educational administration, and *wherever the men are*. For wherever the men are is where the money and policy-making are.

Develop Your Career

There are three basic steps in your career development. The first is to learn about yourself—to assess your own skills, values, and interests. The second is to learn about work—to locate your career possibilities. And the third step is to find the educational pathways that will lead you to where you want to go.

What Skills Can You Call Your Own?

The purpose of your education is to learn what you like to do and how well you can do it. At the same time, you learn what you don't like and what you don't do well. For example, in the classroom you learn how much mathematics and foreign language you can master. In addition to learning such content skills, you also learn transferable skills—how well you read, study, speak, and write. You apply these skills to all the subjects you learn and also to all career situations.

You learn what your skills are not only by grades, test scores, pay, and promotions, but also by your own evaluation. Although your school grades may predict how well you will do in college, they don't necessarily measure all the skills you have learned. You can't possibly tell what you are going to accomplish in life merely by your school grades and achievements. For example, if you rank fourth in your mathematics class right now, that doesn't mean that you will be fourth in money-making ability in your age group twenty years from now. Grades in high school and college *do not* predict who will be happiest, most miserable, richest, poorest, or most powerful, either in work or in family life.

To find out more about your skills, take a look at your everyday actions—not only what you say you like or don't like, but the things you actually *do* with your time. Think about the subjects you study in school, the tasks you perform at work, the things you do at home that really excite you, that make you feel special and make the time run fast. Notice what activities make you feel good, and what activities make you feel lousy and make you feel you can't wait to get them over with. Think about how your activities are related to having fun, to making money, to school or work or community achievement. Then, notice what skills are needed for the activities you love. Is time-management one of them? Is decision-making important? Is being your own boss and taking the initiative a part of your enjoyment? Do you get along with almost anyone, or much more with one group of people than another? Do your activities involve getting others to participate with you? Do they involve staying with a project after you've lost your initial enthusiasm? Here are a few more pertinent questions:

- Do you prefer to work in a particular situation or location?

- Do you prefer to work with particular types of people?

- Is money your main goal? Is power?

- Do you think you would like a job that is short on money but long on prestige?

▶ Would you like a job where you can be left to work on your own?

▶ What kind of physical surroundings do you prefer where you work?

▶ Do you mind traveling, or working occasionally at night and on weekends?

As you learn about yourself, you will notice how you relate to others. You will discover your ability to get along with other students, your family, and your co-workers; your leadership abilities in class and on the job; and your ability to get along with authority, such as your boss, your teachers, your coach, and your parents. Of course, your skills, interests, and values will change. In fact, many work and school experiences often bring about major changes in how you feel and act. But even bearing these changes in mind, you still can learn a lot right now about your skills in school, at home, and at work.

Reading Tells You a Lot about a Career

I Can Be Anything: A Career Book for Women is about work. The "career clusters" in this book describe many different jobs and career possibilities. Read about several careers that sound as if they describe your interests. When one career in a cluster interests you, read about the occupations related to it as well. Using the clusters in this way may help you find new ideas.

Sometimes people in a business-oriented family tend to look only at business careers, or people with relatives working in the military and government tend to examine only those fields. Or perhaps someone in your family has told you "you ought to be" a nurse, or a teacher, or a computer operator, and you may not like the idea. You may reject it before you seriously consider whether the career is a good one for you or not. Explore career possibilities that *you* have in mind, not those your family or friends say you should look at or not look at. After researching these possibilities, you'll either want to learn more about them or will be able safely to eliminate those possibilities.

As you research the careers in *I Can Be Anything,* notice that the average salaries are cited for each career. It is easy to think of the average as the exact salary at which you can expect to start working. For example, in 1981 engineers with a bachelor's degree started at an average of $22,900. What that average figure really means is that some engineers started at $18,900 a year while others started at $26,900. Beginning engineers *averaged* $22,900. For a better idea of the money you can expect in a particular career, you will want to translate the average salary into a range of starting salaries. Within this range, the particular salary you start with will depend on the college you attended, your college record, your work experience, where the job is located, and the type of employer.

If you are a student now, salaries will be even higher by the time you are ready for the job market because of inflation and cost-of-living salary increases. To give you an idea of the future rate of increase, let's look at past salaries for teachers. In 1976, teachers averaged $11,700; in 1981, they averaged $17,725. Remember, when you read "average," that means many workers make less and just as many may make more than the figure cited.

As you choose a career, what does money mean to you? Will your income be high enough to maintain the standard of living you want and justify your education costs? How much will your earnings increase as you gain experience? Like most people, you probably think of "salary" as money. But money is only one type of financial reward for work. Paid vacations, holidays, and sick leave; life, health, and accident insurance; and retirement and pension plans are also part of the total earnings package. Some employers also offer stock options and profit-sharing plans, savings plans, and bonuses.

Which jobs pay the most? This is a difficult question to answer because good information is available only for one type of earnings—wages. Obviously, some kinds of work pay better than others. But, many times, the same kind of work does not always pay the same amount of money. Some areas of the country offer better pay than others for the same type of work. For example, the average weekly earnings of a beginning computer programmer vary from city to city. Generally, earnings are higher in the North Central and Northeast regions of the country than in the West and South. You should also remember that cities that offer the highest earnings are often those in which it is most expensive to live.

Earnings for the same type of work also vary according to the type of organization you work for. For example, Ph.D.

chemists in marketing and production earn more than Ph.D. chemists in industrial research and development; however, those in industrial research earn more than chemistry professors, who also must do research.

Undoubtedly you will wonder what the economy will be like when you enter the labor market. Each career description anticipates your chances for getting a job through the 1980s. These chances are estimates developed by the U.S. Department of Labor, and they are based on the following general assumptions about the future of the economy and the country:

▶ Energy prices will not rise dramatically to alter the growth of the Gross National Product (GNP).

▶ The institutional framework of the U.S. economy will not change radically.

▶ Current social, technological, and scientific trends will continue.

▶ No major events, such as widespread or long-lasting energy shortages or war, will significantly alter the rates of industrial and economic growth.

▶ Federal grants-in-aid to state and local governments will decline.

▶ Federal expenditures will decline as a proportion of the Gross National Product.

Finally, you should remember that job prospects in your community or state may not correspond to the description of employment outlook given here. The outlook in your area may be better—or worse—for the particular job you are interested in. The local office of your State Employment Service is the best place to ask about employment projections in your area.

Looking at all the possibilities, then, find one or two or three careers that sound interesting enough to read about and research further. Reading in detail about a career is a reliable way to acquire accurate information about that career. Some people make their choices only on information provided by the mass media. A detective or doctor or trial lawyer on television often provides a romantic picture of his or her career. None of the beginning drudgery and dirty work that all jobs demand, nor the long hours away from the family, may come through in a television or otherwise stereotyped version of a career.

After reading the career descriptions that interest you, write to the professional groups cited for more information. Look in your school library for some of the recommended readings listed for each job, or send away for readings if your library does not carry them. Notice in particular the trade magazines cited for each career. If you want the inside story of what people in a career are reading, thinking about, and actually doing, read their trade magazine! *The Wall Street Journal, Variety,* and *Veterinary Economics* are where you will find out what the financial, theater, and vet people are really like. It isn't academic theory but the business of the job itself that you'll find in the trade magazines. In addition to learning what people in a field are doing, you can't beat the trade magazine as raw material for a job interview. For example, nothing will impress a book publisher more than hearing you discuss facts about his or her business you acquired from reading *Publishers Weekly;* or a physician, if you can talk about the latest research published in the *New England Journal of Medicine;* or a banker, if you have the latest economy reports from the *American Banker;* or an urban planner, if you are aware of recent urban trends in *City.* If your school library doesn't have the trade magazines you are interested in, check your community library or a local college library. For those of you who don't have a library resource, publishing addresses are cited at the end of each career description. Write for one issue to find out what's going on in the fields you are considering.

What Do Others Think about Their Work?

Talking to people who are willing to discuss their work is an excellent way to find out about a career you are interested in. One good place to find people to interview about their work is in your own family. Ask your parents, aunts, uncles, and their friends to help you find some people who are already in the career you are thinking about entering. Talk with those people. If a securities salesperson is what you want to be, find a stockbroker and ask her what it's like to be in securities. Does it sound like you? Ask another person what it's like to be in that field. How much of the job does she really like? What parts of the job does she hate and wish were over as soon as she starts them? Listen to everything you hear from others as it relates to you, because *you* are the one who will be selling and either enjoying the hustle and competition or getting an ulcer by the time you finally make the sale. Let others you talk to know about your interest in their work.

In addition to your family, many of your teachers or co-workers will be good sources for finding people in careers that you are ready to research. Clergy, youth-group leaders, and many people in your community, including the alumnae from your school, will want to help with career development. Some of them already have specific programs to help, while others are looking for ways to help. Ask them if they know a forester, a computer systems analyst, or a foreign service officer you can meet and interview in your career research. Don't wait until you are choosing a college major or hunting for a job to talk with others about their work. The more experience you have talking with people in careers that interest you, the more background you'll have for your decisions ahead. Not only will your interview experiences be good training for future interviews, they will also have value right now in teaching you more about work and the ways that work will fit into your life.

Even if you don't know someone, but you have read about his or her interesting work in the paper, go ahead and write to that person, saying that you are interested in learning about his or her job or in working with the person during the summer or school holiday. Usually, people are flattered about your interest. In this way, you can learn how to make your own opportunities for future interviews and jobs. Students are in a good position for exploring. You have a positive image, and people aren't threatened that you will take over their job. So, make the most of your learning status to learn about careers from the people already doing well in them.

When you have the names of people to interview, call them. Tell them you would like to talk with them for a specific amount of time, so they will know you won't keep them too long from their work. Say, for instance, that you are interested in being a computer programmer and want to talk about what the job is like with someone who knows. Ellen J. Wallach, career-development specialist, suggests that you make an appointment, then have the following questions in mind to help begin the interview:

▶ How did you get into this career?

▶ How did you view the work before you got into it? Is your view different now? How is it different?

▶ What do you like *most* about your work?

▶ What do you like *least* about your work?

▶ Why did you choose this type of work?

▶ What are the greatest pressures, strains, and anxieties about your work?

▶ What special problems might someone new to the job have in adjusting to it?

▶ Would you make the same career choice again? Why?

▶ Besides the environment in which you work, where else could someone perform your work?

▶ Are there careers related to your work?

▶ How much time do you spend with your family? Is this amount what you expected to spend when you began working in this career?

▶ How much time do you spend with hobbies?

▶ How do your family and friends fit into the lifestyle of your career?

▶ What are the greatest "highs" about this work—what really turns you on about it?

At the end of the interview, advises Wallach, always ask the following questions: "Is there anyone else you know who also does your kind of work who might be willing to speak to me? May I use your name when I call?" And when you get home, write a short thank-you note to the worker for sharing his or her time and work with you. This follow-up is a must.

Throughout your career-research process, remember that everything you learn counts. Even though you decide that a given career isn't what you had thought it was before your research, you are still ahead to have the accurate information. You may learn about new careers indirectly, and your follow-up from reading and interviews may lead you in directions you didn't plan on taking. The more information you finally have for your career decision, the more sure you can be of your decision — at least for this phase in your life.

Test Your Interest through Work Experience

Choosing and changing work experiences are pathways or directions toward your career development. Actual work experience provides opportunities where you can try out your school knowledge in a work situation.

Once you get a career idea that makes sense for you, use your summer vacation, after-school time, and weekends for a trial run in that career, whether it's paid work or volunteer work. Work at a car agency if you are interested in sales, or in a hospital if you are interested in health care. Work with a children's group in a day camp or child-care center if you are interested in education, or in a bookstore or publishing house if the book business interests you. Try a summer job in a bank or real estate office if finance is your interest.

Even though the kind of work you are likely to get is the lowest level in that field and, therefore, reserved for beginners, the menial tasks become meaningful if you apply what you learn to your own career development. Even if you are doing a repetitious job that takes no thinking, you can look around at the whole system and notice what the next step up is for people who have permanent jobs and can get promotions. Who is your boss? Who is her boss? Who is the top boss? Do any of those jobs look interesting? For example, a summer job in a real estate office may consist of painting front doors on homes to be sold. But you can look around and see the hours kept by other salespeople, listen to the kinds of questions clients ask and the answers salespeople give, and notice which salespeople are making the most money, which are putting in the most time, and which are living a life you would like to live.

Getting ahead in a job is like learning to walk or to ski. You've got to put so many hours and so many miles into the learning, no matter who you are, or how fit you are, or how well-qualified you are. When you start summer work, or an after-school job, or your first full-time job, you will probably start at the bottom. Setting goals is what people do who really want to get ahead. It's especially important when you just begin a job and it turns out that the job isn't everything you had hoped it would be.

Men have always known about career goals. They are taught to plan their college years, their work experience, their priorities at work and home, their moves, promotions, and acceptance of one job over another with an eye toward whatever goal they have set. As they achieve their goals, and as they change and learn more skills and see their own potential more clearly, they set new ones.

Women are just beginning to learn about career goals. Their early career goals usually ended with marriage or a baby. They tend not to make decisions and plan a strategy for fulfilling a career goal at an age when they can do most about such a goal—in school or during the first few years of a job. They credit "luck" for the good jobs they do get, rather than their qualifications or skills. They seldom plan to be in the right place at the right time for terrific jobs; and if they happen to be, that also is "luck."

Letitia Baldridge, executive, feminist, president of her own New York City public relations firm, writer of books and a weekly column, is an outstanding woman. She is 6 feet 1 inch tall. But even more outstanding for a woman is the fact that she has persistently set career goals and methodically fulfilled them.

When Tish Baldridge graduated from college she wanted to work in Europe for the State Department. She was told that she needed secretarial skills in addition to her Vassar undergraduate degree. She clearly saw the necessity for the skills that would eventually get her where she wanted to be, so it was worth it to her to go back to school for a crash course in secretarial skills in order to start work at the State Department. Continuing to set her goals, she advanced to being the social secretary to the U.S. Ambassador in Italy, Clare Booth Luce. After coming back to the U.S., she became Tiffany's first woman executive. From there, she went to the White House, where she was Jackie Kennedy's social secretary as well as President Kennedy's protocol officer. From her experience and contacts that she made working for others, Tish went into business for herself, starting a public relations company in Manhattan. She was well-established in her career before she married at 35 and had 2 children. Because of her career achievements, she could be flexible in her work to be with her babies, and she could afford child care and domestic help. Of all the outstanding things you can learn from Tish Baldridge, the most helpful to you is her example of how a woman can set her own goals and plan the necessary strategy to achieve them.

Setting career goals is necessary not only for women who want to end up in their own business, but also for those teachers who want to be administrators, those engineers who want to direct a project, those reporters who want to get top assignments, and those volunteer women who want to be policy makers.

Your work may not always seem related to where you want to end up. But when you see how everything about a job counts, including motherhood, then your present work activity takes on new meaning. When a mother understands what she learns from raising children, then the time spent with them becomes more meaningful. Your purpose in career exploration and development is to help you determine all the possible directions for your future.

Keep Your Options Open

Four-year college students can put off specific or specialized career decisions longer than two-year community college or technology students can. If you are a four-year student, or if you are taking time out from school or a job to raise children, take advantage of this extra time and explore your options as best you can. Keep in mind that all the technological and economic changes in the job market you've heard about in the past five years are still going on. All the changes in you that you've noticed are still going on, too. In other words, in the next few years, it can be a whole new ball game. If you stick with assessing your own skills, getting in tune with your values and interests as they change in your family place or workplace, and if you keep your career options open for new directions, you can't go wrong.

ART, ARCHITECTURE, AND DESIGN

PERFORMING ARTS
Actress
Dancer
Musician

ARCHITECTURE
Architect
Landscape Architect

DESIGN
Commercial Artist
Industrial Designer
Interior Designer
Photographer

About these careers Creativity and the ability to communicate, along with luck and drive, are necessary to succeed in the arts and design careers. This cluster of careers represents 887,200 jobs. That is about 0.9 million out of a total national work force of 102.1 million workers.

Even in good times, the number of performing artists always exceeds the number of job openings. The difficulty of earning a living as a performer is one reason why many artists earn their living through teaching or routine jobs, such as waiting on tables and word-processing, that will support them while they continue to study and audition for performing-arts work.

Evening work is a regular part of the performing artist's life. Rehearsals may be held late at night and on weekends and holidays. When performances are given on the road, weekend traveling is often necessary. Besides the traveling required in the performing arts, many artists have to take any casual work they can find when a show closes and while waiting for another job. Travel, irregular hours, and unemployment are all very hard on family and social life.

A college degree counts less in the performing arts than in any other career. More important to artists are the professional schools of acting, dance, and music, which are located in the major cities where the work opportunities also exist. A professional school whose goal is to turn out the best musician, or actress, or dancer is the best place for your training. In order to find a professional school, write to the professional association at the end of the particular career description that interests you and ask for a list of approved schools.

Architects and designers spend long hours at the drawing board in well-equipped offices. New graduates usually begin as junior drafters in architectural firms, where they are closely supervised. Junior members of a firm are often asked to work overtime to meet a deadline and to do routine and tedious work that no one likes to do, until they gain experience and have paid their "professional beginner's dues."

Architect and landscape-architect education require a four-year or five-year program. Commercial art, interior design, and photography require a two-year or three-year professional or specialty school. Write to the professional association in the design career that interests you for a list of approved schools and colleges.

ACTRESS

*Entertains people through her interpretations
of dramatic roles on the stage and in film.*

What's It Like to Be an Actress?

Actresses agree that professional acting is not a "nine-to-five" job, but fills every aspect of your life. Rehearsals, performances, learning lines, and taking classes in acting, dancing, and singing are all part of your involvement in the theater and film. The best way to experience what it is like to be an actress is to serve as an apprentice in summer stock theater productions. The lives of an acting company on the road and in summer stock are very close. Everyone eats, sleeps, and works together, and the particular group you work with makes a difference to everything you do in your life. Theater arts major at Ohio State University, Diane Elaine Wondisford, spends her summers getting experience in summer stock as a production stage manager. "I am trained as a theater director," explains Wondisford, "and I enjoy it most because it allows me to fill any stage with life, with countless good scripts mounted in a cooperative effort with other theater artists." She advises students who are interested in professional theater and film to attend a college that is a member of the League of Professional Training Schools and offers a Bachelor of Fine Arts (B.F.A.) degree in acting, directing, and design.

What Education and Skills Will I Need?

High school: College preparatory course and as much acting experience as possible.

College: A theater arts or dramatics major offers acting experience in local productions as well as in summer stock. Acting experience is more important than the number of years in college. It can be the best way to establish recognition in your community as you build your acting record for future jobs.

Personal skills: Dramatic talent, the patience and commitment to wait for work, and physical stamina for long rehearsals often under lights are needed to be an actress.

How Many Women in the Field and Where Do They Work?

There are 21,000 actors and actresses working in stage plays, film (including television), industrial shows, and commercials. Half of them are women. In the winter, most of the theatrical job opportunities are in New York City. In the summer, many stock companies employ actresses in the suburbs and resort areas. Motion pictures and films for television are made in Hollywood, although there are a few studios in New York and Chicago. The main networks for television and radio are in New York and Los Angeles, with some opportunities in Chicago. Occasionally, local television and radio stations employ actresses.

$ $ $ $ $

All professional actresses belong to unions. In 1980, the minimum salary for a Broadway actress was $475 a week. Off-Broadway paid from $153 to $317 a week. Motion pictures offer a minimum of $259 a day for roles and $68 a day for "extras." Most actresses get little if any unemployment, since they seldom have been employed long enough in any state to meet the eligibility requirements. The Actors Equity Association surveyed their 26,000 members and found that 22,000 of them earned less than $5,000 a year.

What Is the Future for Women?

Making a living in the theater and film is often nearly impossible and almost always difficult. New York City is flooded with young, talented, well-trained people looking desperately for the few jobs available. Even though more residential theaters are being organized, and more local television stations are beginning, the increasing number of young people entering acting each year offsets the new opportunities. Dinner theaters provide the fastest growing job openings in the country for actresses. The expanding public broadcasting system and cable television are other good possibilities for work. It is difficult for a woman to leave the theater in order to raise a child and then try to return at a later date, because she loses contacts in the theater. A community nonprofessional theater can offer a good way for a professional actress who leaves work for a few years to stay in contact with the theater. Most successful actresses don't leave the theater to raise children but continue to work as they share or hire childcare.

RELATED CAREERS
disc jockey   narrator
comedian   radio announcer
director   television announcer

WHERE CAN I GET MORE INFORMATION?
Professional Groups
American Theater Association
1000 Vermont Avenue, NW
Washington, D.C. 20005

The American National Theater and Academy
245 West 52 Street
New York, NY 10019

League of Professional Theater Training Programs
1860 Broadway, Suite 1515
New York, NY 10023

Trade Journal
Variety
154 West 46 Street
New York, NY 10036

DANCER
*Expresses ideas and emotions through
her body movements.*

What's It Like to Be a Dancer?
Dancers work together as a chorus in dance productions for the stage, movies, and television. Some are selected for special numbers, and a very few top artists do solo work. The few dancers who become choreographers create new ballets or

dance routines. Others become dance directors who train dancers in new productions. Teachers usually teach in a professional dancing school or in colleges and universities.

Michele (21) and Janine (17) Ceballos, two sisters from New York City, started taking ballet lessons at 6 years old and focused on dance at the age of 11. Both are professional dancers and have lived their lives in the dance world. They took high school courses through correspondence work and attended a special high school for performing artists, freeing them to take dance classes all day. As young women growing up in the world of professional dance, what do they like least about dance life? Michele says, "The lack of money. The conditions we work under are a disgrace but even worse is the amount of talent that isn't developed from lack of money." And Janine doesn't like the constant competition among dancers, the shortage of jobs for dancers, and the dieting. Janine has just been chosen to train for a Belgian ballet company and will leave home in the fall. Michele lives with a friend, sharing or taking turns earning the money, both doing the domestic work. They will move to Chicago, where she has a new job with the Chicago Ballet Company. It's her turn to pay the bills while he studies. Michele plans to have a baby at 28 when, she says, her dance career will be "strong enough to take some time off or not good enough to continue." What do they like best about their careers? "It's physical, creative, and constantly growing and demanding. I am never bored. It's a beautiful profession," says Michele. And Janine adds, "The good things in my work outrun the bad. I love it a lot. I like having control over my body and moving and working hard. I like working closely with a teacher, relating to him or her and listening to the music. I love dancers. They are nutty people, but interesting! I love the thought of being in a professional company, working with great choreographers and helping them express their ideas through us."

What Education and Skills Will I Need?

Professional training: Performers begin their training by the age of 7 for ballet and by 12 or younger for other kinds of dance. Professional training includes 10 to 12 lessons a week for 11 or 12 months a year and many hours of practice. By 17 or 18 years of age, the dancer is prepared for audition.

Professional school or high school: A good professional school

DANCER

is very important for the training it offers and for the connections it has for employment. In addition to dancing, students study music, literature, and history. An alternative to professional school training is a high school program that leads to a dance major in college, sometimes within the physical education or theater arts department. This option can lead to performing or to teaching. Professional schools require teachers to be experienced performers.

Personal skills: A dancer must have agility, coordination, grace, a sense of rhythm, and a feeling for music; also, self-discipline, patience, good body build, physical stamina, and the ability to work as part of a team.

How Many Women in the Field and Where Do They Work?

Half of the 23,000 dancers and dancing teachers are performers on stage, screen, and television. Eighty-five percent of all dancers are women, but in ballet and modern dancing 50 percent of the dancers are women. Performers work primarily in New York City, although there are now major dance companies in Los Angeles, San Francisco, Chicago, Houston, Cincinnati, Miami, Hartford, Minneapolis, Seattle, Boston, and Philadelphia. Rarely can dancers perform after 30 or 35 years of age.

$ $ $ $ $

Performers belong to a union that sets their contracts and salaries. In 1980, starting dance salaries in ballet and stage production was around $500 a week. College dance teachers with a master's degree receive the same salary as other instructors, usually beginning at $15,000 a year. (See "College Professor.")

What Is the Future for Women?

Very competitive. The supply of qualified dancers far exceeds employment opportunities. Excellent health and unusual physical vitality are always needed. A first job in Broadway shows is rare for women over 25, unless they have had experience.

RELATED CAREERS
> dance therapist   choreographer
> dance teacher   dance critic
> acrobat

WHERE CAN I GET MORE INFORMATION?
Professional Groups
American Guild of Musical Artists
1841 Broadway
New York, NY 10023

Ballet Society, New York State Theater
1865 Broadway
New York, NY 10023

Trade Journal
Dance News
119 West 57 Street
New York, NY 10019

MUSICIAN
*Expresses ideas and emotions through
the music she plays.*

What's It Like to Be a Musician?

Violist Barbara Steg, who has a graduate degree from the Oberlin Conservatory, says, "A performing musician spends most of her lifetime involved with music. Playing, thinking, and listening to music becomes a way of life. In addition to the performances are the daily hours of practice, music selection, group practice, and organization of concerts—all time-consuming duties of the musician." Conducting is the last male stronghold in music and, until 1975, almost no women were seen or heard conducting major musical groups. Sarah Caldwell, conductor and director of the Boston Opera Company, is leading the way for women and, in 1975–1976, she began to accept conducting engagements with major American orchestras. Music teachers usually teach vocal music, instrumental music, or classroom music appreciation and often give individual lessons to students. Large churches hire full-time music directors and organists, and smaller churches employ school music teachers or local people to take these jobs as part-time music opportunities.

What Education and Skills Will I Need?

Professional training: Professional musicians usually start studying an instrument at an early age (elementary school), with intensive training in private lessons. They audition for symphony orchestras, chamber groups, and other professional music groups whenever they are ready.

High school: Preparation for college, with as much music training as possible.

College: High school and college music teachers usually major in music in college and meet particular certification needs according to the state in which they teach.

How Many Women in the Field and Where Do They Work?

There are 127,000 performing musicians, mostly employed in New York, Chicago, Nashville, Miami Beach, Las Vegas, Los Angeles, and New Orleans. About 23 percent of the musicians are women. Some are in symphony orchestras and very few women are working in dance bands or rock groups. Women represent about one-fourth of the total players in major orchestras. It wasn't until the late 1960s that the New York Philharmonic Orchestra hired its first permanent woman player; today, only 9 out of 106 New York Philharmonic musicians are women. To date, there are 10 women with the Boston Symphony; 16 with the Los Angeles Philharmonic; and 25 with the Atlanta Symphony.

$ $ $ $ $

Musicians belong to the American Federation of Musicians (AFL-CIO); concert soloists belong to the American Guild of Musical Artists. In 1980, major symphony orchestra musicians earned from $350 to $600 a week. In the high school system, music teachers receive the same salary as other teachers.

What Is the Future for Women?

All music jobs are extremely competitive. There are many more talented musicians of all kinds—classical, pop, teachers, performers—than there are jobs. The best job opportunities are in instrumental teaching in the public school. However, a talented musician can get a performing job. Violist Barbara Steg decided she wanted to change her music career after 25 years in education. She auditioned for major orchestras, sent tapes to others, and was hired by the Orchestra of Vera Cruz, Mexico, where she plays major concerts in Mexico including a weekly symphony concert in Mexico City.

RELATED CAREERS

arranger	music teacher
composer	music therapist
copyist	music salesperson
music critic	radio music producer
music librarian	TV music producer

WHERE CAN I GET MORE INFORMATION?

Professional Groups
American Federation of Musicians
1500 Broadway
New York, NY 10036

Music Educators National Conference
1902 Association Drive
Reston, VA 22091

Trade Journals
Billboard
One Astor Plaza
1515 Broadway
New York, NY 10036

Rolling Stone
745 Fifth Avenue
New York, NY 10022

ARCHITECT

Plans and designs buildings and other structures.

What's It Like to Be an Architect?

An architect meets and discusses with her client the purpose, costs, and preferences for style and plan of a structure to be built. She considers the local building and zoning laws and makes a preliminary drawing of the building to show the client. The final design is a working one that includes details of the plumbing, electrical, and heating systems. The architect helps her client select a building contractor and continues to represent her client until the structure is completed and all structural tests are made. Self-employed architects work on a variety of products, from homes, churches, and office buildings to renewal projects, college campuses, new towns, and urban planning. Margaret Zirkel Young, age 34, designs, manages, and supervises construction of high-rise urban complexes for a Chicago firm. Young believes that many more women who are interested in design would be happy in architecture if they were advised early to go into the field, and if they could see more women architects at work.

What Education and Skills Will I Need?

High school: Preparation for college, with an emphasis on mathematics, physics, and art.

College: There are 87 accredited schools of architecture offering a five-year program for a Bachelor of Architecture degree or a six-year program for a Master of Architecture degree. After three years of experience, an architect takes a state examination for a license to practice.

Personal skills: Capacity to solve technical problems, ability to work independently, artistic skills, and good business sense are necessary for architects.

How Many Women in the Field and Where Do They Work?

About 4.4 percent of the 79,500 architects are women. Forty percent of the architects are self-employed, although only

ARCHITECT

26 percent of the women are principals or partners, and most of the others work for architectural firms. The majority of architects are employed in seven cities: Boston, Chicago, Los Angeles, New York, Philadelphia, San Francisco, and Washington. Houston, Dallas, and Phoenix are attracting new businesses and architects.

$ $ $ $ $

In 1980, architects started at over $15,000 per year. With three years experience, they averaged $20,000 a year. In 1981, the average salary for all architects working for the federal government was $32,000 a year.

What Is the Future for Women?

Jobs will be competitive through the 1980s because graduates are outnumbering the job opportunities. If you are interested in mathematics, drawing, and art, consider this profession where part-time opportunities and the ability to work out of your home are both possible advantages for the family woman. Women earning degrees in architecture have increased from 5.3 percent in 1970 to 20 percent in 1980.

RELATED CAREERS
civil engineer   building contractor
urban planner   landscape architect
industrial designer

WHERE CAN I GET MORE INFORMATION?
Professional Group
The American Institute of Architects
1735 New York Avenue, NW
Washington, D.C. 20006

Trade Journal
Architectural Record
McGraw-Hill Publications Company
Box 430
Hightstown, NJ 08520

LANDSCAPE ARCHITECT

Combines design with nature to develop a composite landscape project.

What's It Like to Be a Landscape Architect?

Landscape architects design outdoor areas that are functional as well as artistically pleasing. Working with architects, engineers, and city planners, they consider the nature and purpose of a project, the funds available, and the resource conservation of the site. Sue Evans, mother of two teenagers, works for a real estate firm that constructs housing developments. Her first job with the firm was to study the map features of a housing development, such as the slope of the land and the position of roads, walkways, and trees. She considered the sunny parts of the site at different times of the day and the soil texture of the land. Then, as part of a design team with the project architect, she drew up landscape plans for the development. After the plans were approved, she outlined in detail a working drawing with the list of building materials and the methods of construction. Her plan developed and approved, Evans is now in the process of inviting landscape contractors to bid for the work. While her children were younger, she worked with city planners on a nine-to-five job, where she always was sure of when and where she was going to be. Evans finds her present job more challenging, interesting, and better paying, even though her hours are longer. She moves around a lot looking at new sites and keeping an eye on the contracted work in progress.

What Education and Skills Will I Need?

High school: Preparation for college, with biology, botany, art, mathematics, and mechanical drawing.

College: Take a four-year or five-year college program in landscape architecture in one of the 40 approved colleges. Thirty-eight states require landscape architects to be licensed. To qualify for a license, you must have a college degree, two to four years of experience, and you must pass a state examination.

Personal skills: Landscape architects need talent in art and design, an interest in nature, and the ability to express their thoughts creatively with details.

How Many Women in the Field and Where Do They Work?

There are 15,000 landscape architects and less than 5 percent are women. Most landscape architects are self-employed or work for architectural or engineering firms. Government agencies employ 40 percent of all landscape architects.

$ $ $ $ $

In 1980, landscape architects began at $13,500 to $18,000 per year. In 1981, those with the federal government started at $15,900 to $19,700. Average salaries with experience were from $24,700 to $35,000.

What Is the Future for Women?

Jobs are expected to be very good through the 1980s. The increased demand results from the growing interest in city and regional environmental planning. Many women share this interest in city and regional environmental planning and also have an interest in art, design, and nature. If you combine those interests with making money, you could be a landscape architect.

RELATED CAREERS
architect
environmental planner
urban planner

WHERE CAN I GET MORE INFORMATION?
Professional Group
American Society of Landscape Architects
1733 Connecticut Avenue, NW
Washington, D.C. 20009

Trade Journal
Landscape Architect
Society of Landscape Architecture
1500 Bardstown Rd.
Louisville, KY 40205

COMMERCIAL ARTIST

Creates the artwork for publications, films, textiles,
greeting cards, and industrial products.

What's It Like to Be a Commercial Artist?

Valerie Bessette, art director and production manager of *Skating Magazine,* has a Bachelor of Fine Arts in graphic design. She has had all kinds of jobs leading up to this one and urges young women interested in commercial art to take any design job they can get for the experience and see where it goes. For instance, Ms. Bessette first worked on brochures and photography for a landscape architect, then taught art for one year in public school, and then worked in a design studio on packaging and ads. Next, she was the art director of a small ad agency before her present job in Boston. Bessette also enjoys building her free-lance work so she can do a variety of work as well as make more money.

Ann Babcock, staff artist for an educational television station, describes her job: "I draw, do paste-ups, cut-ups, collages, and print promotional work on camera cards that are photographed and made into slides for television. As it turns out, I do everything requiring a pen and a little imagination. This is a nine-to-five job but wholly unlike other nine-to-five jobs, since the atmosphere of a quality television station is very stimulating and not at all routine."

The majority of commercial artists work on a team of artists under the supervision of an art director. One member of the team is the advertising artist, who creates the concept and design for promotional ideas to be used in mass media. Other members of the team are the layout artists, who draw a rough visual sketch for the design; the renderers, who make pastel or wash drawings of the design; letterers, who add the writing to the design; illustrators, who sketch a finer form of the design; and paste-up and "mechanicals" artists, who cut and paste together the basic parts of the final design, using ruling pens and drafting tools. In a small office, many of these jobs are done by the same person. Other commercial artists specialize in fashion illustrations, greeting cards, book illustrations, package design, textile design, painting, and industrial design.

What Education and Skills Will I Need?

High school: Preparation for an art school or a fine arts major in college. Art schools require an art aptitude test and an example of your work. Get as much art training and experience in high school as possible.

College: A two-year art school or a four-year college art program will prepare you for the better commercial art jobs. As in all the arts, demonstration of your ability and talent is more important than a degree.

Personal skills: Artistic talent, imagination, a distinctive style, and the capacity to translate ideas into visual concepts are needed to be a commercial artist.

How Many Women in the Field and Where Do They Work?

About 120,000 people work as commercial and graphic artists and designers. Thirty-five percent of them are women. They are employed in the major cities of New York, Chicago, Los Angeles, Boston, and Washington, but some are employed in every city. The majority of the artists are staff artists, working for advertising agencies, commercial art studios, and advertising departments of stores and companies. There are a considerable number of free-lance commercial artists working part-time in order to spend the rest of their time on fine arts.

$ $ $ $ $

Artists in entry level paste-up or layout jobs often make as little as minimum wage. Art directors, designers, and well-known free-lance illustrators earn from $30,000 to $40,000 a year and more.

What Is the Future for Women?

Chances for work and promotions will continue to be very competitive through the 1980s. Women with exceptional artistic talent will continue to find the best jobs in the textile industry and as fashion illustrators for department stores. Some jobs are needed more than others, and free-lance artists will find work as will paste-up and mechanical artists.

COMMERCIAL ARTIST

RELATED CAREERS
industrial designer   set designer
interior designer   fashion designer

WHERE CAN I GET MORE INFORMATION?
Professional Groups
The Graphic Artists Guild
30 East 20 Street, Room 405
New York, NY 10003

National Art Education Association
1916 Association Drive
Reston, VA 22091

National Association of Women Artists
156 Fifth Avenue
New York, NY 10010

Trade Journal
Illustrator Magazine
500 S. Fourth Street
Minneapolis, MN 55415

INDUSTRIAL DESIGNER
Designs or arranges objects and materials to optimize a
product's appearance, function, and value.

What's It Like to Be an Industrial Designer?

Josie Erickson wanted to have an art career, but she never thought of industrial design until her art professor suggested it as an alternative to the overcrowded art field. Now, working for a manufacturing company outside of Chicago, she tells what the job is like. "I work on a team with managers, engineers, production specialists, and sales and market research personnel to look at the feasibility of design ideas for products. We consider a product's visual appeal, convenience, utility, safety, maintenance, and cost to the manufacturer, distributor, and consumer.

After our team selects the best design for a product, I make a model of it, often of clay so that it can be easily modified. After any necessary revisions, I make a working model, usually of the material to be used in the finished product. The approved model then is put into production. When I learned that all industrial designers experience the frustration of having many designs rejected, I began to find my job a real challenge. I like working with the team, and I like the business side of learning more about how to market products. I pride myself in combining practicality with catchy design in order to get my ideas on the market. I am single and I like to work overtime when the pressure is great in order to finish a design. I'm not sure that I would stay with this particular company if I had young children. There are many different kinds of work opportunities, including free-lance work, that I will seriously consider when I start my family."

What Education and Skills Will I Need?

High school: Preparation for college, with courses in art, drafting, and mathematics.

College: Take one of the 33 college programs for industrial design that are approved by the Industrial Designers Society of America.

Personal skills: Creativity, artistic and drawing skills, ability to see familiar objects in new ways, ability to work with people who are not designers, and an interest in business and sales are needed for success.

How Many Women in the Field and Where Do They Work?

Of the total 10,000 industrial designers only 1,000 are women. Most designers work for large manufacturing companies or for design consulting firms in New York, Chicago, Los Angeles, and San Francisco.

$ $ $ $ $

In 1980, beginners started at $15,000 a year. Designers with 2 years experience averaged $18,000 a year.

What Is the Future for Women?

Jobs will be competitive for college graduates of industrial design. When the economy is in recession, the markets for new products shrink.

RELATED CAREERS
architect
fashion designer
commercial artist

WHERE CAN I GET MORE INFORMATION?
Professional Group
Industrial Designers Society of America
1717 N Street, NW
Washington, D.C. 20036

Trade Journal
Industrial Design
717 Fifth Avenue
New York, NY 10022

INTERIOR DESIGNER
*Plans and supervises the design and arrangement
of building interiors and furnishings.*

What's It Like to Be an Interior Designer?

Carol Durfee is an interior designer at a Denver, Colorado, architectural firm and has a Bachelor of Fine Arts in architecture from the Rhode Island School of Design. She spends her day talking with field supervisors about space planning for current construction, and with salesworkers about new products and colors. She attends meetings with clients, visits construction sites to check progress and quality, and spends afternoons in local shops looking at draperies, carpets, and furnishings. She often meets with building committees to present her plans to clients. Interior designers work closely with architects to check their plans with the blueprints and building requirements.

Doris Kaufman, interior designer in Boston and a professional member of the American Society of Interior Design, is in business for herself. After an hour or two of conference with a client, she takes the client from design showroom to design showroom to shop. Late afternoon is fabric-shopping time in the closed-to-client design center. Kaufman likes this least about her work. What she likes best is the constant change of pace and the variety—from designing the interior of a small house to model apartments for a seventy-story project, then to an office, an apartment, and a showroom, all in different periods. Kaufman keeps up-to-date with professional lectures and courses and enjoys the stimulation of being with other interior designers. "The satisfaction of liking my completed work is the ultimate reward of the job."

What Education and Skills Will I Need?

High school: Preparation for art school or a degree in fine arts.

College: A college degree in architecture or a three-year professional art school program is required to be a professional member of the American Society of Interior Design. This membership is necessary for the best jobs.

Personal skills: Artistic talent, color sense, good taste, imagination, good business judgment, and the ability to work with detail are needed to be a successful interior designer.

How Many Women in the Field and Where Do They Work?

Half of the 35,000 full-time interior designers are women. The majority work in large cities, in large department and furniture stores, for hotel and restaurant chains, for architects, and for home furnishing magazines. Others are in small businesses of their own or in partnerships.

$ $ $ $ $

In 1980, many art school graduates began at $8,000 to $14,000 a year. Experienced interior designers with a reputation in their area earn from $15,000 to $25,000 a year, while nationally known designers make over $50,000. In addition to salary, many designers earn a commission based on their sales of rugs, draperies, furniture, and other materials used in their design.

What Is the Future for Women?

Talented art school graduates with good business ability will get the few jobs through the 1980s. Like most creative work, jobs are very competitive as many young people flock to the cities where the largest number of jobs are.

RELATED CAREERS
exhibit designer
display worker
fabric designer

WHERE CAN I GET MORE INFORMATION?
Professional Group
American Society of Interior Design
730 Fifth Avenue
New York, NY 10019

Trade Journal
Interiors
130 East 59 Street
New York, NY 10022

PHOTOGRAPHER

*Takes pictures as an artistic or technical
occupation, such as portrait photography,
commercial photography, and photojournalism.*

What's It Like to Be a Photographer?

Just as a writer uses words, a photographer uses a camera to portray people, places, and events. Some photographers specialize in scientific, medical, or engineering photography, and their pictures enable thousands of people to see a world normally hidden from view. Others specialize in photojournalism, in portrait or commercial photography, or work in industry. Photojournalism combines photographic ability with newspaper work. Most photographers own several cameras of various kinds depending on their speciality. Rosanna Nelson has been in a portrait business in partnership with her husband, John, for 30 years in a small city. They have two galleries in neighboring suburbs and are successful because they have put in long hours and always have been careful in their work. Nelson wants young people to know that "if you're going into the photography business, you will need to know about business management and how to use the camera. Photography has come of age in the last fifteen years, with technology and materials enabling people to do more creative work. With the tools available, there's no limitation on creativity."

What Education and Skills Will I Need?

Professional training: Education required varies from on-the-job learning to courses leading to a degree in photography. The future belongs to the photographer whose training and experience enable her to do more than other photographers can do. Preparation for a career in photography must include knowledge of the field in which photography is to be applied. Economics, geography, international affairs, and journalism are important fields for the photojournalist. A career in advertising photography requires knowledge of art and design and some background in advertising.

Personal skills: Photographers need good eyesight, artistic ability, and manual dexterity. News photographers need the ability to see the potential for a good photo in a situation and act quickly; portrait photographers need the ability to help people relax. Original ideas are necessary for success in free-lance work.

How Many Women in the Field and Where Do They Work?

Of the total 91,000 photographers, 23 percent are women. Half of all photographers are in the portrait and commercial art studio businesses. Salaried photographers work for the government, television broadcasting, newspapers, magazines, private industry, and advertising agencies. Over 40 percent of all photographers are self-employed.

$ $ $ $ $

In 1981, beginners earned from $250 to $335 a week; experienced photographers averaged $440 a week. Photographers in business for themselves and with a national reputation make much more than these figures.

What Is the Future for Women?

Portrait photography is a very competitive business. The newspaper, business and industry, law enforcement, and scientific fields are expected to need more photographers through the 1980s. The well-trained people with strong technical backgrounds will have very good opportunities.

RELATED CAREERS
commercial artist   painter
illustrator   sculptor

WHERE CAN I GET MORE INFORMATION?
Professional Group
Professional Photographers of America, Inc.
1090 Executive Way
Des Plaines, IL 60018

Trade Journal
Popular Photography
Davis Publishing
1 Park Avenue
New York, NY 10016

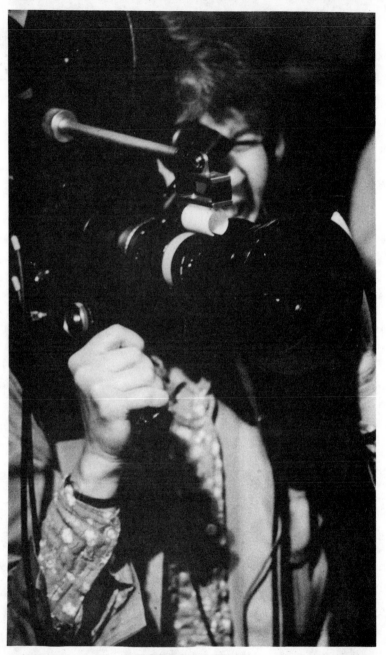

PHOTOGRAPHER

BUSINESS: ADMINISTRATION AND MANAGEMENT

Administrative Secretary
Business Executive
Funeral Director and Embalmer
Hotel, Motel, Restaurant Manager
Personnel and Labor Relations
Purchasing Agent
Retail Buyer

About these careers   There are 9.4 million managers and administrators in business and business-related jobs. Your chances for getting into a business-management training program in a major corporation are competitive, even with a college degree. A Master of Business Administration (MBA) is your best bet for the top management programs. People in business come from all college majors and backgrounds. Many are from liberal arts programs, with majors in economics, accounting, statistics, and law.

In spite of the women's movement, there are almost no women in top business management. For young women trying to get ahead, "Learn the business from top to bottom, establish a 'winner' reputation, and plan to spend long hours at work. Be prepared to spend 25 years getting to the top," warns the Chief Operating Officer of the Equity Life Assurance Society.

Owners and managers of small businesses, such as restaurants, lodgings, and funeral homes, usually work very long hours. They can be on call 24 hours a day 7 days a week because these are service businesses. Almost one out of five managers are self-employed. However, the number of self-employed managers is declining, and this trend is expected to continue through the 1980s.

The major department stores have formal training programs in merchandising for their management trainees. These programs usually last from 6 to 8 months and combine classroom instruction with store operations and policies to provide the fundamentals of merchandising and management. To be promoted to merchandise manager, most assistant buyers need 5 years of experience and exceptional ability. Many managers advance further into executive jobs in large retail stores or chains. Retail managers often work more than 40 hours a week because of sales conferences and travel.

Graduate study in industrial relations, economics, business, or law provides sound preparation for work and advancement in labor relations. Corporations are just beginning to get into the graduate education business. The 1980s will see more and more corporate educational institutes where you can learn the specific business management, engineering, selling, and investment skills you need for changing careers and advancement. You can get a master's degree at Arthur D. Little's graduate Management Education Institute in Cambridge, Massachusetts, or a master's degree in a computer specialty at the Wang Institute. Wang offers one of the few software engineering degrees in the world. Merrill Lynch, Pierce, Fenner & Smith has opened its own college for stockbrokers. McDonald's Hamburger University teaches management, personnel, finance, and taxation. Both IBM and the American Telephone and Telegraph Company spend millions of dollars to educate their full-time employees in skills needed on the job as well as in management skills for advancement. When you are planning advancement through education, be sure to check the company you work for, or want to work for, first. Women can take a lesson from men, who have traditionally expected the company they work for to train them at corporate expense.

ADMINISTRATIVE SECRETARY

*Processes and transmits information to the staff
and to people in other organizations; attends to
business activities, depending on the nature of
the employer's business.*

What's It Like to Be an Administrative Secretary?

The computer revolution is changing the role of administrative secretary. The secretarial days of Dolly Parton in the movie *9 to 5*, when an executive secretary assumed many of the responsibilities and duties of a vice president but was paid only a secretarial salary with no chance for advancement, are numbered. Word processors, or computers with typewriter-like keyboards, are taking over the routine reports and other clerical chores of the secretary. Their use has just begun and is rapidly growing. At least one million word processors have been installed in small and large offices, and another million and a half will be installed by 1985. Instead of spending 20 percent of her day typing, the typical administrative secretary will spend only 10 percent in the years ahead. Word processors are expected to give secretaries more time and opportunity to perform administrative tasks now completed by managers. When this happens, some experts believe today's serious shortage of secretaries may subside and the gap in wages between executive and secretary may narrow. But the leaders of Working Woman, an organization of 12,000 office workers dedicated to improving the lives of secretaries, are not so sure. Their organization negotiates with companies for the opportunity to enter the corporation under two different categories: career secretary or professional secretary. The purpose is to make sure that women will be considered for advancement more directly in line with their career goals, rather than to let bosses get away with their traditional point of view, "Once a secretary, always a secretary." Women who want to use the secretarial entry level as a springboard to learn a business will find the word processor an advantage. Bernard Schwartz, Director of Communication of the International Information/Processing Association says, "Word processing is a good field for career-minded women. Many of our 14,000 members started out as secretaries. Today, some of them are earning as much as $50,000 a year because word processing was a career path to management. In the 1980s, more secretaries will have such opportunities."

What Education and Skills Will I Need?

High school: Preparation for business college, secretarial school, community college, or college.

College: Take one or two years of specialized training in the secretarial field of your choice, or take secretarial courses along with another major in a college or correspondence school. Computer science and word processing are a must for the better jobs leading to management.

Personal skills: Secretaries must have an interest in accuracy, detail, organization, and an ability to follow through on assigned work.

How Many Women in the Field and Where Do They Work?

There are 2.7 million people in occupations requiring secretarial or stenographic skills and 98 percent of them are women. Half of all secretaries work in public service organizations, such as schools and hospitals. The other half work in banks, insurance companies, real estate firms, and business and industrial companies.

$ $ $ $ $

In 1981, graduates of the Katharine Gibbs School started at $10,400 to $15,600 a year. Women with a second language and some word-processing training start at the highest salaries. The field of publishing, however, is so swamped with bright liberal arts graduates from the most prominent colleges that they begin at much less—from $8,000 to $11,000 a year as editorial assistant/secretary in New York's major publishing houses. Secretarial salaries vary with the location and the job. For example, in 1980, secretaries in the Northeast averaged $13,364 a year; in the North Central, $14,066; in the West, $14,586; and in the South, $12,818. A general secretary averaged $11,856 a year; a bilingual secretary, $12,844; a legal secretary, $13,572; and an administrative or executive secretary ranged from $13,416 to working for the top executive of a company at $19,812.

What Is the Future for Women?

The demand for qualified secretaries is expected to increase through the 1980s. Secretarial schools graduate only two-thirds of the secretaries needed to fill 305,000 openings each year. The rise in paperwork, especially in finance, real estate, and health, creates a demand for more secretaries just as fewer women are going into the field.

RELATED CAREERS
bookkeeper
office manager
administrative assistant

WHERE CAN I GET MORE INFORMATION?
Professional Groups
National Secretaries Association
2440 Pershing Road, Suite G–10
Kansas City, MO 64108

9 to 5
YWCA
140 Clarendon Street
Boston, MA 02116

Working Woman
National Association of Office Workers
1224 Huron Street
Cleveland, OH 44115

Trade Journals
Working Woman (newsletter)
National Association of Office Workers
1224 Huron Street
Cleveland, OH 44115

Word Processing Report
Geyer-McAllister Publishers
51 Madison Avenue
New York, NY 10010

SECRETARY

BUSINESS EXECUTIVE

*Directs or plans the work of others in order to
run a business at a profit.*

What's It Like to Be a Business Executive?

Virginia Dwyer is the first woman to be appointed Vice-president and Treasurer of the American Telephone and Telegraph Company, the world's largest corporation and the largest private employer in the United States. She is one of the very few women in the world in top management. That she is smart, ambitious, and loves her work was the first basic necessity for her promotions. It is interesting to learn that Dwyer was not sure of her future until she was in her late 30s. She was taking a master's degree and couldn't decide whether to go into the academic world or to stay in business. When she was 39, she moved up to department chief at Western Electric; at 44 she was promoted to assistant manager of economics; at 47 she became a corporate economist. When she was 50, Dwyer was named chief economist and director of accounting research, her last position at Western Electric until she moved to AT&T, where she started as pension-fund manager and administrator of company assets. Within eight years she was promoted to her present top management position.

Dwyer's strengths are her beliefs that a top manager must allow people to accomplish results and that delegation of responsibility is an absolute necessity. She says that she is a candid person and that she "tries to build good personal relationships with people because I think the most effective way to accomplish tasks in the business world is through development of communications techniques. It's essential in management."

What Education and Skills Will I Need?

High school: Preparation for college in whatever major that interests you, taking as broad a program as you can do well. Participate in extracurricular activities that teach such management qualities as leadership, assertiveness, and sensitivity to others. Athletics are especially important for learning teamwork and competitive skills that are absolutely necessary in management.

College: Most executive training programs recruit liberal arts students. Ability to think and make decisions, computer skills, and an interest in a particular training program are special qualities the corporations are looking for. A Master of Business Administration (MBA) is an ideal education for management.

Personal skills: Directors of training programs hiring college graduates as potential managers for their corporations look for "self-starters" who are able to use their initiative, who have an observing eye to see what needs to be done, who can work well with others, who like responsibility, and who have high standards of fairness. They must have thoroughness, not necessarily brilliance, and persistence to be good in their job. "My best quality as Store Chief of Fifth Avenue's Henri Bendel," says Geraldine Stutz, "is being a finder and nourisher of talent. I help people perform more bravely than they think they can."

How Many Women in the Field and Where Do They Work?

About 10 million salaried persons manage the nation's business enterprises. For all the talk about women in top management, female students should realize that women hold fewer than 1 percent of the top management posts, and as little as 6.4 percent of all middle-management positions in the country. Women now make up 25 percent of all business school graduates.

$ $ $ $ $

In 1980, college graduates entering management trainee programs received $15,000 to $21,000 a year. Middle management salaries range from $25,000 to $50,000 in major corporations. Women are not paid equal salaries in most management jobs. Carol McLaughlin, a graduate of Wharton, found that after $7\frac{1}{2}$ years out of Wharton, men averaged $23,000 a year while women averaged $17,000. Just as bad, men averaged a staff of 30 people reporting to them while women averaged two or three. Salaries tell a lot about where the women are. In 1981, 4,173,000 men earned over $25,000 in business and industry, while only 140,000 women earned that much—less than 3 percent of all women who work outside the home. When you think about middle- and top-management salaries, be aware that salaries are fast becoming only a small part of what is known as the "executive compensation package," or perks. For example, a salary of $50,000 a year usually is accompanied by an additional $20,000 in rewards. And the executive with a salary of $200,000 a year may earn as much as $100,000 more a year in bonuses, long-term incentives, fringe benefits, and perks. Also important for women to know is that a designer of executive compensation packages for more than 25 major corporations noted that *not one* of the corporations had a woman high enough on the executive ladder to qualify for special treatment. He says the main reason that women are not in on the perks is because most women executives run "nonprofit centers" such as personnel or public relations, rather than managing profit centers such as factories or sales divisions. If you want to be in on the money, remember that the money is where the men are—in the "profit centers" of management.

What Is the Future for Women?

Business manager is one of the fastest growing occupations in the country. From 1960 to the late 1970s, the number of business managers increased four times as fast as all other workers. The best opportunities for women are in those big corporations where women hold management positions and where women are trained in executive training programs. According to *Savvy*, these corporations are: American Express, Atlantic Richfield, AT&T, Chemical New York, Connecticut General, Continental Illinois, Control Data, Digital Equipment, Equitable Life Assurance Society of the United States, General Mills, Hewlett-Packard, Honeywell, IBM, Johnson & Johnson, Quaker Oats, and Security Pacific. These companies give maternity leaves and promises of career advancement for women. But big business is not for the woman who intends to stop working outside the home for 5 or 6 years to raise children; it is for those who want to work full-time, regardless of their family situation. Women who are interested in managing their own business but are raising a family often begin a business at home. As their business and family grow, they can be more flexible and can control their particular lifestyle.

RELATED CAREERS
      hospital administrator   sales manager
      hotel-restaurant manager   marketing manager

WHERE CAN I GET MORE INFORMATION?

Professional Groups

The American Management Association
135 West 50 Street
New York, NY 10020

Women Entrepreneurs
3061 Fillmore Street
San Francisco, CA 94123

Trade Journals

Business Management
22 West Putnam Avenue
Greenwich, CT 06830

Fortune
Time-Life Building
New York, NY 10020

MBA
MBA Enterprises
373 Fifth Avenue
New York, NY 10016

FUNERAL DIRECTOR AND EMBALMER

A funeral director helps families with business arrangements necessary for the funeral service and burial; an embalmer prepares the deceased for viewing and burial.

What's It Like to Be a Funeral Director and Embalmer?

Judy Rizzo, licensed embalmer in her family's undertaking business, says that "a funeral director arranges for the deceased to be removed to the funeral home, obtains the information needed for the death certificate, and discusses the details of the funeral with the deceased's family. An embalmer replaces the deceased's blood with a preservative fluid, then applies cosmetics to the body to give it a natural appearance, dresses the body, and places it in the casket selected by the family. Embalming is a sanitary and preservative measure required by law."

The funeral director arranges the time and place of the funeral service, the clergy and organist, selection of the casket and clothing, and provision of burial or cremation. She also makes arrangements with the cemetery and places obituary notices in the newspapers. The director attends to the floral displays, provides cars for the family and pallbearers, receives ushers, and sees guests to their seats. Also she may serve a family for months following the funeral until all Social Security and insurance claims are settled. Helen Scruggs, a funeral director from Roxbury, Massachusetts, says, "Few occupations require the tact, discretion, and compassion called for in the work of a funeral director. Families of the deceased are under considerable emotional stress and are often bewildered by the many details of the occasion. Funeral directors must be sympathetic, but they also must know the veteran's laws, Social Security laws, and how to deal with people who have no money. The big disadvantage in a small business is that you are on call 24 hours a day. But what I like best about my work," says Mrs. Scruggs, "is that it's a challenge to help people when they're at their lowest ebb in life."

What Education and Skills Will I Need?

High school: Preparation for school of mortuary science, with high school courses in biology, chemistry, speech, and psychology. Work in a part-time or summer job in a local funeral home while in high school.

College: Half of the states require one year of college before the one-year training in mortuary science offered at 35 accredited mortuary schools. For the list of accredited schools, write to: American Board of Funeral Service Education, 201 Columbia Avenue, Fairmont, West Virginia 26554. A license is needed to practice embalming, and an apprenticeship of one or two years must be served; an examination is required by each state.

Personal skills: Composure, tact, ability to communicate easily with the public, and a desire to comfort people in sorrow are needed for success as a funeral director.

How Many Women in the Field and Where Do They Work?

Of the 45,000 persons licensed as funeral directors and embalmers, 2 percent are women. Most funeral workers are employed in small family-owned businesses with 2 or 3 workers. Karen Martin, 21, is a funeral director in New Hartford, New York. After graduating and passing her licensing exam, she interviewed about 100 funeral homes around New York in search of a full-time job. She is now on call at one home and director of another. Martin has always wanted to be a funeral director, and even though her friends thought she was "crazy," she persisted and now loves her work.

$ $ $ $ $

After one year of training, apprentices started from $150 to $250 a week in 1980. Directors and embalmers earned from $15,000 to $30,000 a year, and owners of the business earned more than $50,000.

What Is the Future for Women?

The number of mortuary school graduates has about equaled the number of jobs available. Traditionally, women have not gone into the funeral business unless their father or husband was already in it. Every community in the United States is served by a funeral business. If you have the personal skills for the work, you should seriously consider this career that pays very well for only two years of education.

RELATED CAREERS
small business manager
family business owner
minister

WHERE CAN I GET MORE INFORMATION?
Professional Group
National Funeral Directors Association, Inc.
135 West Wells Street
Milwaukee, WI 53203

Trade Journal
The Director
135 West Wells Street
Milwaukee, WI 53203

HOTEL, MOTEL, CLUB, OR RESTAURANT MANAGER

Manages food and lodging establishments and satisfies guests for a profitable business.

What's It Like to Be in a Food-Lodging Career?

Hotel managers decide about room rates and credit policy, direct the kitchen and dining rooms, and manage the housekeeping, accounting, and maintenance departments of hotels. They are also responsible for any problems that guests or hotel staff may have. The job depends on the size of the hotel. Large hotels and chains offer more specialization. A manager of a small hotel or a self-employed hotel owner often does all of the jobs, including front-desk clerical work, advertising, and personnel.

Many opportunities for experienced managers can be found in club and restaurant management. For instance, a country club in Wichita, Kansas, pays their manager $50,000 a year plus a car and other benefits. Cooking has always been a very acceptable female business, and many women have owned and run their own diners and restaurants. When Cindy Ayres of Philadelphia was divorced, she looked for work in the area she loved best—cooking. Starting at $60 a week, she was up to $225 in two years, with experience in restaurant cooking, menu planning, and ordering. She followed her dream and opened her own restaurant, after borrowing money from friends and the Small Business Administration for the initial investment. Now working 16 to 20 hours a day, Ayres is just where she wants to be—owner and chef of, "the best new inexpensive restaurant in town."

What Education and Skills Will I Need?

High School: Preparation for college or business college. Summer work in resorts, hotels, and restaurants will help you gain experience and find out what the job is like.

College: Major in hotel administration, or go to a community college or take a correspondence course for hotel-motel management. Training programs for the large hotels look for graduates of hotel and restaurant administration. Small hotels and owner-manager lodges and restaurants do not require a degree, but they do require interest, motivation, an original idea, and capital.

Personal skills: Initiative, self-discipline, and the ability to organize and concentrate on detail are needed in food-lodging careers.

How Many Women in the Field and Where Do They Work?

There are 84,000 hotel and motel managers, and more than 40,000 of them are owner-managers. In addition, there are 707,000 restaurant and bar managers, and 40 percent of them are women.

$ $ $ $ $

A beginning graduate from a hotel school starts in the training program of a large hotel at $13,500 a year. In 1981, hotel general managers ranged from $20,000 to $80,000 a year. Hotel food and beverage managers earned from $16,000 to $40,000 a year.

What Is the Future for Women?

Job opportunities for the college graduate who has specialized in hotel administration will be very good through the 1980s. Small lodges and restaurants in cities and resort areas are often started by young people. Even though a competitive field, many original ideas have made a living and a satisfying lifestyle for the owners.

RELATED CAREERS
apartment manager
office manager
sales manager

WHERE CAN I GET MORE INFORMATION?
Professional Groups
The American Hotel and Motel Association
888 Seventh Avenue
New York, NY 10019

Club Managers Association of America
7615 Winterberry Place
P.O. Box 34482
Washington, D.C. 20034

Council on Hotel, Restaurant, and Institutional Education
Human Development Building, Room 118
University Park, PA 16802

Trade Journals
Hotel and Motel Management
Sun-Times Building, Room 534
401 North Wabash Avenue
Chicago, IL 60611

Nation's Restaurant News
2 Park Avenue
New York, NY 10016

PERSONNEL AND LABOR RELATIONS

*Personnel workers try to hire and keep the best
employees available for the success of a business
or for government. Labor relations workers
handle union-management relations in
unionized firms.*

What's It Like to Be in Personnel and Labor Relations?

"I interview and test people, match them to jobs, and follow up on people after they are in their jobs. I try to help the employee be as satisfied as possible with our company. It is a fascinating job if you like working with adults, with the varied interests of workers and management, and enjoy being a 'middle person,'" says Janet Woodruff, personnel counselor with a telephone company. She adds, "I help to develop new recruiting and hiring procedures, new methods for selecting the qualified applicant, and new methods of evaluation after the person is on the job. The increase in midlife career changes and the number of older workers who don't want to retire as early as before make personnel a fascinating career." Other personnel people counsel employees, formulate personnel policy, advise their company on personnel matters, classify jobs, plan wage and salary scales, and conduct research in personnel methods. One of the few blacks in business administration, married with a young son, Gail Royston Joyce went into personnel and is now Director of Personnel at the Hyatt Regency Hotel in San Francisco.

Labor relations workers advise management on collective bargaining sessions, participate in contract negotiations with the union, and handle labor relations matters that occur every day.

What Education and Skills Will I Need?

High school: Preparation for college, with emphasis in English and social studies.

College: Personnel people come from a great variety of college majors. Some have been in business administration, psychology, sociology, or education. Most companies look for college graduates with the personal characteristics they think would be good for the company.

Personal skills: Ability to speak and write effectively, work as a member of a team, see opposing viewpoints, and work with people of all different levels of education are necessary skills in personnel and labor relations.

How Many Women in the Field and Where Do They Work?

There are 178,000 people in personnel and labor relations careers, and about 49 percent of the personnel workers are women. Two-thirds of personnel and labor relations people work for private industry and the others work for government agencies.

$ $ $ $ $

In 1980, beginners started for private industry from $14,800 to $21,900 a year. Companies employing 500 employees paid personnel directors from $27,719 to $49,730 a year.

What Is the Future for Women?

Employment opportunities will be best with the federal government and specialized fields in personnel, such as psychological testing and labor relations. Opportunities for liberal arts graduates to start in personnel jobs are very limited and competitive. Most companies advance someone within their company to personnel jobs. A woman who goes to the city to find work in personnel for an advertising agency, television, or other big company will find the competition very stiff. The best chances for the competive labor relations jobs will be for graduates with a master's degree in industrial relations or economics or with a law degree.

RELATED CAREERS
employment counselor
career counselor
psychologist

WHERE CAN I GET MORE INFORMATION?
Professional Group
American Society for Personnel Administration
30 Park Drive
Berea, OH 44017

Trade Journal
The Personnel Administrator
19 Church Street
Berea, OH 44017

PURCHASING AGENT
*Negotiates and contracts to purchase equipment,
supplies, and other merchandise for a firm.*

What's It Like to Be a Purchasing Agent?

A purchasing agent, sometimes called an industrial buyer, is responsible for getting the best dollar value for supplies she has to buy for her firm. She buys raw materials, office supplies, furniture, and business machines. A purchasing agent checks on deliveries to be sure the work flow of the firm isn't interrupted because of lack of materials. She works with other departments within the company, such as engineering and shipping, in order to coordinate the supplies with who needs them. Cheryl Arnold, purchasing agent for a machine manufacturing firm, says that developing a good business relationship with her suppliers is crucial for cost savings, favorable payment terms, and quick delivery on emergency orders. She builds her supplier market by comparing listings in catalogues, trade journals, and from telephone suppliers. Arnold meets with salespeople to look at their samples and attends demonstrations of equipment. Often, she invites suppliers to bid on large orders and then selects the lowest bidder who can meet her firm's requirements for quality and delivery date. Seven years on the job, Arnold sees purchasing with market forecasting and production planning as a step to a management job in manufacturing.

What Education and Skills Will I Need?

High school: Preparation for college. Large firms hire college graduates for their training programs.

College: Many purchasing agents come from backgrounds in engineering, accounting, and economics. Understanding the computer and its uses is a necessity in a purchasing job.

Personal skills: Skill in analyzing numbers and technical data, ability to work and get along with others, and memory for detail are all necessary skills for a purchasing agent.

How Many Women in the Field and Where Do They Work?

There are 172,000 purchasing agents and over half work in manufacturing firms. Others work for government agencies, hospitals, and schools.

$ $ $ $ $

In 1980, purchasing agents started at $12,000 to $14,000 a year. Experienced agents earned $25,000 a year, and managers made over $50,000 a year.

What Is the Future for Women?

Job opportunities are good, especially for the technically trained college graduates in electronics, communications, and industrial machinery. Two-year graduates have good opportunities in small firms.

RELATED CAREERS
   retail buyer
   procurement services manager
   wholesaler

WHERE CAN I GET MORE INFORMATION?
   Professional Group
   National Association of Purchasing Management, Inc.
   11 Park Place
   New York, NY 10007

   Trade Journal
   Purchasing
   C–M Business Publications
   205 East 42 Street
   New York, NY 10017

RETAIL BUYER

*Purchases merchandise for her firm to resell
at a profit.*

What's It Like to Be a Retail Buyer?

Buyers must be able to assess the resale value of goods after a brief inspection and make a purchase decision quickly. They must be familiar with the manufacturers and distributors who handle the merchandise they need. They also must keep informed about changes in existing products and the development of new ones. To learn about merchandise, buyers attend fashion and trade shows and visit manufacturers' showrooms. They are aware of their stores' profit margins and try to select merchandise that will sell quickly at well above the original cost.

Helen Galland, President of Fifth Avenue's Bonwit Teller, is one of only seven women to be head of a retail organization. (The others are Geraldine Stutz of Henri Bendel; Martha Phillips, founder of Martha's; Hilda Kirschbaum of Petrie; Hanne Merriman of Garfinckel; Pamela Grant of Goldwater's; and Barbara Armajani, Chief Operating Officer of Powers Dry Goods.) Galland started her executive climb as an assistant buyer of millinery thirty years ago. After fourteen years in millinery, she became a merchandise manager for accessories; six years later, a vice president; and five years after a move to another company, she returned to Bonwit's as president. She works hard, always finishing the day's work even if it takes until 2:00 A.M. and starting fresh the next day. From the very first taste of retailing at New York University's School of Retailing while working full-time at Lord and Taylor, Ms. Galland, a family woman, says, "I was excited about retailing. It's creative; you can see the results of your efforts almost immediately. It's never dull and there are many crises."

What Education and Skills Will I Need?

High school: Preparation for business school, art school, merchandising program, or liberal arts degree.

College: Take a two-year or four-year course that includes business, computer science, marketing, fashion, merchandising, and art. Prepare for a department store training program for buyers, such as the prestigious Bloomingdale's program.

Personal skills: Buyers must be able to work fast, be good planners, and be able to communicate with salespeople, buyers, and sellers all at the same time.

How Many Women in the Field and Where Do They Work?

There are 150,000 buyers and merchandising managers. Half of them work for clothing and general department stores in major cities, and 43 percent of them are women.

RETAIL BUYER

$ $ $ $ $

In 1980, most buyers earned between $19,000 and $28,000 a year.

What Is the Future for Women?

Jobs will be competitive through the 1980s, since it's a glamorous field and many college graduates go after it. Assertive, fast-working people who like to hustle are the ones getting these jobs.

RELATED CAREERS
comparison shopper
merchandise manager
manufacturer's sales representative
wholesale trade sales representative

WHERE CAN I GET MORE INFORMATION?
Professional Group
National Retail Merchants Association
100 West 31 Street
New York, NY 10001

Trade Journals
Marketing Times
380 Lexington Avenue
New York, NY 10017

Women's Wear Daily
7 East 12 Street
New York, NY 10003

BUSINESS: ADVERTISING AND MARKETING

Advertising
Market Researcher
Public Relations

About these careers There are 286,000 jobs, or about one-quarter of a million, in advertising, public relations (PR), and marketing. Many employers prefer college graduates who have liberal arts training in journalism or in business. However, there is no correlation between a particular educational background and success in advertising.

Advancement is very competitive in these jobs, especially for women, who traditionally have not held top management positions. Advertising is a glamorous and popular career, with many highly qualified young people seeking jobs in the field. Copywriters and account executives may advance to more responsible work in their specialities, or to managerial jobs. Some exceptional ad and public relations people become partners in an agency or establish their own agency.

People in advertising work under great pressure. They are expected to produce quality ads in as short a time as possible. Sometimes they must work long and irregular hours in order to make last-minute changes and meet deadlines. Advertising can be a satisfying career for women who enjoy variety, excitement, creative challenges, and competition. Unlike people in many other careers, advertising workers experience the satisfaction of having their work in print, on television, or on radio, even though they themselves remain unknown to the public.

As assistants and junior analysts in market research gain experience, they may assume responsibility for specific marketing-research projects, or advance to supervisory positions. Outstanding workers become market-research directors or vice-presidents in marketing and sales. Market-research people usually work in modern, centrally located offices. Some public relations and market researchers do a considerable amount of traveling, especially those employed by independent firms.

ADVERTISING
*Persuades people to buy a firm's products
or use a firm's services.*

What's It Like to Be in Advertising?

Madison Avenue advertising in New York City is one of the most glamorous careers in the country. It is a creative and imaginative job where the salaries can be the highest. The commodity is the person's talent and the person must produce the copy, thought, and business that will maintain the client's product. The career of advertising includes a number of different positions: advertising managers, who are responsible for planning budget and overall supervision; creative workers, such as writers, artists, and designers, who develop and produce advertisements; people with business and sales ability, who handle the arrangements for broadcasting the ads on radio and television, publishing them in newspapers or magazines, or mailing them directly.

What Education and Skills Will I Need?

High school: College preparatory program, with as much work in language as possible. Writing and skills with the written word must be learned exceptionally well. Working on school publications, learning to be a good observer, noticing how people respond, and selling are experiences that will be helpful in advertising.

College: Most advertising agencies prefer a liberal arts student with a major in advertising, marketing, journalism, or business. Community college, business college, and art programs can get you started in advertising. The most common way into advertising without a degree is to go through a department store advertising program.

Personal skills: Imagination, creativity, and a flair for language and selling are required for success in advertising.

How Many Women in the Field and Where Do They Work?

Almost half of the 170,000 people in advertising are in New York and Chicago, and about 100,000 of them are employed by advertising agencies. There are few women who become officers in an advertising agency, although some account executives and many copywriters are women. Most women are employed in fashion department stores and in the independent agencies of smaller cities. An exception is Lyn Salzberg, one of the few women in a top management advertising job. A senior vice-president, Salzberg has worked her way up in Dancer Fitzgerald Sample, a major New York City advertising agency she started with 26 years ago. Salzberg loves her work. She loves the challenge of being a woman who has "made it," and she thinks it's worth the constant planning, attention to detail, and long hours it took to get there.

$ $ $ $ $

In 1980, beginners started from $10,000 to $18,000 a year, although those with an MBA often started at $25,000. The top beginning salaries are paid to outstanding MBA graduates, almost always men. Salaries vary with the size of the advertising agency. Advertising executives in a large New York agency often make $40,000 and a few make much more.

What Is the Future for Women?

Competition in advertising is very stiff for everybody and will remain so through the 1980s. A male vice-president of a New York firm says that "women get the work and responsibilities in advertising but seldom get the promotions, titles, and salaries that go with the work." There are few part-time opportunities for women in advertising. People who work in this field find that it leaves little time for children and family responsibilities. Successful women in advertising are those who have the time and freedom from home responsibilities to work irregular hours and withstand the pressure of the job.

RELATED CAREERS
    public relations   lobbyist
    fundraiser   promotion manager

ADVERTISING

WHERE CAN I GET MORE INFORMATION?
Professional Groups
Advertising Women of New York
153 East 57 Street
New York, NY 10022

American Association of Advertising Agencies
666 Third Avenue
New York, NY 10017

Trade Journal
Advertising Age
J. J. Graham
740 North Rush Street
Chicago, IL 60611

MARKET RESEARCHER

*Plans, implements, and analyzes surveys to learn
more about people's wants and needs.*

What's It Like to Be a Market Researcher?

"Finding out how much money people spend on what products and which services is a fascinating career for anyone interested in why people do things," says Clara White about her first year in market research for a firm in Los Angeles. She takes public opinion surveys, then studies and analyzes the sales of the company and competitive companies. White looks at population changes, people's income levels, and consumer credit policies, which she reports to the Board of her company. This kind of information is used to help management decide on brand names, choose the package and design for their products, choose new locations for the company, and decide on types of advertising needed by the company.

What Education and Skills Will I Need?

High school: Preparation for college, with emphasis on English and mathematics.

College: Business college, community college, or four-year college. Researchers come from business administration, economics, sociology, psychology, and liberal arts programs, with a variety of majors.

Personal skills: Market researchers should be resourceful in analyzing data, assertive, and able to write clearly.

How Many Women in the Field and Where Do They Work?

There are 29,000 market researchers. In most cases, men hold the top professional levels, while women are at the junior professional levels. In addition, there are thousands of part-time workers, mostly women, who take surveys and interview consumers wherever they live. The majority of market researchers are employed by manufacturing companies, advertising agencies, and market research firms in New York and Chicago.

$ $ $ $ $

In 1980, college graduates started from $12,000 to $17,000 a year. Experienced market researchers such as senior analysts made over $27,000 a year. Directors who had more than 15 years' experience averaged $50,000 a year.

What Is the Future for Women?

The best job opportunities will go to persons with skills in statistics and computer science. Chances for work will be good through the 1980s. New job opportunities are expected in health care facilities, banks, and accounting firms.

RELATED CAREERS
economist   urban planner
political scientist   social welfare research worker

WHERE CAN I GET MORE INFORMATION?
Professional Group
American Marketing Association
250 Wacker Street
Chicago, IL 60606

Trade Journal
Marketing News
222 South Riverside Plaza
Chicago, IL 60606

PUBLIC RELATIONS
*Develops and distributes persuasive
materials in order to create a favorable
public reputation.*

What's It Like to Be in Public Relations?

Public relations people plan publicity that they think will be most effective for a company or product, communicate with the people who would use the publicity, write press releases for newspapers and magazines, and write brochures and pamphlets about the company or product. They arrange special speaking engagements for company officials and often write speeches. They work with films, slides, video, and all types of audio-visual equipment. Their work is often under tension and pressure of deadlines and last-minute newspaper releases. Public relations workers must be knowledgeable about all media and decide what is the most effective way to communicate their ideas. They must be imaginative, able to promote their own ideas, and able to sell these ideas to other people. Public relations executive Jacqueline Ceballos is an active feminist in New York City, the mother of four children, and founder of her own PR firm, Ceballos and Philipes. Ceballos finds that the difficulties in the PR business are "dealing with corporate clients who often do not fully understand or agree with your plans; having to change your concept to please them; working on projects that bring in good money but do not stimulate you one bit; wasting valuable time with people who don't have the money for public relations or know they will not use your firm but are getting ideas from you; and trying to run the business end of the company while also handling the accounts and disagreements with a partner. Like a marriage, partnership has its difficult moments. But the ever-challenging work offsets the difficulties. The variety; the excitement of introducing programs, products, and people to the world; the creative work involved in planning programs; the fulfillment felt in helping to expand horizons for women—these are what public relations is all about."

Nini Finkelstein, the publicity coordinator for Ringling Bros. Barnum & Bailey Circus, urges women to find a PR area that fascinates them. "It's impossible to do this kind of work if it's not something you'll enjoy. When the circus is at Madison Square Garden in New York, I'm there for ten weeks, often on my feet 14 hours a day. If I didn't like it, my feet would hurt!" cautions Finkelstein.

What Education and Skills Will I Need?

High school: Preparation for junior college or four-year college.

College: Major in English, journalism, or a field that interests you and that you want to relate to public relations. Public relations people come from a wide variety of college majors, including liberal arts and the applied arts. Writing skills are mandatory.

Personal skills: Self-confidence, outgoing personality, assertiveness, understanding of human behavior, enthusiasm, and imagination are important for success.

How Many Women in the Field and Where Do They Work?

Over one-fourth of the 87,000 public relations workers are women. Women are employed mostly by department stores, hospitals, hotels, and restaurants. Half of all public relations people work in New York, Los Angeles, Chicago, and Washington.

$ $ $ $ $

In 1980, college graduates began in public relations from $10,000 to $13,000 a year. In 1981, the average salary for top experience was $38,000 a year.

What Is the Future for Women?

PR jobs are very competitive because thousands of college graduates that go to the city look for jobs with glamor, like PR. Chances will be best for enthusiastic people with good academic records and some media experience.

RELATED CAREERS

advertising careers   fundraiser
lobbyist   account executive

WHERE CAN I GET MORE INFORMATION?

Professional Group
The Information Center
Public Relations Society of America, Inc.
845 Third Avenue
New York, NY 10022

Trade Journals
PR Quarterly
305 East 45 Street
New York, NY 10017

Jack O'Dwyer's Newsletter
271 Madison Avenue
New York, NY 10016

BUSINESS: COMPUTER OPERATIONS

Computer Programmer
Systems Analyst

About these careers   Computer careers are expected to
be the most rapidly growing occupational group in our economy
through the 1980s. The world is on the verge of a computer revolution
—a revolution as inevitable and sweeping in its effects as the
industrial revolution. At its heart is an extraordinary development of
modern technology: the microprocessor, the ultracheap, amazingly
small computer that processes huge amounts of information in a
fraction of a second. Christopher Evans, a renowned computer
scientist, writes in his book, The MicroMillennium, "The computer
revolution will have an overwhelming and comprehensive impact,
affecting every human being on earth in every aspect of his or her
life. It will run at a gallop in the next twenty-five years. Once the
revolution is under way, it will be unstoppable."

Employment in computer careers is conservatively expected to
rise 85 percent in this decade. Most college graduates will be in the
following jobs: systems analyst and programmer, sales, operations,
and management.

Most of the growth in the computer industry will result from
advances in computer capabilities. There are three major areas of
new technologies: hardware—the machinery that is getting smaller,
cheaper, and faster; software—the programs or instructions that tell
the hardware what to do, and the language the instructions are
written in; and applications—the kinds of work computers can
perform.

Employment is clustered around major cities. The education and
training of computer personnel will continue to be inadequate for the
demand. The shortage of computer personnel is expected to continue
through the 1980s, resulting in higher wages, more job mobility,
increased job security, and generally greater opportunities for these
workers.

On the following page is a list of professional computer job
descriptions to give you an idea of what the college-level jobs are.

COMPUTER CAREERS

1. **Corporate Director of Data Processing:** *The top executive for all computer processing.*
2. **Technical Assistant:** *Member of corporate director's staff; usually head of advanced planning for data processing (DP) function.*
3. **Services Coordinator/User Liaison:** *Coordinates DP activities with other functions or departments.*
4. **Manager of Systems Analysis:** *Analyzes how DP can be applied to user problems; designs effective and efficient DP solutions.*
5. **Lead Systems Analyst:** *Helps plan, organize, and control the activities of the systems analysis section.*
6. **Senior Systems Analyst:** *Confers with users to define DP projects, formulates problems, and designs solutions.*
7. **Systems Analyst:** *Works with users to define DP projects or project segments, or irons out details in specifications.*
8. **Systems Analyst Trainee:** *Usually has some DP experience; expected to spend time learning rather than producing.*
9. **Manager of Applications Programming:** *Responsible for the development of effective, efficient, well-documented programs.*
10. **Lead Applications Programmer:** *Helps plan, organize, and control section activities.*
11. **Senior Applications Programmer:** *Works with program designs or specifications.*
12. **Applications Programmer:** *Works on only one or a few applications.*
13. **Applications Programmer Trainee:** *Learns to program under supervision.*
14. **Programming Team Librarian:** *Keeps track of program revisions.*
15. **Manager of System Programming:** *Plans and directs the activities of the programming section; assigns personnel to projects.*
16. **Lead Systems Programmer:** *Helps plan, organize, and control the activities of the programming section.*
17. **Senior Systems Programmer:** *Specializes in support, maintenance, and use of one or more operating systems; able to work at highest levels of programming.*
18. **Systems Programmer:** *May specialize in the support of one or a few operating system components or subsystems.*
19. **Systems Programming Trainee:** *Has a good background in DP and knows or is learning assembler language.*
20. **Program Librarian:** *Responsible for maintaining the on-line and off-line libraries of production programs in source and object form.*
21. **Manager of Data Base Administration:** *Plans, organizes, and schedules activities of the data base administration section.*
22. **Data Base Administrator:** *Analyzes company's computerized information requirements; coordinates data collection with storage; organizes data.*
23. **Data Communications Telecommunications Manager:** *Responsible for design of data communications networks and installation and operation of data links.*
24. **Data Communications Analyst:** *Specializes in network design, traffic analysis, and data communications software.*

COMPUTER PROGRAMMER

*Writes detailed instructions called programs that
list in a logical order the steps the computer must
follow to solve a problem.*

What's It Like to Be a Computer Programmer?

There are two kinds of computer programmers: *systems programmer* and *applications programmer*. A systems programmer, sometimes called a software systems engineer, gives a particular computer the ability to perform certain tasks. For example, a systems programmer determines which specific computer language will be used and which functions should get priority. An applications programmer uses the language and tasks already established by the systems programmer to write programs that tell the computer exactly what to do. "An applications programmer can work quite independently and at her own pace, and can progress pretty much as fast as she is capable," says Doris Schwartz, a recent college graduate who is a full-time computer programmer with IBM. "Most days we spend an entire day writing a program for the computers, or correcting errors in a program that's already written. If we are in the process of designing a program system (preparing a series of programs, for example to keep track of production and take inventory), we may spend several hours discussing methods and details with our customers. We often run the computers ourselves, testing progress. Attending classes and lectures is important since the field is changing and growing so fast."

What Education and Skills Will I Need?

High school: Preparation for college, with as much mathematics and computer courses as possible.

College: Programmers are hired from community colleges, business colleges, two-year community colleges, and four-year colleges. Most programmers are college graduates. Major in mathematics, computer science, business, or whatever field you want to work in, such as health or engineering.

Personal skills: The work calls for patience, persistence, and the ability to be extremely accurate. Imagination and logical thinking are important for programmers who work out new solutions to problems.

How Many Women in the Field and Where Do They Work?

There are 247,000 programmers and 30 percent are women. The field is expected to grow to 500,000 by 1990. Most of the jobs are clustered around major cities. Insurance companies, banks, utilities, and manufacturing companies hire the majority of programmers.

$ $ $ $ $

In 1980, beginning salaries for applications programmers with a college degree averaged $13,520 a year, and salaries for systems programmers started at $16,380 a year. Experienced applications programmers averaged $20,800, and experienced systems programmers averaged about $23,920. Lead programmers made more.

What Is the Future for Women?

The opportunities are expected to increase 102 percent in the 1980s, as computers are used much more in medicine, education, and data processing services. Most of the increase will be in the high-level jobs, as the simple programming jobs become automatically programmed and stored in libraries. The systems and applications programmers for complex work will be in most demand.

RELATED CAREERS
systems analyst
financial analyst
actuary

WHERE CAN I GET MORE INFORMATION?
Professional Groups
Data Processing Management Association
505 Busse Highway
Park Ridge, IL 60068

Association for Women in Computing
407 Hillmore Drive
Silver Spring, MD 20901

Trade Journals
Computerworld
Box 880
Framingham, MA 01701

Software News
5 Kane Industrial Drive
Hudson, MA 01749

SYSTEMS ANALYST

*Decides how data is collected and prepared for
computers, and how it is processed, stored, and
made available to users.*

What's It Like to Be a Systems Analyst?

Sally Aarons, a mathematics major at Stanford, was accepted in a computer training program by Wang Laboratories. After some work experience in programming, she is back in training as a systems analyst.

Systems analysts are the problem solvers for the computer users. For example, the analyst begins her work by discussing with managers the job they need to perform. She learns exactly what kind of data they need to do the job, what they must do with the data, how quickly they have to process it, and how they currently are collecting and recording the data. In most companies, the systems analyst evaluates the computer equipment already owned by the company in order to determine if it can carry additional data or if new equipment is needed. Next, the analyst develops the system, that is, she decides how the data will be collected and prepared for the computers. If the company decides to adopt the proposed system, the analyst prepares specifications for computer programmers to follow. Systems analysts usually specialize in business, scientific, or engineering applications. The problems systems analysts deal with range from monitoring nuclear fission in a power plant to forecasting sales for a publisher.

What Education and Skills Will I Need?

High school: Preparation for college, with as much mathematics as possible.

College: Systems analysts come from majors in engineering, computer science, accounting, mathematics, and economics. Regardless of the major, most must know programming language. Half of the analysts come from other careers and learn the necessary skills in adult and corporate education courses.

Personal skills: Logical thinking, ability to work with abstract ideas, and ability to concentrate are all needed to be a systems analyst.

How Many Women in the Field and Where Do They Work?

There are about 205,000 systems analysts and that number is expected to grow to 400,000 by 1990. Of the total, 25 percent are women. Most of them started as computer programmers and advanced to systems analysts. They work in urban areas clustered around major cities. Some also work for banks and insurance companies.

$ $ $ $ $

In 1980, beginners earned $17,000, experienced analysts made $24,000, and lead systems analysts earned from $24,500 to $25,750.

What Is the Future for Women?

Sophisticated accounting systems, telecommunications networks, and scientific research have resulted in new approaches to problem solving. Jobs will increase 120 percent through the 1980s. Opportunities are especially good in medical, educational and data processing services.

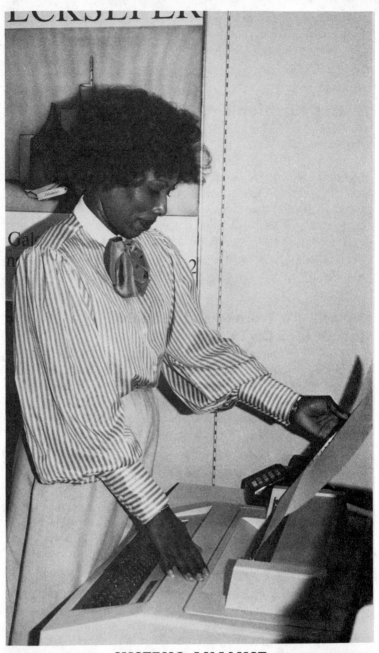

SYSTEMS ANALYST

RELATED CAREERS

financial analyst	research analyst
data base analyst	computer programmer
engineer	

WHERE CAN I GET MORE INFORMATION?

Professional Groups
American Federation of Information Processing Societies
1815 North Lynn Street
Arlington, VA 22209

Association for Women in Computing
407 Hillmore Drive
Silver Spring, MD 20901

Trade Journals
Computerworld
Box 880
Framingham, MA 01701

Software News
5 Kane Industrial Drive
Hudson, MA 01749

BUSINESS: MONEY MANAGEMENT

Accountant
Actuary
Bank Officer
Credit Manager

About these careers   There are over one and a half million jobs in these four money-management careers, most of them held by men. In general, money management requires a college education, and banking requires college and a well-organized officer-training program ranging from six months to one year. Bank trainees may start as credit or investment analysts, or they may rotate among bank departments to get the "feel" of banking.

Advancement in money management depends largely on job performance and on specialized study to pass qualifying examinations in accounting and actuary work. Courses in every phase of banking are offered by the American Institute of Banking, an industry-sponsored school.

Money managers work in well-lighted, attractive, comfortable offices. Since a great deal of bank business and credit business depends on customers' impressions, money managers are encouraged to wear conservative, somewhat formal business clothes. Almost all of them work in one place, although accountants employed by national accounting firms may travel extensively to conduct audits and perform other services for their clients. Most money managers work long hours, often taking their work home, and some are constantly studying at home for the qualifying examinations necessary for advancement. The first ten years in a money-management career limits the time for social and family life outside of work.

ACCOUNTANT

Designs and controls financial records and analyzes financial data.

What's It Like to Be an Accountant?

Accountants prepare financial reports, profit and loss studies, cost studies, and tax reports. The three major accounting fields are public, management, and government accounting. Public accountants are independent and work for themselves on a fee basis for businesses, individuals, or accounting firms. Management accountants, also called industrial or private accountants, handle the financial records of their company and work on a salary basis. Government accountants examine financial records of government agencies and audit private businesses for government regulations. Any of these accountants may specialize in auditing, taxes, cost accounting, budgeting and control, or investments. Sue Jourdon, Certified Public Accountant (CAP) for a small city, likes her work because she has the challenge of revising the city's present accounting system to a computer system. She had a liberal arts college background with summer work in computer programming that she says adds to the excitement of accounting. "The hours are too long during the tax season—10 to 12 hours a day. But," Jourdon adds, "the good pay makes up for it."

What Education and Skills Will I Need?

High school: Preparation for college, with strong ability and interest in mathematics, is necessary for a Certified Public Accountant (CPA) program. Alternatives include a commercial course leading to a business college or community college program in accounting, or correspondence study in accounting, or a college course leading to a business administration major.

College: Accounting is offered in a one-year business college program, two-year community college program, and in four-year colleges. Nine out of ten CPAs are college graduates, have passed the CPA examination in the states in which they work, and have had two years of accounting experience before taking the CPA exam. In the near future, some states may require CPA candidates to have a graduate degree, and computer programming skills are increasingly required.

Personal skills: Aptitude for mathematics, ability to work independently, ability to work with computer systems, accuracy, and a high standard of integrity are necessary in an accounting career.

How Many Women in the Field and Where Do They Work?

Only 4 percent of the 200,000 CPAs and less than 24 percent of the 900,000 accountants in the U.S. are women. More than half of the women accountants are in industrial and commercial jobs, and about 15 percent are in government or nonprofit organizations. Most accountants work in urban centers where the large accounting firms and central offices of big businesses are located.

$ $ $ $ $

In 1980, starting salaries for accountants averaged $16,800 a year. Beginners with a master's degree started at $19,200 a year. Accountants with experience made from $18,400 to $31,900, and chief accountants from $28,300 to $50,100.

What Is the Future for Women?

The 1980s is the decade of the accountant. New tax laws and increased pressure on businesses and government agencies to improve budgeting and accounting procedures will provide all kinds of jobs. Even though accountants are in demand and increasing numbers of women will be hired in professional accounting, tradition and preference for men have limited the number of women who plan accounting careers. Accounting is one of the few careers with plenty of job openings, especially for students who have had some part-time experience. Susan C. Crampton, CPA, the only female accounting partner in Vermont, finds that women are often reluctant to go from middle-level to top positions. Crampton encourages women who are in accounting to disregard their few numbers at the top and to for it!

RELATED CAREERS

appraiser	budget officer
loan officer	financial analyst
bank officer	actuary
underwriter	FBI special agent
securities salesperson	purchasing agent

WHERE CAN I GET MORE INFORMATION?

Professional Groups
National Association of Accountants
919 Third Avenue
New York, NY 10022

National Society of Public Accountants
1717 Pennsylvania Avenue, NW
Washington, D.C. 20006

American Society of Women Accountants
35 East Wacher Drive
Chicago, IL 60601

American Women's Society of CPAs
500 North Michigan Avenue, Suite 1400
Chicago, IL 60611

Trade Journal
Journal of Accountancy
American Institute of CPA
666 Fifth Avenue
New York, NY 10019

ACTUARY

*Assembles and analyzes statistics to design
insurance and pension plans on a
profit-making basis.*

What's It Like to Be an Actuary?

Why do teenagers pay more for car insurance? How much is a life-insurance policy for a woman at age 21? Answers to these and similar questions are provided by actuaries. Actuaries calculate probabilities of death, sickness, injury, disability, unemployment, retirement, and property loss from accident, theft, and fire. They use statistics to construct probability tables in order to develop insurance rates. They usually work for a life insurance or liability insurance company. Actuary Kathy Muleski, of New England Life Insurance Company in Boston, specializes in pension plans, which involve her company's investments. She cautions college graduates to plan on a limited social life for the first few years as an actuary because the required actuarial examinations take 15 to 25 hours a week of home study. Or she recommends—date another actuary and study together!

What Education and Skills Will I Need?

High school: Preparation for college, with as much mathematics as possible.

College: Required, with a good background in calculus, probability, statistics, and computer science. You can major in mathematics, statistics, economics, or business administration. While still in college, you should begin to take the examinations required to become a professional actuary; it takes from 5 to 10 years to complete them after college on the job. There are 17 colleges and universities that offer special training for actuarial careers.

Personal skills: Mathematical ability, and interest in studying and working independently to pass on your own, and ability to do routine, detailed work are needed.

Personal skills: Mathematical ability, an interest in study and working independently to pass on your own, and ability to do routine, detailed work are needed.

How Many Women in the Field and Where Do They Work?

Less than 3 percent of the 10,700 professional actuaries in the U.S. are women. Most actuaries are employed with major insurance industries in five cities: New York, Hartford, Chicago, Philadelphia, and Boston. Private insurance companies employ 70 percent of all actuaries.

$ $ $ $

In 1980, starting salary for college graduates who had not taken and passed any actuarial exams was $13,000 a year. Beginners who had passed one exam started at $17,000; and at $18,000 with two exams. The pay increases rapidly as the actuary completes her examinations and has a few years of experience.

What Is the Future for Women?

Job opportunities are expected to be very good through the 1980s. Because of the rising numbers of insurance policies of all kinds, and the expanding group health and life insurance plans, actuarial employment will increase along with the increase in health occupations. Women who are afraid of mathematics can qualify for actuarial jobs if they deal with their math anxiety and major in mathematics in college. Like all subjects, mathematics is learned. Men are not born with a natural ability to do math!

Keep in mind that the best actuarial jobs go to the graduates who have passed actuarial examinations while they are still in college. Also, knowledge of computers is important. Kathy Muleski says she is presently in a computer program for actuaries sponsored by her company. She encourages others to learn as much as they can about computers as early as possible.

RELATED CAREERS

mathematician financial analyst
statistician engineering analyst
economist

WHERE CAN I GET MORE INFORMATION?

Professional Groups
National Association of Insurance Women
P.O. Box 4694
1847 E. 15 Street
Tulsa, OK 74104

Society of Actuaries
208 South La Salle Street
Chicago, IL 60604

Casualty Actuarial Society
One Penn Plaza
250 West 34 Street
New York, NY 10019

Trade Journal
Risk Management
205 East 42 Street
New York, NY 10017

BANK OFFICER

Banks are in the "money" business and bank officers are responsible for management of the bank's business.

What's It Like to Be a Bank Officer?

Officers in a bank include the loan officer, who makes decisions on loan applications according to the bank's policy; the trust officer, who manages property, funds, or real estate for clients, including financial planning, investment, and taxes; the operations officer, who manages efficient working procedures for the bank; the customer manager, who is responsible for relations with customers and other banks; the branch bank manager, who has full responsibility for a branch office; and the personnel administrators, public relations officers, and operational research officers. It's tough to be in a demanding financial career and have a family. Nancy Jones, Vice-President at Banker's Trust in New York, manages investment portfolios for large institutions. She tells of the stress she feels with two children: "On the bus to work I'm reading the *Wall Street Journal.* Even if I walk ten blocks, I'm thinking about what to do when I arrive. Sometimes I feel like I'm being pulled in all directions." When her first child was born, there was no one at the bank she could talk to. Motherhood can be a lonely place in a so-called "man's working world." One of the attitudes women aspiring to top-level positions have to work on is that their careers must be as important to them as their families. A bank officer in Houston finally realized, "I'd give anything to be able to spend more time with my 2-year old — anything except my career!"

What Education and Skills Will I Need?

High school: Preparation for college, with emphasis on mathematics and economics.

College: Many banking officers majored in business administration, accounting, economics, finance, or banking. The large city banks have training programs, especially for liberal arts graduates who are interested in finance regardless of their college major. A Master of Business Administration (MBA) with computer skills is an "ideal" education for future bank managers.

BANK OFFICER

Personal skills: Ability to analyze detailed information, assertiveness, an interest in making money, ability to win confidence from others, tact, and good judgment are needed to be a success in banking.

How Many Women in the Field and Where Do They Work?

Madelyn Davidson, bank Vice-president, says, "The only two ways a woman will ever become president of a bank is either if she assumes a vacancy caused by the death of her bank president husband who controlled the stock of the bank, or like Claire Gionnini Hoffman, Director of the Bank of America, if her father was founder of the bank." Or if she starts her own bank! Twenty percent of the 400,000 bank officers are women. Most women officers are middle-management rather than top-management, and they are in the trust, personnel, and public relations departments of the bank, rather than in operations or investment.

$ $ $ $ $

Beginning college graduates in a bank officer training program start from $1,100 to $1,300 a month. They start at $1,300 to $1,900 a month with a master's degree, and at $1,400 to $2,400 a month with an MBA. The officers of small town banks advance from positions as tellers and are paid much less than city bankers.

What Is the Future for Women?

The opportunities for good management in banks will continue to be very good. The increased numbers of qualified applicants creates a competitive job market. Bank Vice-president Madelyn Davidson is convinced, however, that in order for women to get these jobs they must choose to educate themselves and prepare for a management job, with purposeful *planning.* She says that the potential bank officer will have to accept the requirement of many hours at work, which calls for a flexible home and family life. Bank officer careers are for the women who want to work full-time, rather than part-time with interrupted work plans.

RELATED CAREERS
  industrial relations director
  city manager
  any business management career

WHERE CAN I GET MORE INFORMATION?
  Professional Groups
  National Association of Bank Women, Inc.
  500 North Michigan Avenue, Suite 1400
  Chicago, IL 60601

  American Bankers Association
  1120 Connecticut Avenue, NW
  Washington, D.C. 20036

  Trade Journal
  American Banker
  525 West 42 Street
  New York, NY 10036

CREDIT MANAGER
*Decides which individuals or businesses are
eligible for credit, according to a credit policy.*

What's It Like to Be a Credit Manager?

In our society, coins and paper money are on the way out. Computerized credit is on its way in. To decide who can receive credit, credit managers analyze detailed financial reports of businesses (commercial credit) or bank records, credit bureau recommendations, and applications of individuals (consumer credit). They are also responsible for establishing their company's credit policy and setting financial standards on the basis of the amount of risk the company can take. Credit managers often work with salespeople in setting up the credit policy.

What Education and Skills Will I Need?

High school: Preparation for a two-year or four-year college.

College: Most credit managers have a college degree in business administration, accounting, or economics in order to get into good training programs. Others have a two-year accounting or business administration college program. Understanding computer systems is crucial for all career levels in credit.

Personal skills: Ability to analyze details and draw logical conclusions, a pleasant personality, and speaking skills are necessary for success as a credit manager.

How Many Women in the Field and Where Do They Work?

There are 55,000 credit managers and 40 percent of them are women. About half work for wholesale and retail trade, and others for manufacturing and financial institutions.

$ $ $ $ $

In 1980, trainees with a college degree averaged from $12,000 to $14,000 a year. Experienced credit managers averaged from $22,000 to $25,000 a year. The top-level jobs paid over $40,000.

What Is the Future for Women?

Jobs will be competitive in credit management through the 1980s. Use of credit has increased very rapidly and it's here to stay. As firms strive to get the biggest sales, there will be a greater demand for skilled credit managers who can establish credit policies strict enough to minimize bad debt losses. Use of computers, telecommunications networks, and centralized credit will limit the growth of jobs.

WHERE CAN I GET MORE INFORMATION?

Professional Group
National Association of Credit Management
475 Park Avenue South
New York, NY 10016

Trade Journal
Credit and Financial Management
National Association of Credit Management
475 Park Avenue South
New York, NY 10016

BUSINESS: SALES

Automobile Salesperson
Insurance Salesperson
Manufacturer's Salesperson
Real Estate Salesperson
Stockbroker
Travel Agent

About these careers   Sales jobs are the place where people with the least amount of education can make the most amount of money. However, high unemployment rates and tough competition for jobs have increased the need for a college degree to get into some sales training programs. There are 6.8 million salespeople and 1 million, or 16 percent, have college degrees. Most salespeople come from a great variety of college backgrounds, although manufacturers' salespeople are often from technical or scientific backgrounds.

Some salespeople, such as those who sell for manufacturers, have large territories and do a lot of traveling. Others usually work in the neighborhood of their "home base."

A beginning salesperson works evenings, weekends, and holidays — whenever the customers and clients are free to buy. She has to hustle to build up her accounts, putting in long hours that are inconvenient for her family and friends. After she has been in the business for ten years or so, and her accounts are well-established, she can meet clients at their mutual convenience — on the tennis court, on the racket ball court, or at lunch.

If you are after big money, building accounts takes tremendous time and energy. If you are interested in sales but decide not to go for the big money, then you can work fewer hours because sales-people are free to set up their own time schedule. More than 25 percent of the 6.8 million people in selling work part-time. Sales provides many opportunities for coordinating a career with parenting, which many mothers need to do until their children are older.

Most sales advancement is in terms of making more money and having more free time because accounts are well-established. But salespeople who have managerial ability may advance to assistant sales manager, sales manager, or general manager. Some managers open their own business or become partners in dealerships or agencies and firms.

AUTOMOBILE SALESPERSON

Sells new and used cars for car dealers.

What's It Like to Be an Automobile Salesperson?

Commission selling, or getting paid by a percentage of the product you sell, is a nontraditional job for women. The higher the price of the product, the fewer the women selling it. For instance, very few women sell cars, real estate, or securities. More than knowing anything complicated about the product, an automobile salesperson has to know how to sell. The main thing to learn is how to "close a deal," that is, how to overcome the customer's hesitancy to buy. Often, a new salesperson begins a sale and an experienced one helps her close the sale. The new salesperson learns how to quote prices and how to give a trade-in allowance for the customer's present car. Salespeople often arrange financing and insurance for the cars they sell. Good salespeople develop and follow leads of prospective customers. Automobile selling is an exciting job because the salesperson deals with $300 to $500 profit on each car, rather than the 30 to 50 cent profit on food items, for example, which most female salespeople deal with.

What Education and Skills Will I Need?

High school: Most salespeople have a high school diploma. Usually, they are trained on the job by sales managers and experienced salespeople. A new-car dealer who employs women to sell cars asks, "Where else can a woman earn from $800 to $1,200 a month with no formal training, other than what she gets on the job?"

College: Many new-car dealers have some college, but business and selling experience count more than a degree.

Personal skills: Sales skills, initiative, assertiveness, enthusiasm for the product, and ambition make a successful salesperson.

How Many Women in the Field and Where Do They Work?

There are an estimated 157,000 automobile salespeople and almost none are women. New-car dealers employ from 1 to 50 salespeople.

$ $ $ $ $

In 1980, salespeople in the automobile industry averaged $18,000 a year. Earnings vary widely depending on geography, experience, and type and size of dealership.

What Is the Future for Women?

With the energy crisis, unemployment in Detroit, and an economic recession, all car-related jobs are going to be hard to predict. Anyone who can prove herself a seller can convince a dealer to hire her on a commission basis that doesn't involve a financial risk to the dealer. If selling cars is what you want to do, you can suggest a work plan to the dealer: after the work hours of another job, or after school, or on weekends. Ask for a few months' trial, and if the dealer makes money, you should have a job. Women who have sold cars have experienced discrimination from other salespeople but not from customers or dealers. So be prepared to compete with the men.

RELATED CAREERS
insurance agent   manufacturer's salesperson
real estate agent   stockbroker

WHERE CAN I GET MORE INFORMATION?
Professional Group
National Automobile Dealers Association
8400 West Park Drive
McLean, VA 22102

Trade Journal
Automobile News
965 East Jefferson
Detroit, MI 48207

INSURANCE SALESPERSON

*Sells policies that protect individuals and businesses
against future losses and financial pressures.*

What's It Like to Be an Insurance Salesperson?

There are 1.6 million people in the insurance field and one-third of them are in sales. An insurance agent sells for one company, usually on a commission basis; an insurance broker sells for several companies. Sheila Lief, insurance broker in a family business, spends the day changing and rating policies, answering clients' questions about coverage, talking to special agents representing their companies, and contacting people about accident reports and new information. She finds the work very stimulating, because of the constant changes in policies and people's needs and because she makes very good money.

Other insurance jobs for college graduates include managers, underwriters, and actuaries. Managers are responsible for the administration of policy accounting, investments, and loans. Underwriters review insurance applications to evaluate the risk involved in insuring an applicant, in order to determine profit for the company. Insurance companies also employ accountants, bookkeepers, and lawyers.

What Education and Skills Will I Need?

High school: Preparation for business college, community college, or four-year college.

College: Major in business administration, personnel, insurance, or liberal arts. Insurance people come from all kinds of educational backgrounds; a degree is not a necessity for sales jobs. All agents and most brokers must be licensed in the state where they plan to sell insurance. Many good insurance people become qualified through correspondence courses in insurance.

Personal skills: Depending on the job, the sales or management or business skills needed for any big business are needed in insurance.

How Many Women in the Field and Where Do They Work?

More than 325,000 agents and brokers sell insurance, and of these, 40,000 are women. One-third of all insurance managers are women, usually middle rather than top management, and 5 percent of the professional workers are women. Every town has agents and brokers. The "home office" people are in the insurance centers of the country: California, Connecticut, Illinois, Massachusetts, New Jersey, New York, and Texas.

$ $ $ $ $

Beginners start at a salary of $1,000 a month for six months before they go on commission. In 1981, life insurance agents with 5 years experience had a median income of $22,000 a year. But thousands of agents and brokers earn over $40,000 a year, and many earn over $100,000 a year.

What Is the Future for Women?

The selling business is a competitive field, with many turnovers in beginning sales positions. Selling is a good opportunity for women who are ambitious and enjoy saleswork. Part-time work and selling at odd hours are good possibilities in insurance. Opportunities in middle management will continue to be good, because the insurance industry is expected to grow.

RELATED CAREERS

real estate agent   car salesperson
manufacturer's company representative   stockbroker

WHERE CAN I GET MORE INFORMATION?

Professional Groups
Insurance Information Institute
110 William Street
New York, NY 10038

National Association of Insurance Women
1847 East 15 Street
Tulsa, OK 74104

Trade Journal
The Insurance Salesman
1200 N. Meridan Street
Indianapolis, IN 46206

Insurance Week
2322 Seattle-First National Bank Building
Seattle, WA 98154

MANUFACTURER'S SALESPERSON

*Sells manufactured goods mainly to businesses
and institutions.*

What's It Like to Be a Manufacturer's Salesperson?

Manufacturers' salespeople, sometimes called sales engineers or industrial salesworkers, spend most of their time visiting their manufacturing company's prospective customers. They also write reports on sales and customers' credit ratings, plan their schedules, make up lists of new customers, handle correspondence, and study their products. Some salespeople promote their products by displays at conferences or by giving demonstrations to companies on how to use their products. Stacey O'Sullivan, salesperson for Digital, sells highly technical computer equipment. She says that, in addition to learning all about her product (software), she also must be able to help prospective buyers with technical problems, show them how to use the software most effectively, and tell them what other software is available for expanding their computer system. It often takes months to negotiate a sale. O'Sullivan loves the challenge of selling and the money she makes in computer software, the fastest growing product in the world.

What Education and Skills Will I Need?

High school: Preparation for college. College graduates are preferred.

College: Many technical or specialized salesworkers are engineers, pharmacists, or chemists. Others come from business or liberal arts majors.

Personal skills: Selling skills, assertiveness, pleasant appearance, interest in the product, and the ability to get along well with people are needed for all saleswork.

How Many Women in the Field and Where Do They Work?

Of the 440,000 salesworkers, more work for food companies than for any other industry. Large numbers also work for printing, publishing, chemical, drug, metal product, and electrical and machine industries. Only 15 percent are women. Joyce White Ferrell says she was born to be a saleswoman. She started selling salve at 10 years old, and gears, sprockets, and universal joints when she graduated from college. Ferrell was the first black woman in the U.S. to be hired in sales at Gillette Safety Razor Division. At age 30, she is the top sales representative for Pro-Line, a black hair care firm.

$ $ $ $ $

In 1980, beginners averaged from $13,900 to $15,400 a year. The highest salaries were in selling electrical equipment, construction materials, hardware and tools, and scientific and precision instruments. The majority of salespeople get paid a combination of salary, commission, and bonus, earning between $21,000 and $24,400 with experience.

What Is the Future for Women?

Job opportunities will be good for well-trained and ambitious people through the 1980s.

RELATED CAREERS

real estate agent   car salesperson
retail buyer   stockbroker

WHERE CAN I GET MORE INFORMATION?

Professional Group
Manufacturers' Agents National Association
P.O. Box 16878
Irvine, CA 92713

Trade Journal
The American Salesman
424 North 3 Street
Burlington, IA 52601

REAL ESTATE SALESPERSON

*Represents property owners who want to sell or rent
residential and commercial properties.*

What's It Like to Be a Real Estate Salesperson?

Real estate brokers show and sell real estate; some handle rental properties as well. Many brokers combine real estate with insurance selling or practicing law.

Broker Sally Miller rents and manages properties, makes appraisals, arranges for loans to finance purchases, and helps develop new building projects. In addition, she manages her office, advertises properties, and supervises her salespeople.

Ruth W. Bennett, associate realtor in a small city, started looking for a career when she was divorced. After three years as an unappreciated secretary, she started working in a real estate office as a secretary, took a night course to get her realtor's license, and did everything she could to learn the business. A year ago, she took the risk of working only on commission and has been constantly surprised at her success and involvement in the work. Like many women, she had been taught that only aggressive men can make big money selling. "I never thought I could make a living in real estate, and then I learned that a great variety of people are buyers and a great variety of people can be successful at selling. It's very exciting to sell in my own way and to find that it works!" Bennett urges women to trust their own talents and ways of doing things.

Mildred Gunther, broker in industrial real estate in New Jersey, urges more women to move from residential selling into industrial selling. In *Savvy* magazine, Gunther is quoted, "In residential selling, you sell houses and co-ops for relatively small amounts of money. The issues are pretty much the same every time. In industrial/commercial selling, you're dealing in millions of dollars, and six-figure commissions are normal. You work with sophisticated executives and heads of companies who have challenging requirements. In residential selling, I hated having to show places seven days a week. Now I deal with nine-to-five types who come to see things on the company's time—and only if they're serious."

What Education and Skills Will I Need?

Professional training: A college degree is not required to be a real estate broker, although a state real estate license is required. More than 200 colleges and many correspondence schools offer one or more courses in real estate to qualify for the real estate examination. Ability to sell is the key to success in real estate, although most women in the field have some college background.

Personal skills: Pleasant personality, assertiveness, enthusiasm, tact, a good memory for faces and names, and ambition are necessary for successful saleswork.

How Many Women in the Field and Where Do They Work?

There are 500,000 full-time real estate salespeople and about one-half of them are women. Part-time people in real estate outnumber the full-time and, in 1980, there were 4 million licensed realtors. Most real estate salespersons are in small businesses and are self-employed.

$ $ $ $ $

Commissions on sales are the means of income in the real estate business. Commissions vary from 5 percent to 10 percent, depending on the type of property and the area of the country. In 1980, full-time real estate agents earned an average of $14,700 a year. Experienced salespersons can earn much more than that.

REAL ESTATE SALESPERSON

What Is the Future for Women?

Jobs in real estate are very competitive and will continue to be so. Shifts in population ages of those needing housing will create some new jobs, and the best chances for this work will go to the well-trained, ambitious people who enjoy selling. The high cost of mortgages has resulted in a tough real-estate job situation.

RELATED CAREERS

car salesperson   securities salesperson
insurance salesperson   manufacturer's representative

WHERE CAN I GET MORE INFORMATION?

Professional Group
National Association of Realtors
430 N. Michigan Avenue
Chicago, IL 60611

Trade Journal
The Appraisal Journal
NAREB
155 E. Superior Street
Chicago, IL 60611

STOCKBROKER

*Sells stocks, bonds, or mutual funds to individuals
and institutions.*

What's It Like to Be a Stockbroker?

A stockbroker, sometimes called a securities salesperson, gets an order for stock and relays the order through the firm's order room to the floor of a securities exchange or to the firm's trading department. After she completes this transaction, the stockbroker notifies the customer of the sale. Other duties include explaining the stock market and trading practices to customers, suggesting purchases and sales, and often managing the money of institutions with millions of dollars to invest. Anita Rozonni is learning the securities business through her secretarial job in a small firm in Newark, Ohio. She finds it an exciting new career and says only in a small firm would she get the great variety of experience with handling the books, making reports to regulatory agencies, taking care of her own customers, and trading as market maker in the firm's stocks.

Mary Calhoun, account executive for Merrill Lynch, Pierce, Fenner & Smith, has been with the firm for two years after she worked seven years as a systems analyst. She advises students who are considering a securities sales career to buy some stock and find out the agonies of losing money before they handle other people's investments. Calhoun works on commission, as most securities stockbrokers do, and what she likes best about her work is that she makes money in direct relationship to how much work (time and energy) she puts into it.

In 1970, women were allowed on the New York Stock Exchange floor as pages for the first time. And it wasn't until 1980 that a woman had a specialist seat on the New York Stock Exchange. Twenty-five-year-old Amy Newkirk was the first. A related investment-sales career is commodities broker. A broker for American Express, Inc., in New York City, Maria E. Healy deals mostly in sugar. A recent graduate of Marymount College, Healy majored in business economics and is fluent in Spanish. She travels three months a year to Latin America, and she loves the excitement of her job, the money she makes, and the business world in general.

What Education and Skills Will I Need?

High school: Preparation for college. Read the financial pages of newspapers in order to learn about daily financial situations, especially the business section of the Sunday *New York Times* and the *Wall Street Journal.*

College: Almost all trainees for stockbrokerage firms are college graduates. They come from many liberal arts majors, although economics and prelaw are the predominant college majors.

Personal skills: Selling skills, ambition, and interest in making money in the financial world are needed for success in the securities business.

How Many Women in the Field and Where Do They Work?

There are 63,000 full-time and part-time stockbrokers and 16 percent of these are women. They are employed by broker-age firms, investment bankers, and mutual funds firms. Most brokers work for a few large firms who have offices in large and small cities all over the country. The jobs that pay the most money are underwriters or investment bankers. None of the ten largest underwriting firms has a woman senior vice-president, vice-president of corporate finance, president, or full partner. Leslie N. Hammond is one of the few women with a seat on the New York Stock Exchange. She was the third. Now there are twelve women out of a possible 1,366 seats. When Hammond came to the floor in 1977, after five years with Merrill Lynch, she said the hardest part was that no one was used to a female voice—they just didn't hear her!

$ $ $ $ $

Depending on the size of the firm, trainees start at $900 to $1,200 a month, until they are licensed and working on commis-sion. In 1980, full-time stockbrokers who sold to individuals averaged $40,000 a year, while brokers who sold to institutions averaged over $88,000.

What Is the Future for Women?

Jobs will be competitive, but there will be work for the well-trained successful salespeople. During a recession and economic downturn, jobs are tight, but in the long run the opportunities will be good. The career opportunities for women will be best for the holder of an MBA who gets into business for a few years and then into a brokerage house training program. Rosemarie Sena makes over $100,000 a year as a Vice-president on Wall Street by managing funds for corporate investors. A graduate of an MBA program, Marian S. Adams at age 27 is Vice-presi-dent of a New York City securities firm that handles a $300 million account.

RELATED CAREERS
insurance agent   securities trader
real estate agent   commodities broker

WHERE CAN I GET MORE INFORMATION?
Professional Groups
Financial Women's Association
New York, NY 10005

New York Stock Exchange
11 Wall Street
New York, NY 10005

Securities Industry Association
20 Broad Street
New York, NY 10005

Trade Journal
Wall Street Journal
Dow Jones
30 Broad Street
New York, NY 10004

TRAVEL AGENT

*Organizes, schedules, and sells travel services
to the public.*

What's It Like to Be a Travel Agent?

The travel agent is a dealer in dreams, other people's dreams, and in the course of a day she plans many round-the-world trips, vacations, special event trips, as well as the routine business trips for regular customers. A travel agent must possess a great deal of specialized knowledge about climate, accommodations, fares, places of interest, tariffs and customs laws, currency exchange, and sources of references for new information. When an anthropologist schedules a trip to Taute, New Guinea, the agent supplies exact information regarding connections and time changes from airline to airline as well as time zone to time zone. The agent must know that when the anthropologist ends up in a mission plane in Lumi, walking through the bush is the only means of transportation left to get to her destination! Travel agencies are service agencies. Good will and good client relations are vitally important to make a profit in these services. Knowing details, excursion rates, and suggestions for making trips convenient and comfortable are imperative for a successful agent.

What Education and Skills Will I Need?

Professional training: Most travel agents have some college background, although it is not a requirement. Some travel agents took courses in special schools and correspondence schools, and other agents learned while on the job.

Personal skills: Sales skills, business ability, interest in details and accuracy, and a pleasant personality that can accept people changing their plans are necessary to a successful travel agent.

How Many Women in the Field and Where Do They Work?

There are 52,000 travel agents in the U.S. and Canada. About one-fourth of the agents are self-employed. Most agencies hire from 1 to 40 agents, about one-half women. The urban and resort areas employ the most number of agents.

$ $ $ $ $

Since the jobs are competitive and so many young people want to work in the travel industry, beginners start low. In 1980, travel agents earned from $9,500 to $18,000 a year. People often go into this career for the fringe benefits, which include vacations at reduced rates and transportation and hotels at a discount. Often, agents are invited for free holidays to see and recommend the facilities of an airline or resort hotel.

What Is the Future for Women?

The travel industry is a very competitive field, since it is one of the glamor careers where many qualified people apply each year. The surest way to get a start is to be qualified to take any job any small agency offers you and work toward a promotion after learning the job.

RELATED CAREERS
> airline reservation agent   tour guide
> rental car agent   salesperson

WHERE CAN I GET MORE INFORMATION?
> *Professional Group*
> American Society of Travel Agents
> 711 Fifth Avenue
> New York, NY 10022
>
> *Trade Journal*
> Travel Trade
> 605 Fifth Avenue
> New York, NY 10017

COMMUNICATIONS

Cable TV
Radio Broadcasting
Television Broadcasting
Writer

About these careers   Responses such as, "I'm a writer,"
or "I'm in TV," to the question, "What do you do for work?" almost
always is an envied reply. Communications careers are glamorous,
and because they are, the competition for most jobs is tough, with
many more jobseekers than there are job openings. Some people are
attracted by the image of media jobs — the opportunities to meet
public figures, to appear before nationwide audiences, to attend
special events. It is often difficult to see the hard work required when
looking at the glamorous aspects of communications careers.

Communications is a process that begins with observing what is
happening, analyzing and interpreting that information, and
transmitting it to an audience through a variety of media. The field
includes a broad range of careers that have to do with research,
writing, editing, and production; it encompasses educational,
medical, business, speech, joke, screen, and fiction writing; and
interpreting, translating, public relations, advertising, and many
other specialities.

Specialties that take the place of mass media are becoming the
new media. The three major television networks have lost viewers to
cable television with its 30 choices in all kinds of specialties that a
viewer can watch with just the flip of a switch at any time of day or
night. Big newspapers are closing while small specialized local
newspapers and magazines are thriving. Specialization means more
jobs that require more depth of knowledge in particular areas.

The intellectual skills acquired during college are important for
a communications career. Acute powers of observation and the
ability to think clearly and logically are necessary traits, because
people in communications need to understand the significance of
the events they observe. A feeling for language enables newspaper
reporters and broadcast journalists to breathe life and meaning into
the overwhelming number of events that occur every day. A knack
for drama through the spoken word makes radio and television
announcers attractive to audience of all kinds. Even though the
competition is tough, there will be jobs through the 1980s for talented
people who have acquired appropriate education and experience.
The willingness to "start at the bottom" will help get the job. A
combination of talent, education, motivation, imagination, and
"luck" helps too.

CABLE TV

*Plans, prepares, produces, and sells
cable television programs.*

What's It Like to Be in Cable TV?

"You have to be hungry, ambitious, and energetic to compete in this industry," says Vivian Horner, Vice-President of program development for Warner Amex Cable in New York. Cable television is the fastest growing communications career in the country. At present, cable television is in 14.5 million American homes and is likely to spread like wildfire during the early 1980s. Industry experts say there soon will be 40 million cable subscribers. Because of this new and expanding industry, many jobs are being created where none existed before. Michael Dann, Senior Program Advisor at ABC Video Enterprises in New York, says that women's chances of getting into cable television compared to their chances of getting into commercial television are 1,000-to-1 better.

The fierce competition in cable television today is in winning the franchise, or exclusive right, to deliver cable in cities, towns, and boroughs. When a cable company is competing for franchise rights, from ten to fifty people may be working to study the locality and prepare a bid. The franchise team must determine the needs of a community and develop a responsive programming package. "Working on a franchise team is a good way to enter and learn the industry," says Judie Carroll, Director of Franchise Proposals at Warner Amex Cable. However, in a few years when most cities become franchised, there will no longer be a need for the team.

Other major jobs in cable are the same as broadcasting: marketing, sales, and operations. Lorrie Secrest, Associate Producer at Qube of Columbus, Ohio, has been in cable television for four years and won four awards for her documentaries. She is active in the women's professional group, American Women in Radio and Television, where she is President of her Ohio chapter. She urges women to describe their skills and tasks rather than to use their titles, and to change jobs as often as necessary for advancement.

What Education and Skills Will I Need?

High school: Preparation for college and a communications or business major, with as much writing, speaking, and reading as you can get in high school.

College: Major in communications, radio and television, journalism, theater arts, business, or a related area. Most women (85 percent) in radio and television have attended college, and 27 percent of them have a master's degree.

Personal skills: A well-modulated speaking voice, a reasonable command of the English language, plus knowledge of dramatics, sports, music, and current events are important for the entertainment side of cable television. Programming careers require interest and skills in business.

How Many Women in the Field and Where Do They Work?

There are 34,000 jobs in the cable industry and 31.9 percent are held by women, but most of those women are in office, clerical, operative, and service positions. Women hold only 5.7 percent of office management, professional, technical, and sales positions in the cable industry. The cable employment projections are that the current number will more than double in the 1980s to over 65,000 jobs.

$ $ $ $ $

Selling is a major job in cable, as subscriber fees are the major source of income. Salaries of entry-level salespeople range from $12,000 to $20,000, depending on geographic location. Members of a franchise team for a major cable company make from $25,000 to $40,000 a year. Experienced account executives can earn $30,000 and up.

Operations is the business-management side of the cable industry. An operations manager oversees capital expenditures, customer service, accounts payable and receivable, installation and maintenance, and other administrative functions. Salaries for entry-level operations range from $12,000 to $15,000 in small systems and go up to $60,000 in major cities.

What Is the Future for Women?

Along with computers, cable television is the fastest growing industry. Like other communications careers, it is a glamorous field with many talented, ambitious people applying for jobs. Getting in on the ground floor means a wonderful advantage to learn with the growth of the industry.

RELATED CAREERS
commercial and public radio broadcasting
commercial and public television broadcasting
business management
sales

WHERE CAN I GET MORE INFORMATION?
Professional Groups
Women in Cable
2033 M Street, NW, Suite 703
Washington, D.C. 20006

The National Cable Television Association
918 16th Street, NW
Washington, D.C. 20006

American Women in Radio and Television, Inc.
1321 Connecticut Avenue, NW
Washington, D.C. 20036

Trade Journals
Cable Vision
Titsch Publishing, Inc.
1130 Delaware Plaza
P.O. Box 4305
Denver, CO 80204

Multi-Channel News
Fairchild Publishing, Inc.
P.O. Box 18248
Denver, CO 80218

THE TOP TEN CABLE COMPANIES

Teleprompter Cable TV
888 Seventh Avenue
New York, NY 10019

American Television and
   Communications Corp.
160 Inverness Drive, W
Englewood, CO 80150

Tele-Communications, Inc.
5455 S. Valentia Way
Denver, CO 80222

Cox Cable Communications
219 Perimeter Center Parkway
Atlanta, GA 30346

Warner Amex Cable
   Communications, Inc.
75 Rockefeller Plaza
New York, NY 10019

The Times Mirror Co.
Times Mirror Square
Los Angeles, CA 90053

Storer Broadcasting Co.
1177 Kane Concourse
Miami Beach, FL 33154

Viacom International
1211 Ave. of Americas
New York, NY 10036

Sammons Communications
Box 225728
Dallas, TX 75265

UA-Columbia Cablevision
315 Post Road, W
Westport, CT 06880

RADIO AND TELEVISION BROADCASTING

Plans, prepares, produces, and presents radio and television programs.

What's It Like to Be in Radio and Television Broadcasting?

The glamor and excitement of radio and television make broadcasting careers attractive to about 200,000 people who are employed in this career. Whether in commercial or public broadcasting, *radio and television directors* plan and supervise individual programs or series of programs. They coordinate shows, select artists and studio personnel, schedule and conduct rehearsals, and direct on-the-air shows. Often, they are assisted by entry-level associates who work out details, arrange for distribution of scripts and script changes to the cast, and help direct the shows. They may assist in timing and make arrangements for use of props, makeup service, artwork, and film slides. *Announcers* probably are the best known workers in the industry. They introduce programs, guests, and musical selections, and deliver most of the live commercials. In small stations, they also may operate the control board, sell time, and write commercial and news copy. *Musical directors* select, arrange, and direct music for programs, following general instructions from program directors.

News gathering and reporting are key aspects of radio and television programming. *News directors* plan and supervise coverage of all news and special events. *News reporters* gather and analyze information about newsworthy events for broadcast on radio or television programs. They may specialize in a particular field, such as economics, health, or foreign affairs, and often report special news events from the actual scenes where the events occur. *News writers* select and write copy for *newscasters* to read on the air. In many stations, the jobs of news writer and newscaster are combined. In addition, broadcasting stations have video and film editors, engineering technicians, salespeople who sell time to advertisers who sponsor the programs, and general administrators. National Public Radio (NPR) is an increasingly popular medium, where 1.6 million listeners have been tuning in every weekday evening for 90 minutes to hear Susan Stamberg on *All Things Considered,* public radio's oldest and most popular program. According to *Savvy,* Stamberg started in radio by hosting programs for a local public station. Then, in 1971, she moved on to NPR as a tape editor and occasional reporter. Her promotion to the anchor spot of *All Things Considered* came when the show's host went on vacation. Asked to replace him, Stamberg took over with such aplomb that "even the control room applauded." *Savvy* explains, "It is Stamberg's voice, in part, that makes listeners tune in. Comfortingly maternal, ready to laugh, eager to understand, with its unmistakable New York City accent — it's a voice that seems to inspire devotion."

What Education and Skills Will I Need?

High school: Preparation for college and a communications major, with as much writing, speaking, and reading as you can get in high school.

College: Major in communications, radio and television, journalism, theater arts, or a related area. Most women (85 percent) in radio and television have attended college and 27 percent of them have a master's degree.

Personal skills: A well-modulated speaking voice, a reasonable command of the English language, plus knowledge of dramatics, sports, music, and current events are important. Careers in announcing require a dramatic personality with special style. Programming careers require an interest in business and detail as well.

How Many Women in the Field and Where Do They Work?

There are 120,000 full-time and 30,000 part-time staff employed in commercial broadcasting; 50 percent are in radio. Women make up 25 percent of the broadcasting staff. They work in 7,000 commercial radio stations and 700 commercial television stations in the U.S. In addition, there are 700 educational radio stations and 220 educational television stations. There are about 3,150 cable television systems who hire about 9,500 workers. A combination of the women's movement, laws for equal employment, and a multimillion-dollar antidiscrimination suit against NBC has helped women get broadcasting jobs. This is a very important breakthrough because it means that, when little girls' families watch the news, they will learn that women can tell about serious and important things, too.

$ $ $ $ $

In 1980, beginning announcers made from $150 to $160 a week in small stations. Salaries in public broadcasting still are not competitive with commercial broadcasting.

What Is the Future for Women?

Radio and television are two of the most popular careers of today. The professional level jobs are very competitive and every spring thousands of liberal arts graduates attempt to get the few jobs available. Traditionally, most women (90 percent) started in radio and television careers with typing and shorthand jobs. The small local stations are the least competitive and offer the most diverse experience in communications for the beginner. Walda Roseman, age 36, is National Public Radio's highest-ranking female executive. She is Senior Vice-president for National Affairs and Planning. From the beginning, National Public Radio has hired women in nontraditional areas at a commendable rate. *Savvy* points out how women at NPR compare to women in broadcasting in general:

	NPR	Industry-wide
On-air and production	33%	25%
Management	33%	20%
Technical	25%	9%

RELATED CAREERS
commercial and public radio broadcasting
commercial and public television broadcasting
cable television

WHERE CAN I GET MORE INFORMATION?
Professional Groups
American Women in Radio and Television, Inc.
1321 Connecticut Avenue, NW
Washington, D.C. 20036

National Association of Broadcasters
1771 N Street, NW
Washington, D.C. 20036

Trade Journal
Broadcasting
1735 Descales Street, NW
Washington, D.C. 20036

WRITER

Writes clear and meaningful copy for newspapers, magazines, books, technical and trade brochures, and advertising.

What's It Like to Be a Writer?

"I write stories, put on headlines, check copy, mark pictures, dummy pages, check teletype setters and composing room, open stacks of mail, and answer the phone, which rings constantly," says Maggie Maurice, a daily newspaper feature editor in a small city. "It's an 8-to-6 or an 8-to-7 o'clock day." A daily newspaper has a fast pace and a deadline atmosphere not found in other writing jobs. Beginning reporters are assigned civic, club, and police court proceedings. As they gain experience, they may report more important events. Reporters may advance to reporting for larger papers or press services.

Magazine writers write features or are magazine researchers, interviewers, and co-writers. Magazine production is similar to newspaper production in that they are both dependent upon advertising for profits. The magazine personnel work closely with their advertising agency. The pace on a magazine staff is faster than on a book publishing staff because magazine personnel have weekly or monthly deadlines. There are many other kinds of writers. Fashion writers write about fashion for department store ads, trade publications, advertising agencies, and newspaper columns. Radio and television news writers put the news programs into short sentences for listening purposes rather than for reading purposes. The major networks have a staff of writers for their newscasters. Technical writers rewrite technical and scientific articles for use by nontechnical people, or by people in other scientific fields. Nancy Franklin writes for the "soaps." She writes two scripts each week and is paid over $800 a week. As she writes, she gets very involved with her story and characters who constantly grow and change. She is a driven woman, auditioning for plays and television commercials, as well as writing. What is she after? Financial independence!

What Education and Skills Will I Need?

High school: Preparation for college, with as much language skills and experience as you can get. Any part-time or summer work on a local newspaper will help you find out what some writing jobs are like. Work on as many school publications as you can while in high school.

College: Writers come from journalism, English, and liberal arts majors, and a great variety of other programs. Most commercial writers have a college degree; however, college is not a necessity to be a successful writer. Writing and communication skills, together with a special writing style and interesting experiences, are what counts.

Personal skills: Writing skills, imagination, curiosity, resourcefulness, an accurate memory, and the ability to work alone or in a bustling environment are necessary for most writing jobs.

How Many Women in the Field and Where Do They Work?

Of the 57,000 reporters and correspondents for newspapers and other media, 16,000 are women. Women have only 4.4 percent of the directing editorships of newspapers with circulations of 25,000 and over. That means that there are a total of 1,554 male news executives and only 71 female news executives.

There are 20,000 technical writers in electronics and aerospace industries and very few are women. There are also 110,000 writers and editors for books, magazines, journals, newsletters, radio, television, and movies. Most women in writing occupations are in book publishing and the fashion industry. Others work for women's magazines, or write the women's page or "Living Section" of daily newspapers. Almost all book publishing jobs are in New York City, while newspaper jobs are in almost every town in America. The many women in the book publishing companies find the intellectual environment they are looking for and a place to use their college education. The general attitude toward publishing houses is explained by a Vassar graduate, "Publishing houses are civilized places to work."

$ $ $ $ $

In 1980, newspapers reporters who worked under union contracts started around $250 a week. Reporters with experience averaged $406 a week, and top-level reporters made $616 a week. Beginning salaries for writers and editorial assistants

WRITER

ranged from $12,000 to $16,000 in 1980. Experienced editors made up to $31,000 a year and top-level editors earned over $50,000. Book writers seldom earn enough to live on without other income.

What Is the Future for Women?

The writing jobs in urban centers are glamorous and competitive. Each fall, thousands of English and journalism majors look for writing jobs in New York and other major cities. *Every* bit of experience counts, and if you can publish while in college or work during the summers, you will have a headstart on the competition. Best chances for newspapers are in the smaller towns. Most technical writers enter the work after several years in technology or engineering.

RELATED CAREERS

journalist	translator
copy writer	fiction writer
nonfiction writer	biographer
screen writer	

WHERE CAN I GET MORE INFORMATION?

Professional Groups
American Newspaper Publishers Association
Box 17407
Dulles International Airport
Washington, D.C. 20041

The American Society of Magazine Editors
575 Lexington Avenue
New York, NY 10022

Women in Communications, Inc.
P.O. Box 9561
Austin, TX 78766

Trade Journals
Publishers Weekly
1180 Avenue of the Americas
New York, NY 10036

Editor and Publisher — The Fourth Estate
850 Third Avenue
New York, NY 10022

Journal of Technical Writing and Communications
Baywood Publishing Company
1 Northwest Drive
Farmingdale, NY 11735

EDUCATION

College Professor
College Student Personnel
Early Childhood Educator
Elementary School Teacher
High School Teacher
Librarian
Museum Personnel
Physical Education Teacher
School Principal
School Counselor
Special Education Teacher

About these careers Education careers require more
education for less pay and have the bleakest outlook for future jobs
than any other career cluster. The field is extremely competitive
because of the oversupply of new teachers graduating from colleges,
the decreased funding for education, the numbers of experienced
teachers being laid off and looking for other educational jobs, the
declining birthrate and school enrollments, and the closing down
of the Department of Education on the federal level.

There are 2.5 million teachers plus professors and librarians
represented by the career descriptions in this group and all of these
careers require a college education. Most of the jobs require a
master's degree or a doctorate for professional certification or
promotion.

Every state offers an education major in their college or
university. Write to your State Department of Education in your state's
capital and inquire which schools offer this major. If you choose to go
to a liberal arts college instead of majoring in education at a state
college, there are several options for becoming certified to teach
elementary or secondary education, including summer school, a
master's degree program, and correspondence courses.

If you are still convinced that education is the field for you, your
best bet is to specialize. Specialize in inner city teaching,
vocational and technical education, bilingual education, math,
science, or education for the disabled, gifted, or disadvantaged.
The computer industry has been draining the math teacher supply
and, therefore, creating a big demand in public schools and colleges.
Physical science is the only field with teacher shortage and funds for
the job. Bilingual and special education have shortages but local
school districts have cut these budgets because they are receiving
very little federal money.

COLLEGE PROFESSOR

Assists students in college-level learning and in getting degrees.

What's It Like to Be a College Professor?

"College teaching is not an occupation but a way of life. The involvement with the subject you are teaching, the reading of professional literature in your own field, and the discussions with students and colleagues becomes your point of view for living," writes Gail Bucknell, Associate Professor of Ecology at Northwestern University. College professors who teach full-time average 8 to 12 hours a week in the classroom. Higher-ranked professors who advise graduate students and are actively engaged in research may spend only 4 to 6 hours a week in actual classroom teaching. Outside the classroom, much of all professors' time is spent in preparing for teaching, grading student work, and keeping up with the subject matter. Most professors carry on research projects and write for their professional journals. Summers may be spent teaching summer school, doing research projects, or on vacation. Dr. Marguerite Carroll, Professor at Fairfield University, finds that her most creative and productive time is spent at home in her own office. Therefore, her writing, reading, professional correspondence, and editing of professional manuscripts are done from early morning until as long as she can stay there.

What Education and Skills Will I Need?

High school: Preparation for college, with as strong an academic program as you can handle well.

College: Preparation for graduate school in whatever major you show the most ability and interest. Your graduate work does not have to be in the same field as your undergraduate work, although usually it is related. As you learn more about your academic abilities and interests, your major field may change. Plan to get your Ph.D. if you want to be a college professor.

Personal skills: A professor needs to be curious about learning and able to share her enthusiasm and interest in her subject with her students. She must like details and be persistent to follow through on academic research and writing.

How Many Women in the Field and Where Do They Work?

One-third of the 691,000 college professors are women. They are mainly in nursing, home economics, and library science. Less than 10 percent of the women are in engineering, physical sciences, law, and agriculture. Half of all female college professors are employed in eight states, each with college enrollments exceeding 2,000,000: California, Illinois, Massachusetts, Michigan, New York, Ohio, Pennsylvania, and Texas.

$ $ $ $ $

In 1980, a college instructor with a nine-month contract averaged $15,179. Based on the same contract, an assistant professor made $18,900, an associate professor made $23,199, and a full professor made $30,738. Beginning teaching salaries are much less than the average, and women do not receive equal pay for equal jobs in most colleges. The American Association of University Professors reports that, on the average, women college professors earned about $3,000 less than men in 1975. Another survey found that women are no better off than they were in 1969. While 21 percent of the men under age 35 have reached the rank of associate professor, only 8 percent of the women have. Only 12 percent of women faculty are full professors, compared to 31 percent of men faculty. Within each rank, women receive lower pay, with the highest rank having the greatest disparity.

What Is the Future for Women?

College teaching jobs will be very competitive through the 1980s. With the oversupply of Ph.D.s and the decreased college enrollment in the past few years, there is no demand for teachers or professors in most fields through 1985. In education alone, there are 119,000 Ph.D.s more than number of jobs available for them. One area in higher education that is growing is continuing education for adults, who attend community colleges part-time and at night. That's where the jobs will be.

RELATED CAREERS

college administrator   dean of students
college librarian   admissions officer
career counselor

WHERE CAN I GET MORE INFORMATION?

Professional Group
American Association of University Professors
1 Dupont Circle, NW, Suite 500
Washington, D.C. 20036

Trade Journal
AAUP Bulletin
AAUP
1 Dupont Circle, NW
Washington, D.C. 20036

COLLEGE STUDENT PERSONNEL

*Help students meet their personal, social,
housing, and recreational needs.*

What's It Like to Be a Dean of Students?

Claire Fulture, Dean of Students of Long Island University, says, "The Dean is responsible for individualizing education for the students in her college. She can be responsible for counseling students, advising student government officers, residence halls programs, an orientation program for new students, sororities, student honoraries, and communications between faculty and students. These activities become very meaningful when helping students take advantage of all the educational opportunities on campus. I get very involved with the students. For young college students, it is usually their first time away from home, and they are at the age when they are finding out who they are, what they can do, and what they can become. Adult students have different concerns. Often, adults are combining family life with student life and a job on the side!" Personnel has to catch up with all of these needs.

What Education and Skills Will I Need?

High school: Preparation for college, with a broad range of academic subjects.

College: Many students prepare for graduate school with a major in social sciences or education. A master's degree is required for student personnel in higher education and a doctorate for the better universities and top career jobs.

Personal skills: Ability to work with people of all backgrounds and ages; emotional stability while under pressure from students, parents, and faculty; patience when working with conflicting viewpoints.

How Many Women in the Field and Where Do They Work?

Of the 50,000 college student personnel workers, one-third are women. The jobs they hold include Dean of Women, Dean of Students, Residence Hall Dean, Counselor, Financial Aid Officer, Foreign Student Advisor, Student Union Worker, Student Government Specialist, and Activities Director. Every two-year and four-year college in the country hires student personnel workers.

$ $ $ $ $

In 1981, the average salaries of student placement directors was $20,671.

What Is the Future for Women?

Competition for jobs is expected through the 1980s. Because of the tight budgets of all higher-education institutions, many jobs in personnel have been cut. The rise in the number of student services could mean more demand for specialized college personnel workers, but lower residential enrollments will keep jobs down and make them hard to get.

RELATED CAREERS

high school counselor	industrial personnel manager
school administrator	school psychologist

WHERE CAN I GET MORE INFORMATION?

Professional Group
American College Personnel Association
Two Skyline Place
5203 Leesburg Pike
Falls Church, VA 22041

Trade Journal
Journal of College Student Personnel
1607 New Hampshire Avenue, NW
Washington, D.C. 20009

EARLY CHILDHOOD EDUCATOR

Teaches children from two through five years old.
Day-care workers also take responsibility for infants.

What's It Like to Be an Early Childhood Educator?

An early childhood educator, or child-care worker, works with small groups of children in an unstructured situation for a few hours a day. The program usually consists of reading to the children, painting, working with clay and crafts, free play, music, dance, teaching colors and numbers, and talking about community services, transportation, and families. Day-care and child-care centers often run from 7:00 A.M. until 7:00 P.M., and children come and go according to the hours their parents work. As more two-career families send their preschool children to these centers, jobs increase for professionals in this crucial field. Day-care Director Mary Marshall says, "You learn how delightful human beings can be when you work with young children as they learn, are curious, and show their many interests. Early childhood education is just beginning to get the recognition it deserves for its importance in child development."

What Education and Skills Will I Need?

High school: Preparation for college.

College: You can prepare for early childhood education with a two-year program in a community college, or a degree program in a four-year college, or an advanced degree. Most nursery schools are private, and a degree is not required for teaching. Many nursery schools are informal cooperatives where the children's parents are involved in teaching and planning school programs. Day-care centers and government programs for early childhood education increasingly will require degrees; master's degrees will be necessary for administration of these programs.

Personal skills: Ability to be firmly low-keyed to allow children to express themselves in a learning environment; an avid interest in the growth and development of small children; and the ability to be relaxed in an active setting.

How Many Women in the Field and Where Do They Work?

Ninety percent of the 239,000 nursery and kindergarten teachers are women. Most communities have several morning and afternoon nursery-school sessions and day-care centers.

$ $ $ $ $

Salaries vary more than any other teaching job because the school may be in a parent's home and dependent upon how many children attend. College graduates working in public and university nursery schools begin around $10,000, about the same starting salary for elementary teachers.

What Is the Future for Women?

Two-career families with children have created the need for more day-care and early-childhood care. The government has responded very slowly and often not at all on a federal level. However, as parents make this issue a priority, day-care will be forthcoming for children from all economic levels. There will be an increasing number of opportunities for qualified people to establish and run both part-time and full-time early-childhood education centers.

RELATED CAREERS
elementary school teacher
industrial training manager
salesperson

WHERE CAN I GET MORE INFORMATION?
Professional Group
National Association for the Education of Young Children
1834 Connecticut Avenue, NW
Washington, D.C. 20009

Trade Journals
Day Care and Child Development Reports
Plus Publications
2814 Pennsylvania Avenue, NW
Washington, D.C. 20007

Young Children
1834 Connecticut Avenue, NW
Washington, D.C. 20009

ELEMENTARY SCHOOL TEACHER

*Teaches science, mathematics, language, and
social studies to children in kindergarten
through sixth grade.*

What's It Like to Be an Elementary School Teacher?

Everyone has been to elementary school and has seen what it's like to be a teacher. Sylvia Fine, a beginning teacher of first-grade gifted children in Queens, New York, finds the work intellectually and emotionally draining. "Anyone can do the job," says Fine, "but to do it well requires a lot of daily planning, round-the clock dedication, and a great deal of self-confidence and assurance, which you don't always get from the students or parents." What she likes best about teaching is helping children make connections between ideas and information they have learned.

Elsie Braun, an experienced fifth-grade teacher, shares a

teaching job with her husband. When asked what advice she would give to students planning their careers, she says, "How do you prepare a young person for a time in life when they will begin to get tired of a career? I don't think I would suggest what my husband and I are doing as a place for young people to start a career. I think they need a little more distance in order to develop their own working style and identity. I do think people can anticipate the need to change a career at some point in life, though. What we are doing offers a possible variation. For me, it has meant that I can go on doing work that I enjoy and am good at, without the crushing fatigue and stress I was feeling the last few years I was teaching full-time." The Braun teaching team earns one salary, which is a variation on the usual work pattern. They doubt if they would have done that twenty years ago. What does Ms. Braun like best about her job? "I love being with the kids."

What Education and Skills Will I Need?

High school: Preparation for college, with as broad a program as possible. Most elementary teachers teach all subjects, including music, arts, and physical education. So, be prepared!

College: Four years of college with a major in elementary education is required. A teaching certificate is awarded by every state, and many states require a fifth year of preparation for a permanent certificate. Plan your fifth year or master's degree in a special area of education, such as administration.

Personal skills: Dependability, good judgment, and enthusiasm for young children are needed.

How Many Women in the Field and Where Do They Work?

Elementary school teaching is the largest professional field for women. Of the 1.6 million elementary school teachers, 83 percent are women, and an additional 60,000 women are principals and supervisors. They teach elementary school in every city, town, and village in the United States.

$ $ $ $ $

Salaries are determined by level of education, years of experience, and location of the job. Most states have a minimum starting salary. The average salary for all elementary teachers in 1981 was $16,879 for a ten-month contract.

What Is the Future for Women?

Overcrowded! The decline in elementary school enrollments and the over-production of teacher graduates have caused a very competitive situation for teaching jobs through the 1980s. Many graduates cannot find a teaching job. The best possibilities for jobs are in the inner city and rural areas, and in specialization to work with the disabled. Some predict the job market will improve with a higher birth rate in the 1980s.

RELATED CAREERS
administrator   training manager
public relations representative   salesperson

WHERE CAN I GET MORE INFORMATION?
Professional Group
National Education Association
1201 16th Street, NW
Washington, D.C. 20036

Trade Journal
Today's Education
NEA
1201 16th Street, NW
Washington, D.C. 20036

HIGH SCHOOL TEACHER
*Teaches a specific subject in junior or senior
high school, grades 7 through 12.*

What's It Like to Be a High School Teacher?
"If you are one of the lucky people who believe in adolescents, who enjoy watching and helping young people in their everyday lives, there is nothing as rewarding as teaching them,

being with them, and helping them every day in school," writes mathematics teacher Susan Lee Sung from Los Angeles. High school teachers teach four or five classes a day and supervise study halls, lunch cafeteria, and activities. As a student, you have a better idea of what a high school teacher does than you have about any other occupation—you can see them at work all the time! You certainly notice which teachers enjoy their work, which make the most sense to you. If you want a career like that of the teachers who are really reaching you, you have a good example before you of what their life is like. Talk to them!

What Education and Skills Will I Need?

High school: Preparation for college, with as broad a program as possible.

College: Major in the subject you wish to teach, or a related subject if you are planning to attend graduate school. Each state has its own certification system; many require a master's degree for permanent certification. There are several ways for you to do graduate work, including summer school, evening school, and correspondence courses. You might plan your graduate work in administration, where women are needed and where you can make more money and participate in policy making.

Personal skills: Good teachers have a desire to work with young people, an interest in a special subject, and the ability to motivate others and relate knowledge to them.

How Many Women in the Field and Where Do They Work?

There are 12 million secondary school teachers, and half of them are women. But, most high school administrators and supervisors are men. Teachers teach in every community in the country, a big advantage for a person who wants a job that is available anywhere.

$ $ $ $ $

Salaries vary with educational background, experience, and job location. In 1981, the average salary for a high school teacher was $17,725. Most states now have a minimum salary for a beginner with a bachelor's degree.

What Is the Future for Women?

Overcrowded! The United States is oversupplied with high school teachers and will be through the 1980s. The best chances for getting jobs are in mathematics and natural and physical sciences.

RELATED CAREERS

administrator   training manager
public relations representative   salesperson

WHERE CAN I GET MORE INFORMATION?

Professional Group
National Education Association
1201 16th Street, NW
Washington, D.C. 20036

Trade Journal
Today's Education
NEA
1201 16th Street, NW
Washington, D.C. 20036

LIBRARIAN

*Selects and organizes collections of books and other
media and provides people access to information.*

What's It Like to Be a Librarian?

Elizabeth Dow, elementary school librarian, trainer of a dog-sled team, and married to a high school football coach tells us about her day. "Several classes come into the library. I read a story to them or tell them about some books, or give a lesson on some skill needed to use a library well. Between classes, I have my choice of buying new materials, cataloging recently bought materials, preparing lessons for classes, chasing down the answer to some technical problem (for example, finding the missing shelf-list card for a book), organizing a unit of materials to go to a classroom, helping students who come to the library in search of information or just wanting a book, weeding out old unusable or outdated material, repairing books, keeping up with invoices, purchase orders, and packing slips, deciding what to do about material that has been gone too long, figuring out why a machine isn't working, and going through the mail. And then there is always recess, where I keep up with what's being taught in the classrooms."

Students planning a career as a school librarian should know what the job is like. Dow says, "It helps if one has a high tolerance for being interrupted and for the imperfections of other people, a real desire to help other people, a capacity for remembering trivia, a sense of organization, a capacity for keeping a lot of loose ends in mind, and a sense of humor. Since one is usually the only librarian in a school, there is a certain loneliness about the job. Nobody else really understands the joy of discovering the perfect Dewey number for an item that has been nagging at your head. One will rarely develop the real closeness that exists between teacher and child. No one uses the library to the capacity that the librarian knows is possible. People forget to express appreciation that they feel, so one must intuit appreciation. And people do not express dissatisfaction, so one must intuit that also. You need to be more or less self-actualizing. The difficult part of the job is the routine work: carding, shelving books, dunning people for overdue items, taking inventory, and so on. On the other hand, there is no end to what needs to be done, so if you are sick of doing something dull, you can always drop it and do something else for a while. The part of the job that makes it all worthwhile is connecting the perfect library item with a student at the exact moment the student needs it. This could be the right story, item of information, or curiosity stimulator. Seeing the click in the children's eyes and knowing I've expanded their world or met their need is a great high."

What Education and Skills Will I Need?

High school: Preparation for college, with as broad a program as possible. Verbal and language skills are important to develop.

LIBRARIAN

College: Strong liberal arts program to prepare for a graduate degree in library science. A reading knowledge of one foreign language is often required, and computer science is increasingly essential to the job.

Personal skills: Good librarians have a strong intellectual curiosity and an interest in helping others to use library materials.

How Many Women in the Field and Where Do They Work?

There are 135,000 full-time professional librarians, and another 10,500 audiovisual specialists who work in school media centers. Eighty-five percent are women. In addition, there are many part-time and nongraduate-degree librarians working in the public libraries all over the country. More than half of the professional librarians are public school librarians, one-fourth are public librarians, and one-fifth are college and university librarians.

$ $ $ $ $

In 1980, a graduate school librarian started at $13,127 a year. Beginning technical librarians in private industry averaged $14,500 a year, and those with five years' experience averaged $21,300 a year. Most school librarians are paid on the regular teacher's salary scale for their school.

What Is the Future for Women?

The large number of library school graduates and the declining school population make it a competitive field. Information management outside the library setting is expected to offer excellent opportunities for library school graduates.

RELATED CAREERS
archivist
publisher's representative
book critic
museum curator
information scientist

WHERE CAN I GET MORE INFORMATION?
Professional Groups
American Library Association
50 East Huron Street
Chicago, IL 60611

Special Libraries Association
235 Park Avenue South
New York, NY 10003

Trade Journal
Top of the News
50 East Huron Street
Chicago, IL 60611

MUSEUM PERSONNEL

*Create museum exhibits and manage the work of
a museum. There are museums of art, natural
history (plants, animals, minerals), history
and industry.*

What's It Like to Be
in Museum Personnel?

As a professional museum worker for the Wadsworth Atheneum in Hartford, Connecticut, and for the Cloisters of the Metropolitan Museum of Art, in New York, Janet K. Schloat leads museum tours for schools, churches, and adult groups. She takes care of slide collections, helps curators, gives evening lectures, takes museum slides to schools for presentations, helps with library research work and helps curators install new exhibits. Curators of a museum design and install exhibits, revise old exhibits, and prepare budgets for the museum programs. They are experts in a particular field. For example, natural history museums have anthropologists, botanists, and geologists as curators on their staffs.

MUSEUM PERSONNEL

What Education and Skills Will I Need?

High school: Preparation for college, with emphasis on art and social sciences.

College: Most people in a museum career majored in art history; some majored in anthropology. A few universities give graduate degrees in museum management.

Personal skills: Creativity, an interest in history and art, and the ability to teach others is needed for success in museum careers.

How Many Women in the Field and Where Do They Work?

There are about 30,000 museum workers, with more being women than men. The pay is very low for the level of education required and the amount of job responsibility. Most curators work in the major cities where the large museums are — New York, Chicago, Los Angeles, and Boston.

$ $ $ $ $

In 1980, college graduates started at $12,000 to $14,000 a year, with small advances coming very infrequently.

What Is the Future for Women?

In spite of the low pay, beginning jobs for college graduates are very competitive. Art history graduates love their work in the museums and thousands of new graduates apply each spring all over the country for the few museum openings. An advanced degree with some part-time or summer experience is the best chance for the new graduate to enter the field.

RELATED CAREERS
   librarian
   anthropologist
   art designer

WHERE CAN I GET MORE INFORMATION?

Professional Group
American Association of Museums
2233 Wisconsin Avenue, NW
Washington, D.C. 20007

Trade Journal
Museum News
AAM
2233 Wisconsin Avenue, NW
Washington, D.C. 20007

PHYSICAL EDUCATION TEACHER

Teaches physical education and health to students from kindergarten through college.

What's It Like to Be a Physical Education Teacher?

Teaching girls a physical activity in an informal setting within the school system is a very rewarding career. A physical education teacher is often very tuned in to her students, their needs and problems, and the development of their lives. Teaching any subject can be helpful to students, but a physical education teacher is often called upon to help other staff members, the guidance department, and the administration to know more about the behavior of a student. A physical education teacher gets to know her students well because sports and after-school activities offer a different type of learning situation. The teacher usually plans her own physical education program, with an emphasis on sports, dance, group exercises, or field sports according to her own interests, the community she is in, and the facilities available. With new laws, now there must be equal budgets for girls' and women's sports. Weekend skiing, biking, and hiking outings also can be part of a physical education program.

What Education and Skills Will I Need?

High school: Preparation for college, with an emphasis on science and mathematics. Participate in as many sports as possible.

College: Major or minor in physical education. A master's degree is needed for certification in many states, and always for college teaching. Anatomy, physiology, and health courses are required for a physical education major.

Personal skills: Physical education teachers must be athletic, able to encourage those who are not athletic, interested in the total development of children, fair-minded, and able to encourage youth to practice good health habits.

How Many Women in the Field and Where Do They Work?

Every high school and most elementary schools have a woman physical education teacher. Summer work is always available for camp and playground jobs and administration of these recreational facilities.

$ $ $ $ $

Physical education teachers receive the same salaries as all other teachers within a particular school system. In 1981, most high school physical education teachers averaged $17,725 a year.

What Is the Future for Women?

As in other teaching jobs, there are many more teachers than jobs now and through the 1980s. The best chances for work will be in special schools, inner-city schools, and rural schools. There is a great turnover, as many physical education teachers leave the profession for related work in recreation, physical therapy, and guidance. This career takes more than a love of playing sports. It is an educational career, and sports are the medium for teaching students. Sports are one place where girls and women can learn about leadership, aggression, and competition, with everyone's approval. If you are interested in the development of young people, teaching physical education can be a unique career today with the new equality standards in sports for women.

RELATED CAREERS

teacher

athletic director

coach

athletic trainer

WHERE CAN I GET MORE INFORMATION?

Professional Group
Health, Physical Education, Recreation
1201 16th Street, NW
Washington, D.C. 20036

Trade Journals
Coaching: Women's Athletics
P.O. Box 867
Wallingford, CT 06492

Scholastic Coach
50 West 44 Street
New York, NY 10036

SCHOOL PRINCIPAL

*Manages, directs, and coordinates the activities
of a school, college, or university.*

What's It Like to Be a School Principal?

"I do everything I can to free the classroom teachers to create the best possible learning environment for their students. This means that teachers are free from concern about classroom size, heat, furniture, teaching aids, transportation, lunches, and interruptions," says Iris Delany, Principal of a small city school in West Virginia. "I like being responsible for our school policy and philosophy, and for hiring teachers who I think will work well in our system and with each other." Women should be in on the policy making rather than having only men hold the positions of principal, superintendent, dean, and president. If more female college graduates would get their master's degree in administration rather than in guidance or special education, they would be prepared for advancement into administrative jobs. It doesn't make sense that women are interested in every educational job except the best paid and most responsible ones in the school—the administration jobs.

Principal Marjorie L. Cook spends her days visiting classes, then she does the administrative work after school when the students have left. She likes being with the students and teachers most of the day so that educational policy and programs come directly from classroom needs. Cook finds being the person in charge an exciting and always changing experience.

What Education and Skills Will I Need?

High school: Preparation for any college major that relates to teaching or education.

College: Major in any subject you wish to teach in school or college. If you want to be a college dean, college president, or large-city high school superintendent, prepare for a master's degree and work toward your doctorate in administration.

Personal skills: Interest in the development of children, business ability, and the ability to communicate with many diverse ideas and people are necessary.

How Many Women in the Field and Where Do They Work?

In the late 1970s, only 2 percent of the 127,000 secondary principals and assistants were women. Today, only 13 percent of more than 173,000 school administrators are women, and statistics show women are losing two percentage points a year in the administrative race.

A female school superintendent is very rare, even though teaching is a so-called "woman's profession." Out of 700 superintendents in New England, only 12 are women. The city of Chicago has its first black female superintendent of schools, Ruth Burnett Love, former head of schools in Oakland, California. Many states in the country have no female superintendents. The number of women in college administration is just as low as in elementary school and high school administration. Less than 5 percent of the country's colleges and universities are headed by a woman—and this includes women's colleges. It was as late as 1978 when Hanna Holborn Gray became the President of the University of Chicago, the first woman president of a major private research university.

$ $ $ $ $

School administrators usually get paid some percentage more than whatever the teachers make in any given school. A superintendent with a master's degree in a small rural area earns about $20,000 a year, and a superintendent with a doctorate in a large urban area earns $45,000 a year. In 1981, an elementary school principal averaged $27,923, and a high school principal averaged $32,231.

What Is the Future for Women?

The employment outlook is competitive for administrators as it is for all educators through the 1980s. The need for elementary school administrators may increase somewhat in the late 1980s as the birthrate rises. Women, however, will have a better chance at the few jobs than will men because the law is now trying to balance the employment ratio of women to men by getting more women into these jobs. Several women's groups have brought cases to court for discrimination against promoting women to school administrative jobs. These court decisions in favor of women and your preparation in graduate school will help bring about better career opportunities in education administration for women.

On the university level, Smith College, the nation's largest women's liberal arts college, finally hired its first woman president in 1975. Vassar College had its second woman president in 1977, over 30 years after the first.

RELATED CAREERS
   teacher
   director of agencies
   management career in government
   management career in business

WHERE CAN I GET MORE INFORMATION?

Professional Group
National Education Association
1201 16th Street, NW
Washington, D.C. 20036

Trade Journal
Nation's Schools
McGraw-Hill, Inc.
230 West Monroe
Chicago, IL 60606

SCHOOL COUNSELOR

*Helps students gain a better understanding of
their interests, abilities, and personality
characteristics in context of their
educational development.*

What's It Like to Be a School Counselor?

According to Grace Butterweck, School Counselor in a Westchester County, New York, high school, "I spend half of my day with students, individually or in small groups; about a fourth of the day talking with parents and teachers, on the phone and in conferences; and the other fourth in administrative work, with records, college and work applications, and correspondence. After-school hours also are important, since students and teachers like to drop by the guidance office informally with questions or for visits. Many evenings are involved attending school activities. It is important to the students to have their counselors attend sports, social, and cultural activities." A counselor is responsible for helping students with their educational and career development. She gives students information and helps them relate that information to all of their educational choices. In this way, she provides students with a basis for good educational decision making.

What Education and Skills Will I Need?

High school: Preparation for college. Most school counselors teach a subject before going into counseling.

College: A master's degree in guidance and one to five years of teaching are required by most states to be a certified school counselor. A doctorate is required for big-city administrative careers in guidance.

Personal skills: Successful counselors have an interest in helping others take responsibility for themselves, and an ability to work with other educators, parents, and teachers who may have varying opinions on students' development.

How Many Women in the Field and Where Do They Work?

About half of the 53,000 full-time school counselors are women, and most counselors work in the large public secondary schools.

$ $ $ $ $

Salaries vary with the school system, but usually counselors are paid more than classroom teachers and less than administrators. In 1981, the average salary for counselors was $20,600. Experienced counselors in the major suburbs earned about $26,000. Counselors often work eleven months a year.

What Is the Future for Women?

The future is bleak through the 1980s. The decline in the school population and the cuts in public school budgets are making guidance jobs very competitive.

RELATED CAREERS
  psychologist
  social worker
  parole officer
  rehabilitation counselor

WHERE CAN I GET MORE INFORMATION?
Professional Group
American School Counselor Association
Two Skyline Place, Suite 400
5203 Leesburg Pike
Falls Church, VA 22041

Trade Journal
Guidepost
ASCA
Two Skyline Place, Suite 400
5203 Leesburg Pike
Falls Church, VA 22041

SPECIAL EDUCATION TEACHER
*Teaches disabled children who are unable to learn
in large classroom situations without special
related services some of the time; or teaches
disabled children who learn best when they are
separated into small groups all of the time.*

What's It Like to Be a Special Education Teacher?

Special educator Carol Rich spends her day assessing students who have been referred for special education by classroom teachers, instructing disabled children in small groups, tutoring some children on a one-to-one basis, and supervising teacher's aides. She spends a lot of time consulting with classroom teachers about the students who leave their classrooms for tutoring but return and are "mainstreamed" for most of their school day. She also evaluates tests and is a regular member of a team for developing the Individualized Educational Program (IEP) for disabled children.

Rich finds the endless paper work a hassle, because she always must be after the classroom teachers to fill out the forms

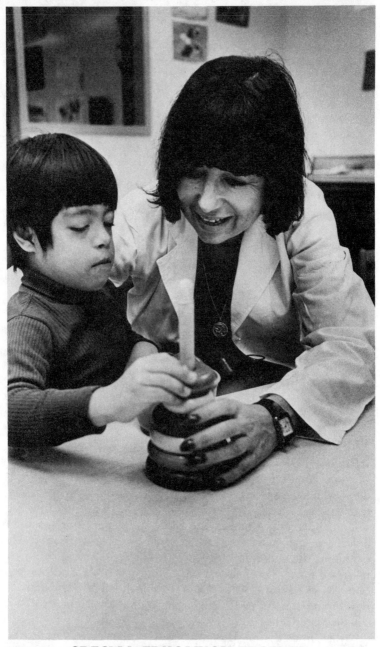

SPECIAL EDUCATION TEACHER

required by law. Her most satisfying experience comes from helping students develop positive changes in their self-images, as they learn to see themselves in terms of their abilities.

What Education and Skills Will I Need?

High school: Preparation for college, with an emphasis on subjects that interest you.

College: Major in any subject, or in education, elementary education, or special education, and prepare for a master's degree. Most states require a master's degree for certification, although you can begin teaching with a bachelor's degree.

Personal skills: Patience in handling slow progress, ability to work with disabled children and their parents, ability to see accomplishment in things that might seem small.

$ $ $ $ $

Salaries vary with the community and the school system. They are the same as salaries of other teachers within the school system, usually averaging $17,725 a year with experience.

What Is the Future for Women?

The good opportunities that existed for special education teachers in the 1970s have been drastically changed because the federal government has decreased funds for education. Now, local schools often consider this teaching an "extra."

RELATED CAREERS

rehabilitation counselor	occupational therapist
social worker	reading specialist

WHERE CAN I GET MORE INFORMATION?

Professional Group
National Education Association
1201 16th Street, NW
Washington, D.C. 20036

Trade Journal
Teaching Exceptional Children
Council for Exceptional Children
1411 South Jefferson Davis Highway, Suite 900
Arlington, VA 22202

GOVERNMENT

City Manager
Community Planner
Foreign Service Officer
Civil Service
Health and Regulatory Inspector
Law Enforcement
Lawyer
Military Careers
Peace Corps Volunteer

About these careers   Until very recently, the U.S.
Government was the nation's largest employer. Today, there are
14.5 million civilian workers in local, state, and federal government
jobs. This means that one out of every six employed persons in our
country works in government. One third of all government workers,
or 4.6 million, are college graduates. In addition, there are 2.2
million military men and women on active duty.

Although government employment has been a major career for
college graduates in the past, job opportunities in government will
be declining rapidly through 1990. If there are jobs, they are
projected to occur in state and local agencies, who are getting more
responsibilities back from the federal government.

Preparing for a career with the government is different from
preparing for most career clusters, because the government hires
about every kind of career described in this book. Therefore,
accountants, physicians, teachers, nurses, and purchasing agents
are all careers that can be government careers. They require a great
variety of educational backgrounds.

The government-related careers described in this cluster, such
as city manager, community planner, and lawyer, require graduate
work. For example, a master's degree in public or business
administration is becoming increasingly important for those who
want to be a city manager.

Volunteer jobs in the Peace Corps are limited to two years and
do not necessarily lead to paying jobs that are directly related to
that experience.

Beginning lawyers who are engaged in legal-aid work usually
receive the lowest starting salaries. New lawyers starting their own
practice may earn little more than expenses during the first few
years. When a case is being tried, lawyers often work long hours and
are under considerable pressure. In addition, they must keep up with
the latest laws and court decisions. However, since lawyers in
private practice can determine their own hours and workload, many
stay in practice well past the usual retirement age.

People who work for the government find maximum security in
terms of regular pay, regular work, vacations, a good retirement
plan, and excellent health insurance.

CITY MANAGER

Administers and coordinates the day-to-day operations of the city.

What's It Like to Be a City Manager?

Planning for future growth, controlling air and water pollution, and combating rising crime rates demand the services of a good city manager. City managers also are in charge of tax collection, law enforcement, public works, and preparing the city's budget. They are responsible to the community's elected officials who hire them. Besides attending to the daily activities of the city, they study long-range problems of traffic, housing, crime, and urban renewal and report their findings to the elected council. They often work with citizens' groups and give reports to special city committees. Many of the citizens' group meetings are held after work hours.

What Education and Skills Will I Need?

High school: Preparation for college, with group experience in as many school activities as interest you.

College: Major in business, engineering, recreation, or political science. A master's degree in public or municipal administration is necessary for the better jobs.

Personal skills: Ability to quickly isolate problems, identify their causes, and find solutions; good judgment; and self-confidence are needed for this job, as well as skills in working well with others.

How Many Women in the Field and Where Do They Work?

There are 3,300 city managers plus many more assistant city managers and department heads. This is a new and growing career. Over three-quarters of the city managers work for small cities with less than 25,000 population. There are almost no women in city management. For the first time, women are getting elected as mayors of major cities. See "Political Scientist," page 298.

$ $ $ $ $

Starting salary for new college graduates is $18,000 a year as assistant city managers. Average salary for experienced managers is $33,000 a year, ranging from $28,000 in small cities to $70,000 in cities with populations of 500,000 to 1 million.

What Is the Future for Women?

Jobs will be competitive through the 1980s, with many more graduates than jobs. The best opportunities are in the South and the West.

RELATED CAREERS

business administrator	school administrator
hospital administrator	airport manager

WHERE CAN I GET MORE INFORMATION?

Professional Group
International City Management Association
1140 Connecticut Avenue, NW
Washington, D.C. 20036

Trade Journal
Nation's Cities
National League of Cities
1612 K Street, NW
Washington, D.C. 20006

COMMUNITY PLANNER

*Develops plans and programs for orderly growth
and improvement of urban and rural communities.*

What's It Like to Be a Community Planner?

Carol Thomas describes what it's like to be planning consultant in a business, faculty member of the graduate school at the University of Rhode Island, and mother of two children. "The morning is devoted to administration—corresponding primarily with municipal planning boards; answering inquiries about subdivisions, zoning decisions, and site location; and preparing material for meetings. The afternoons are used for spe-

COMMUNITY PLANNER

cific projects. These include basic studies, such as data collection, economic base and regional analysis, population studies, and map preparation; planning recommendations for land-use allocation, utilities, municipal facilities, housing, open spaces, recreation, and beautification programs; and planning implementation of the budget, subdivision regulations, and citizen information programs. The usual work includes making master plans, reviewing work completed by other staff members, and reading professional journals and publications. Several evenings a week are devoted to professional meetings and meetings with planning boards and civic groups."

What Education and Skills Will I Need?

High school: Preparation for college, with an emphasis on mathematics, computer science, and social sciences.

College: A beginning job requires a master's degree in urban or regional planning, which is offered in 70 colleges and universities. To prepare for graduate school, major in architecture, engineering, economics, social science, or public administration.

Personal skills: Planners must be able to think in spatial relationships and to visualize plans and designs, be flexible in solving problems, and be able to cooperate with others who have different ideas.

How Many Women in the Field and Where Do They Work?

Ten percent of the 23,000 community planners are women. The majority of community planners work for the government in agencies such as city, county, or urban regional planning organizations. In addition to their regular job, many planners do part-time consulting work with a private firm or developer.

$ $ $ $ $

In 1981, beginning salary for a community planner with a master's degree working for the federal government was $18,600 a year. Consultants are paid on a fee basis according to their regional or national reputation. Directors of planning earned an average salary of $27,000 a year.

What Is the Future for Women?

The employment outlook will become more competitive through the 1980s. An oversupply of graduates and cuts in government spending will limit the job opportunities dramatically. Geographic mobility and willingness to work in small towns are important for many job seekers.

RELATED CAREERS
planning engineer
city manager
architect

WHERE CAN I GET MORE INFORMATION?
Professional Group
American Planning Association
1776 Massachusetss Avenue, NW
Washington, D.C. 20036

Trade Journal
City
National Urban Coalition
2100 M Street, NW
Washington, D.C. 20037

FOREIGN SERVICE OFFICER
Serves in the overseas arm of the United States'
foreign relations activities.

What's It Like to Be a Foreign Service Officer?

Foreign service officers protect and promote the welfare and the interest of the United States and the American people. Working in the Department of State, they are responsible for advising the President on matters of foreign policy; for conducting relations with foreign countries; for protecting the political, economic, and commercial interests of the United States overseas; and for offering services to Americans abroad and to foreign nationals traveling to the United States. Genta A. Hawkins, Foreign Service Officer, appointed by the President and confirmed by the U.S. Senate, writes about her first assignment to the Embassy. "As consular officer, I issued visas to tourists, diplomats, and businesspeople coming to the U.S.; helped Americans in distress; witnessed marriages; signed birth certificates; and renewed passports. When I was a member of the economic section, I traveled extensively throughout the Ivory Coast to find worthwhile projects and to assess their progress. I served as escort officer for a group of American journalists, and for an American folk group who toured the country. Most evenings were filled with official obligations. Dinners and diplomatic receptions were held at the beautiful presidential palace. My current assignment in Washington consists of writing speeches and articles, planning conferences, and acting as a liaison with private agencies. The evening responsibilities of a young foreign service officer in Washington are not as rigorous as in the field, but there are occasional receptions at the embassies and welcoming ceremonies for visiting heads of state on the White House lawn."

In 1982, Rozanne Ridgway was the top-ranking woman in the foreign service, serving as special assistant to Secretary of State Haig. She won her credentials as chief U.S. delegate for negotiating fisheries treaties.

What Education and Skills Will I Need?

High school: Preparation for college, with emphasis in the social sciences, history, government, and foreign language.

College: Foreign service officers come from liberal arts colleges, with majors in English, foreign languages, international relations, history, government, economics, or law. A master's degree is not a requirement, but most officers do have an advanced degree. Of the junior officers appointed in 1980, 57 percent had master's degrees, 11 percent had law degrees, and 11 percent had doctorates. The average age was 28 to 30, and most had a few years of professional experience. Some 38 percent possessed skills in one foreign language, and 16 percent had skills in two or more foreign languages. Everyone applying for an appointment must take the written examination, which is given once each year in December, in about 150 cities. Applications must be made by late October.

Personal skills: Representatives of the U.S. government must have a good physical appearance, be tactful, and have a pleasant personality, in addition to the ability to study and solve problems.

How Many Women in the Field and Where Do They Work?

Although only 560 (14.8 percent) of all career foreign service officers are women, about 30 percent of all *new* officers are women. They are stationed in Washington, or in any of the 150 countries where the U.S. has some 3,400 foreign service posts. Foreign service officers serve as administrative, consular, economic, and political officers in more than 230 U.S. embassies and consulates in over 140 nations.

$ $ $ $ $

In 1980, beginning salaries ranged from $17,000 to $25,000 a year. Salaries for women in the mid-level hiring program start at $30,000. The top salary, which is the same for all federal employees, is $52,750. In addition, there are many fringe, living, and travel benefits.

What Is the Future for Women?

Jobs are very competitive. Only 200 foreign service officers are appointed a year, and thousands of qualified people apply. Almost all of the women are single, and if they marry with the hope of being assigned together, they seldom are. Some ambassadors do marry and live apart, or the husband happens to have a job, such as writing, that he can do anywhere.

RELATED CAREERS
    international business sales
    federal government career
    import business manager

WHERE CAN I GET MORE INFORMATION?
Professional Groups
Board of Examiners for the Foreign Service
Box 9317, Rosslyn Station
Arlington, VA 22209

Foreign Service Careers
Department of State
Washington, D.C. 20520

CIVIL SERVICE

*Federal government jobs represent every kind of
job found in private employment.*

What's It Like to Be in Civil Service?

Four-year college graduates can enter career management, administrative and personnel management, and technical and professional jobs with the government. Two-year college graduates can enter technical assistance careers in economics, administration, writing, data processing, finance, accounting, law, library science, and physical science.

There are two ways to get a federal job. The first and most common is by taking the civil service examination and being placed on a civil service register. Whenever a job opening occurs in a federal agency, the registers are scanned and the names of the best-qualified applicants are sent to the agency. You can increase your chances of getting a federal job by filing in more than one category and by agreeing to move anywhere in the country. The biggest barrier for women is the veteran's preference policy.

The second way to get a federal job is by political appointment. By law, there are over 3,000 high-level jobs that are filled in this way. If you are well known in your field, get in touch with your senator for a recommendation, or with your company for the President's Program for Executive Exchange. If you have not yet made a name for yourself in your career, you can work long and hard on a successful presidential campaign.

A short-term government service can offer you a valuable step up in your career. Carla A. Hills, former Secretary of the Department of Housing and Urban Development, says this about a government term for women. "As you gather experiences, including government experience, you become better at everything you do. It is the breadth of exposure that makes you valuable to an employer. In my view, government is incredibly stimulating, challenging, and broader than most people in the private sector believe. Your responsibilities invariably are greater than your job description." After three years of work in government service, the worker has career status. For example, if a mother leaves her job to raise children, she can return to the same job level rather than competing again for the level she left.

What Education and Skills Will I Need?

High school: Preparation for junior college, business college, nurse's training, or four-year college in any field that interests you.

College: The more education you have, the higher the government career level open to you. Two-year college graduates take the Junior Federal Assistant Examination or the Junior Engineer and Science Assistant Examination to qualify for jobs. Four-year college graduates take the Federal Service Entrance Examination to qualify for trainee-level positions for careers.

Personal skills: Skills needed vary according to the career you select.

How Many Women in the Field and Where Do They Work?

Each year, ten thousand federal jobs requiring college degrees are available and one-third of them go to women. The federal government employs nearly 2 million white-collar workers. Nearly 470,000 of them are general clerical workers. About 150,000 of them work in engineering, 150,000 in accounting, 120,000 in health service, and 45,000 in biological and agricultural service. One in eight federal employees works in Washington; the others work all over the U.S. and abroad.

$ $ $ $ $

Salaries are paid according to the General Schedule (GS) and are set by Congress. The pay scale is set for all government employees in the professions, administrative jobs, and technical and clerical jobs. There are raises within each grade and increases are periodic for each grade. In 1981, graduates of a two-year college without experience started at $12,300 a year; graduates of a four-year college started at $15,900 or $17,700 a year; a person with a master's degree began work at $18,600 a year.

What Is the Future for Women?

Government service employs over 14.5 million workers— that means that one out of six employed persons in the U.S. works for the government! The political trend is to heavily reduce the number of federal employees, so the number of available federal jobs is rapidly declining. Besides no new jobs being opened, thousands of federal employees are job-hunting, which is causing a very competitive situation.

Federal jobs are open to women in every field possible. The largest number of opportunities for a college graduate are in the middle levels of management. Women have been led to believe that in the federal government they can match their responsibilities with titles and salaries that are not yet open to them in private employment. However, even in government, you will find that the higher the job, the fewer the women represented. Only $1\frac{1}{2}$ percent of those earning over $20,000 in the federal government are women. In New York State, although 46 percent of state employees are female, only 1 percent hold top jobs.

RELATED CAREERS
   state and local government
   post office
   military

WHERE CAN I GET MORE INFORMATION?
   Professional Group
   U.S. Civil Service Commission
   Washington, D.C. 20415

Trade Journal
Civil Service Journal
Government Printing Office
Washington, D.C. 20402

HEALTH AND REGULATORY INSPECTOR

Checks compliance with federal health, safety, trade, and employment laws.

What's It Like to Be a Health and Regulatory Inspector?

Health and regulatory inspectors hold a great variety of jobs, such as food and drug inspectors, meat and poultry inspectors, agriculture quarantine inspectors, sanitarians, commodity graders, immigration inspectors, customs inspectors, aviation safety officers, mine inspectors, wage-hour compliance officers, alcohol and tobacco inspectors, and firearms inspectors. Immigration Inspector Paula Rakowski, in her twenties, inspects buses, trains, and planes crossing the American-Canadian border. What she likes least about the job is the offensive attitude people have toward being inspected by a woman. Often, people who are denied admission to the U.S. are abusive in their language, and they resent a woman having the authority to refuse them. What Rakowski likes best about the job is the shift work, which gives her a great variety of days and hours and people to work with. She also likes the interesting people she meets from all over the world.

What Education and Skills Will I Need?

High school: Preparation for community college or four-year college.

College: Most inspectors have two to four years of college plus specialized work experience in the area related to the job they seek.

Personal skills: Inspectors must be responsible, good at detailed work, neat, and have good speaking and writing skills.

How Many Women in the Field and Where Do They Work?

There are over 112,000 inspection officers and only 10 percent of them are women.

$ $ $ $ $

In early 1981, aviation and mining inspectors started at $18,585 a year. Other health and regulatory inspectors and graders started at $12,266 a year. Experienced immunization and customs inspectors averaged more than $20,000 a year.

What Is the Future for Women?

Chances for jobs will be limited through the 1980s. Cuts in government regulatory agencies and spending will result in fewer jobs.

RELATED CAREERS
bank examiner
construction inspector
law enforcement

WHERE CAN I GET MORE INFORMATION?
Professional Group
Interagency Board of U.S. Civil Service Examiners for Washington, D.C.
1900 E Street, NW
Washington, D.C. 20415

Trade Journal
American Industrial Hygiene Association Journal
35 New Street
Worcester, MA 01605

LAW ENFORCEMENT

*Careers, such as police officer or special agent
for the Federal Bureau of Investigation, designed
to preserve law and order by investigating and
apprehending lawbreakers.*

What's It Like to Be in Law Enforcement?

Joyce Hicks, Police Officer in Washington, D.C., is armed with her 38 caliber service revolver when she patrols a high-crime neighborhood on an eight-hour shift. She tickets illegally parked cars, investigates complaints about disorderly persons, breaks up unruly crowds, and fills out a report form covering each activity. Police work involves keeping calm, offering help, and knowing the other agencies in the community that can help people. In large police departments, officers are usually assigned to a specific type of police duty. They go on duty for patrol or traffic, accident prevention, communications systems, or criminal investigation. Women in police work today are refusing to take only traditional jobs for women: working with juveniles, female prisoners, or typewriters.

FBI special agents investigate violations of federal laws, such as bank robberies, kidnapping, frauds and theft against the government, espionage, and sabotage. Until 1972, women were not even allowed in the FBI. There are not many now, but there *are* opportunities.

Sexism is rampant in law enforcement. Two women police officers were the first Americans, civilian or military, to be convicted of cowardice since the Korean War. In *Ms.* magazine, one of the police officers, Katherine Perkins, says, "The men seemed to be so psyched out on this six-foot/two-hundred-twenty-pound image of what a cop should be. It was ridiculous. Any *fool* can shoot a gun. What you really need is intelligence and sensitivity — and that's what women bring to the job."

What Education and Skills Will I Need?

High school: Educational requirements vary with the department and level of job you want. For city police officers and the FBI, prepare for college and play sports to train for the physical qualifications required.

College: Even though a college degree is not a requirement for police work, you will have a better chance to be accepted into training in city and state police departments with a degree. Special agents of the FBI must have a college degree in any subject plus work experience. A law degree helps a lot.

How Many Women in the Field and Where Do They Work?

Only 6,000 of the nation's 495,000 municipal officers are women (mainly in large cities), and one-third of 1,330 law enforcement agencies have women employed. In Detroit, 12 percent of the police officers were female in 1980, one of the highest percentages in the country; 63 percent of those women officers were black. Women have been almost nonexistent in state and federal law enforcement. There are 55,000 state police. Pennsylvania was the first state to hire women for state police duties identical to those performed by men. New York was second, with other states slowly following. In July 1972, the first two women FBI special agents were sworn in. Only 350 (4.2 percent) women are now working as special agents for the 110-year-old U.S. FBI with 7,800 agents.

$ $ $ $ $

In 1980, police officers started from $13,000 to $15,200 a year, depending on the size of the city and their experience. State police began at $14,000 a year. Experienced police made from $18,000 to $20,000 a year. In 1981, FBI special agents started at $20,467 a year.

What Is the Future for Women?

In times of high unemployment, police work is hard to get, but those with college training will have the best chance. Women will have an equal opportunity for the jobs because they are so under-represented and the laws are now against discrimination. The state police and the FBI are glamor jobs and thousands of qualified people apply.

RELATED CAREERS
detective	boarder patrol agent
secret service agent	Internal Revenue Service agent

LAW ENFORCEMENT

WHERE CAN I GET MORE INFORMATION?

Professional Groups
Local and State Police Departments

Director, FBI
U.S. Department of Justice
Washington, D.C. 20535

State Police Headquarters
State Capital

International Association of Women Police
6655 N. Avondale Avenue
Chicago, IL 60631

Trade Journal
National Sheriff
NSA
1250 Connecticut Avenue, NW
Washington, D.C. 20036

LAWYER

Connects the legal system with changing human needs.

What's It Like to Be a Lawyer?

Most lawyers, also called attorneys, work in general practice and handle all kinds of legal work for clients, such as property deeds, making wills, and settling estates. Others specialize in areas of corporate, criminal, labor, patent, real estate, tax, or international law. Because of the oversupply of law graduates, many lawyers have gone into careers outside of legal work. Professional government jobs, political jobs, the FBI, and business and private industry attract law school graduates. Phoebe Morse, Director of Women's Affairs in a State Attorney's office, spends the day consulting with other lawyers, preparing for cases in the state supreme court, preparing witnesses for trial, negotiating settlements, advising state boards and agencies on legal matters, writing regulations, and drafting new laws. What Morse likes best is the opportunity to be directly involved in interesting issues and the flexibility of the everyday work. She urges students who want to be lawyers, "Learn to write well! Being able to express yourself clearly and succinctly, orally and in writing, is the most important skill for a lawyer or a lobbyist. Of course, you must also be able to think clearly, so courses in logic (math and philosophy) are also recommended." Some lawyers become judges. Until September 1981, *no* female lawyer had ever served as United States Supreme Court Justice. Supreme Court Justice Sandra Day O'Connor is the first. Her presence enables other women to aspire to this esteemed, prestigious, top position in law.

What Education and Skills Will I Need?

High school: Preparation for college, with emphasis on verbal and language skills.

College: Prelaw graduates go on to one of the 156 approved three-year law schools, then they must pass the bar examinations in the state in which they will practice. English, history, government, economics, philosophy, and social sciences are important in prelaw. An understanding of society and its institutions is required for law. About one-fifth of all law students are enrolled part-time, usually in night school.

Personal skills: Assertiveness, interest in people and ideas, debating and writing skills, and ability to build trust and confidence in others are needed to be successful as a lawyer.

How Many Women in the Field and Where Do They Work?

Of the 425,000 lawyers, only 14 percent are women. And only 7 percent of the federal judiciary are women. Three out of four lawyers are in private practice, with more than half of them in business by themselves. Since 1972, law schools have been forced to increase their enrollment of women. In 1975, 26.8 percent of the first-year law students were women, a strong increase from 8 percent in 1971. Law schools with fewest women are Brigham Young University, with 5.3 percent; and Gonzaga University, with 6.7 percent. Other schools with few women enrolled are John Marshall Law School, University of Dayton, and South Texas College of Law. Law schools with the highest numbers of women enrolled are University of California at Davis, with 55.6 percent; Northeastern University, with 51.1 percent; and Antioch Law School, with 50.8 percent.

LAWYER

In 1979, 35 percent of all graduates from law school were women.

$ $ $ $ $

In 1980, average beginning salaries for new graduates hired by law firms ranged from $10,000 to $35,000 a year. The average salary for the most experienced lawyers in private industry was over $60,000 a year. In 1981, the federal government started law graduates at $18,600 or at $22,500 a year.

What Is the Future for Women?

Very competitive. Many more graduates than jobs are expected through the 1980s. Graduates at the top of their class from the well-known law schools, and specialists in tax, patent, or admiralty law, will get the salaried jobs. Law is an important area for women to help in human rights, including women's rights, politics, minority rights, and court cases that test compliance to existing civil rights laws. Since women have been discriminated against for so long, many firms and government agencies are actively recruiting women for jobs because they must have more women represented by law.

RELATED CAREERS
  negotiator   legislator
  judge   FBI special agent

WHERE CAN I GET MORE INFORMATION?
  Professional Groups
  The American Bar Association
  1155 60th Street
  Chicago, IL 60637

  National Association of Women Lawyers
  1155 60th Street
  Chicago, IL 60637

  Trade Journal
  Trial
  American Trial Lawyer's Association
  20 Garden Street
  Cambridge, MA 02138

MILITARY CAREERS
*Members of the Army, Navy, Air Force,
or Marine Armed Forces.*

What's It Like to Be in the Military?

Being in the military is like getting paid for job training and work experience. There are over 200 job-training courses in the Army that you can choose *before* you enter the service, such as technical, medical, communications, and electronics courses. The course you can choose depends upon your present level of education and achievement. The only jobs closed to women, by an act of Congress, are those in actual combat and those related to combat (flying, says the Air Force). If the situation changes, it means that women can get the expensive flight training needed to be a commercial pilot that men get from the military. Navy Lieutenant Commander Kathleen Byerly says she doesn't like the thought of combat, but she adds, "I don't know any man who does either, and I would not deny any woman the opportunity to do anything she is capable of doing, including firing a gun." The rights of women in the military have changed in the last few years. Women can now be married, have dependents, get maternity leave whether married or not, and have equal benefits with men for themselves and their dependents.

What Education and Skills Will I Need?

High school: Required for enlisted personnel. Preparation for college in any major to qualify for the officer's training programs.

College: Your major in college qualifies you for the job you wish to select in the service. The military can use any and all types of skills and educational achievement.

Other qualifications: You must be between 18 and 27 years old, a United States citizen, and in good physical condition. There is no restriction on marital status, but you cannot have dependents under 18 at the time you enlist.

MILITARY CAREERS

How Many Women in the Field and Where Do They Work?

Of the 2.1 million people in the military, 110,000 (5.5 percent) are women. Fully 92 percent of ten job categories in the Army—except the infantry, artillery, and other direct combat roles—are open to women. The first female Army base chief, Brigadier General Mary E. Clarke, assumed command of Fort McClellan, Alabama, in May 1978. Ensign Mary Pat Carroll finally shattered Navy tradition in the 1980s as the first woman to take asignment on a Navy vessel other than a hospital or a transport ship. Brenda Robinson joined the Navy in 1978 and today is the first and only black female aviator in the U.S. Navy. By 1984, the Navy plans to have 9 percent of the Navy women (5,130) on ocean-going ships. The Coast Guard was the first service to assign women to sea duty. In 1982, Lieutenant Mary Jane Wixsom was the first female graduate of the Coast Guard Academy to be given command of a cutter. Her crew consists of 12 men.

$ $ $ $ $

In 1980, basic pay and allowances for quarters and food for an officer started at $15,624 a year. Besides salary, officers receive medical and dental benefits, 30 days paid vacation, and special discounts on food and travel.

What Is the Future for Women?

The opportunities for continued education, leadership training, and job training are excellent and are limited only by personal interests and abilities rather than by sex. In the military, job training for both high school and college graduates is increasing, further education is paid for, courses for degrees are given on a full-time or part-time basis. Check into the ROTC programs and the few ROTC scholarships being awarded to women. More than 150 colleges have women enrolled in ROTC programs.

Women were first accepted into military academies in 1976. West Point accepted 100 women cadets, the Naval Academy accepted 80, and the Air Force Academy accepted 100. Since Reagan's administration in the 1980s, there is a trend away from equality for women in the military.

WHERE CAN I GET MORE INFORMATION?

Professional Group

Write to or visit your local recruiting station for the latest official information. Look in your phone book, or write to U.S. Army Recruiting Command, Fort Sheridan, IL 60037. When you are selecting your college, ask about the ROTC programs for women.

Trade Journal

Army Times, Air Force Times, Navy Times,
Marine Corps, Coast Guard
Army Times Publishing Co.
475 School Street, SW
Washington, D.C. 20024

PEACE CORPS VOLUNTEER

Promotes world peace and friendship by providing trained humanpower, creating a better understanding of American people to others, and creating a better understanding of other peoples to Americans.

What's It Like to Be a Peace Corps Volunteer?

Judy Daloz, Peace Corps teacher for two years in Nepal, says, "Living alone and working in a foreign culture helped me realize who I am, what I can do, and what I want to do with my life. The experiences I had gave me a perspective on being a woman, on being an American, on being a human being that I doubt I could have gotten otherwise. Although in the beginning I saw it as an exciting challenge to have the two years in which to affect people's lives in a positive way, in the end I realized my life had been far more affected than the people I was living with." The daily living of Peace Corps volunteers is on the same economy level and in the same style as the people who have invited them. In Ghana, 105 volunteers are currently involved in raising rabbits and keeping bees for food. They glaze pottery, coke charcoal, and patch dams. They teach speech to retarded

children, family planning to medicine men, and plowing with
a bullock to farmers who traditionally used only a hoe.

What Education and Skills Will I Need?

High school: Preparation for college. Any skill or professional achievement can be used to be a volunteer in the Peace
Corps.

College: Most of the volunteers are liberal arts graduates
from college, and a total of 96 percent have attended college.
The Peace Corps is a temporary work experience, and many
volunteers go to graduate school after service. A 13-week training program in the U.S. is required before leaving the country.

How Many Women in the Field and Where Do They Work?

There are only 5,400 volunteers in the Peace Corps, which
is down from 13,000 at its mid-1960s' peak. About 40 percent
are teachers; 25 percent work in health, nutrition, and water
supply; and 18 percent are in food production. Most are college
graduates, 20 percent are married and some of these have children, and they work in the 60 (it used to be 90) countries who
have invited them. These places include Africa, Latin America,
North Africa, the Near East, South Asia, and the Pacific areas.
Over half of the volunteers are from 23 to 25 years old, 24 percent are from 26 to 28 years old, and 8 percent are over 36 years
old. Lillian Carter, best known older woman in the Peace Corps,
joined in her late sixties to work in India.

What Is the Future for Women?

There will continue to be a need for volunteers. Peace
Corps workers return from overseas with an interest in another
area of the world. They have had the opportunity to learn and
use a language and to know the culture and traditions of the
country in which they worked. Many volunteers return home to
take advanced work in college. Of those who do not go to school,
most enter public service. The following skills are needed and
are scarce among applicants: diesel mechanics, engineers, and
forestry, math, and science teachers.

$ $ $ $ $

Travel and living allowances are paid for in the Peace Corps. The living allowance is based on the local conditions where the volunteer is working. In Ghana, volunteers earn $270 a month, more than most other countries because of the high cost of living. Most volunteers accumulate from $1,800 to $2,000 while in the Peace Corps. Before actually returning to the United States, many use this fund for extra traveling.

RELATED CAREERS
    government service
    missionary
    international business

WHERE CAN I GET MORE INFORMATION?
Professional Group
ACTION
Washington, D.C. 20525
Call ACTION toll free at 800-424-8580

HEALTH

ADMINISTRATOR
Health Service Administrator
Medical Records Administrator

PRACTITIONER
Chiropractor
Dental Hygienist
Dentist
Doctor
Nurse
Optometrist
Osteopathic Physician
Podiatrist
Veterinarian

THERAPIST
Occupational Therapist
Physical Therapist
Speech and Hearing Therapist

OTHER
Dietitian
Medical Technologist
Pharmacist

About these careers Today, there are almost 4 million people working in an estimated 200 to 400 individual health-care careers, and the options within each profession have never been greater. Besides doctors, nurses, dentists, and therapists, other careers are behind-the scenes technologists, technicians, administrators, and assistants. Registered nurses, physicians, pharmacists, and dentists make up the largest professional health occupations. Nearly 2 million health jobs are represented in this career cluster.

Hospitals employ about half of all workers in the health field. Others work in clinics, private practice, laboratories, pharmacies, public health agencies, and mental health centers.

Most of the jobs described here require a number of years of preprofessional and professional college work, and a passing grade on a state licensing examination. Only the jobs of dental hygienist and nurse require less than a four-year program to start in an entry-level position.

Working conditions usually involve long hours. Because health facilities such as nursing homes and hospitals operate around the clock, administrators in these institutions may be called at all hours to settle emergency problems. Also, some travel may be required to attend meetings or, in the case of state public health departments and voluntary health agency administrators, to inspect facilities in the field.

Most dental offices are open five days a week and some dentists have evening hours. Dentists usually work between 40 and 45 hours a week, although many spend more than 50 hours a week in the office with technical and business-related work.

Many physicians have long working days and irregular hours. Most specialists work less hours a week than general practitioners.

Veterinarians in rural areas may spend much time traveling to and from farms, and may have to work outdoors in any weather.

Nursing, one of the largest professional-level occupations, has an employment projection of 1.2 million by 1985. The demand for nurses will continue to provide an increasing number of jobs, giving nurses more negotiating power as they plan their time and tasks.

The demand for health care will increase as the population grows older and the public increasingly becomes health conscious. Expansion of coverage under prepayment medical programs that make it easier for persons to pay for hospitalization and medical care also contribute to growth in the health cluster. In addition to jobs created by employment growth, many new jobs will open as a result of turnover and retirement.

Where are there more people than jobs? Besides an oversupply of doctors in many parts of the country, there is an oversupply of people with a master's in public health and in hospital administration, and there are too many general medical technologists.

And where are the jobs? In all areas of nursing, nurse anesthetist in particular; in respiratory, occupational, and physical therapy; in nuclear medicine and radioisotopes; and in emergency room medical care.

HEALTH SERVICE ADMINISTRATOR

Plans programs, sets policies, and makes decisions for hospitals, medical clinics, nursing homes, and other health facilities.

What's It Like to Be a Health Service Administrator?

Lola Peese, administrator of a 100-bed hospital in Mississippi, says, "The work involves coordinating medical staff, nursing staff, and housekeeping within the guidelines acceptable to the board of trustees." Peese does not work directly on the daily operation of the hospital but she does make management decisions that include reviewing budget proposals, making personnel decisions, and negotiating for the expansion of facilities. "The challenge of this management job," explains Peese, "is to keep a working relationship between the medical staff, who compete with each other for profit, and the rest of the hospital staff who are all on salary scales."

Edward H. Noroian, Executive Vice-president of the Presbyterian Hospital of New York City, says, "A hospital is different from other management jobs in that it contains many divisive elements. For the most part, the primary providers of care, the physicians, are not usually employed by the hospital. There are different groups of highly technical employees, a complex physical plant with great energy demands, and a need for fast transfer of information. Furthermore, hospitals are highly regulated. In New York State, more than 160 different regulatory bodies inspect our affairs."

What Education and Skills Will I Need?

High school: Preparation for college, nursing school, or business college.

College: Most women administrators are from a business or nursing background. Hospital administrators in urban areas and in large hospitals are increasingly dependent upon a graduate degree for their jobs. Two-year and four-year degrees in health service administration are offered in 60 colleges and universities. Johns Hopkins University and Columbia University had the highest percentage (40 percent) of women in their health administrative programs. A Master of Business Administration (MBA) or a Master of Public Health (MPH) are the top credentials for this career.

Personal skills: Norman B. Urmy, Administrator of University Hospital and Vice-president of New York University Medical Center, gives this advice about health administration, "Plan to spend 85 percent of your time talking to people, not sitting in your office calling the shots. You'll need an even temper, a liking for people, an ability to tolerate frustration, and a willingness to plan long-term, because great successes demand consensus, and that can take years to achieve."

How Many Women in the Field and Where Do They Work?

About half of the 220,000 health administrators are women, but most of the women hospital administrators are members of religious orders and are employed by religious hospitals.

$ $ $ $ $

In 1980, administrators in state hospitals with 350 to 800 beds averaged $35,000 a year. Experienced administrators in large hospitals earned over $50,000 a year.

What Is the Future for Women?

There are about 17,000 hospital administrators, about 16,000 administrators of long-term-care facilities, about 10,000 public health administrators in regulatory agencies such as federal public health services, plus about 6,000 other jobs in related areas such as fund-raising agencies for various diseases. About 750 true administrative jobs open up each year. Competition for them is very tough, because there are 85 graduate programs who are producing about 3,000 graduates a year. Many administrators urge new graduates to start in a large hospital where they will get experience in many systems, or in a Veterans Administration hospital because they have systems manuals for everything. In these hospitals, you can learn how an organized operation works before you go on to the private sector or to a smaller hospital. Other opportunities for graduates are with the large management-consulting firms that have divisions specializing in health-care consulting.

RELATED CAREERS
business administrator
social welfare administrator
college administrator

WHERE CAN I GET MORE INFORMATION?
Professional Groups
American College of Hospital Administration
840 North Lake Shore Drive
Chicago, IL 60611

Assoc. of Univ. Programs in Health Administration
One Dupont Circle, NW
Washington, D.C. 20036

Trade Journal
Hospitals
AHA
840 North Lake Shore Drive
Chicago, IL 60611

MEDICAL RECORDS ADMINISTRATOR

Trains and supervises workers who verify, transcribe, code, and maintain files on patients' medical histories. Develops systems for documenting, storing, and retrieving medical information.

What's It Like to Be a Medical Records Administrator?

"I compile statistics and make summaries for reports required by state and health agencies. Medical records include case histories of illnesses, doctors' orders and progress notes, and X-ray and lab reports," says Judith MacRae, Director of Medical Records in a city university hospital. MacRae has been working for 6 years and is the supervisor of 24 employees, including librarians and clerical staff. She meets with other department heads of the hospital as part of the management staff and often is required to testify in court about records and procedures.

What Education and Skills Will I Need?

High school: Preparation for college, with emphasis on biological science and computer science.

College: A college degree is required from one of the 44 approved college programs. Programs include anatomy, physiology, hospital administration, and computer science.

Personal skills: Accuracy, interest in detail, ability to write and speak clearly, and discreetness in handling confidential information are needed by medical records administrators.

How Many Women in the Field and Where Do They Work?

There are 15,000 medical records administrators and 6,500 of them are Registered Records Administrators (RRA). Almost all of them are women.

$ $ $ $ $

In 1981, the average salary for registered medical records administrators was $18,000 a year. New graduates started with the federal government at $12,300 a year. Experienced administrators averaged about $23,600 a year, with some earning over $30,000.

What Is the Future for Women?

There will be very good opportunities for employment through the 1980s as health jobs increase. Registered full-time administrators will get the directors' jobs and best salaries.

RELATED CAREERS

hospital-insurance representative
library director
public health educator

WHERE CAN I GET MORE INFORMATION?
  Professional Group
  American Medical Record Association
  875 North Michigan Avenue, Suite 1850
  Chicago, IL 60611

  Trade Journal
  Medical Record News
  AMRA
  875 North Michigan Avenue, Suite 1850
  Chicago, IL 60611

CHIROPRACTOR
*Treats patients by manual manipulation of the
body, especially the spinal column.*

What's It Like to Be a Chiropractor?

Chiropractic is a system for healing based on the principle that a person's health is determined by the nervous system. Most female chiropractors are in private practice and specialize in the treatment of women and children. They treat their patients by massage; the use of water, light, and heat therapy; and prescribing diet, exercise, and rest. Amy Meyer, a chiropractor in Cincinnati, explains that because of the emphasis on the spine and its position, most chiropractors use X-rays for diagnoses and must be skilled in reading X-rays. Chiropractors do not use drugs or surgery.

What Education and Skills Will I Need?

High school: Preparation for college, with as much science as possible.

College: Two years of college are required for admission to the 15 chiropractic colleges approved by the American Chiropractic Association. The degree of Doctor of Chiropractic (D.C.) is awarded after four years of chiropractic college.

Personal skills: Rather than unusual strength, hand dexterity is necessary to be a chiropractor, together with sympathetic understanding.

How Many Women in the Field and Where Do They Work?

Six percent of the 23,000 chiropractors are women. Half of all chiropractors are practicing in California, New York, Texas, Missouri, Pennsylvania, and Michigan. Most are in private practice and three-fourths of them practice alone.

$ $ $ $ $

In 1980, experienced chiropractors averaged $44,000 a year. Beginners earned more than $15,000 a year.

What Is the Future for Women?

The future is good through the 1980s, even with more new graduates coming out of college. Women have a large potential group of patients, since many women and children prefer to be treated by female chiropractors. You can have a part-time practice in your own home with few professional expenses.

RELATED CAREERS

dentist   osteopath
optometrist   podiatrist

WHERE CAN I GET MORE INFORMATION?

Professional Group
American Chiropractic Association
American Building
2200 Grand Avenue
Des Moines, IA 50312

Trade Journal
Today's Chiropractic
P.O. Box 37
Austell, GA 30001

DENTAL HYGIENIST

*Cleans teeth, charts tooth conditions, X-rays teeth,
and teaches patients how to maintain
good oral health.*

What's It Like to Be a Dental Hygienist?

Dental hygienists perform preventive services with patients and teach dental health education. Some hygienists work in public school systems promoting dental health by examining children's teeth and reporting dental treatment needed to their parents. Ruth Mozes, dental hygienist who grew up in Philadelphia but now lives in New York City, tells what it's like to change directions within a career. "My first year in dental hygiene was the most difficult. I felt terribly unappreciated for my diligent but monotonous work cleaning mouth after mouth in a dungeon-like dentist's office. I was introduced as 'the dental hygienist who will clean your teeth and take your X-rays.' The dentist I worked for rarely cared to listen to my interests and I knew I could do better. My ensuing jobs gave me enthusiasm. Working as a school dental hygienist for the local school district was fun. I spoke to each class and many of the students individually, teaching them how to maintain dental health and referring them to the dentist for problems they already had. In private practice, I had a chance to get to know my patients. Because I was responsible for preparing many of them for gum surgery, it was not unusual to see them for six consecutive weeks. I spent half that time teaching them how to care for their mouths to make surgery and postoperative healing more successful. The other half of the time I cleaned the roots of their teeth and their chronically infected gums. After these initial phases of treatment, patients returned for subsequent examinations and maintenance according to our discretion, usually every three, six, or nine months. Since then, I entered an advanced degree program for my B.S. in dental hygiene. In addition to advanced courses in dental hygiene and education, the curriculum provided time for electives in other undergraduate facilities within the university. This year, I was able to begin work toward my master's degree because of a teaching assistantship at the dental school. I am working with the director of one of the clinical programs in a unique position. Most of my responsibilities are administrative; I institute school policies and act as liaison between the director and the students. I still work in a private dental office part-time. I've maintained traditional dental hygiene responsibilities, such as biannual examinations, cleanings, X-rays, and preventive health education for children and adults. Our office philosophy toward preventive dentistry is very progressive, so I've helped to develop programs in blood pressure screening, nutritional analysis and counseling, and more modern systems for keeping patients' records."

What Education and Skills Will I Need?

High school: Preparation for a two-year dental program, with emphasis on science. Most dental hygienist programs require the dental aptitude test for admission. The requirements for admission are usually the same as the four-year college program of the same university.

College: Two-year dental hygienist schools are within a university or college. Degree programs are available for students who want to go into research or teaching. Each state has its own licensing examination.

Personal skills: Manual dexterity, ability to help people relax under stress, and neatness are necessary in dental hygiene.

How Many Women in the Field and Where Do They Work?

There are 36,000 dental hygienists, many of whom work part time. Most of them are women. Three-fourths of the hygienists work in private dentists' office and one-fourth work for public health or school systems.

$ $ $ $ $

In 1980, the average salary for a two-year graduate was from $14,000 to $17,000 a year. Beginners earned less.

What Is the Future for Women?

The opportunities are expected to be very good through the 1980s. The increase in dental education and in the population will create more jobs than the number of hygienists graduating. Many dentists require half-time help or less, providing excellent part-time opportunities for women with children or other things to do.

RELATED CAREERS
nurse	medical technologist
nurse anesthetist	radiologic technologist

WHERE CAN I GET MORE INFORMATION?
Professional Group
American Dental Association
Council on Dental Education
211 East Chicago Avenue
Chicago, IL 60611

Trade Journal
Dental Hygiene
American Dental Association
211 East Chicago Avenue
Chicago, IL 60611

DENTIST

Examines, diagnoses, and treats various oral diseases and abnormalities.

What's It Like to Be a Dentist?

Unusual, for a woman. Not quite five dentists in every 100 are women! Dentists fill cavities, straighten teeth, take X-rays, and treat gums. They clean and examine teeth and mouths for preventive dentistry work. Most of their time is spent with patients, and usually their laboratory work is sent out to dental technicians. Orthodontist Suzanne Rothenberg's mother and father were both dentists. She finds dentistry an exciting career because she can adapt her work to whatever interests her more — patients, research, or teaching. Dentists are independent and can work the hours and days they want. Rothenberg says many young women who have majored in science choose dentistry after they have worked at other jobs.

What Education and Skills Will I Need?

High school: Preparation for a predental program in college, with as much science as possible.

College: Two years of college are required for admission to four years of dental school. Nearly half of the dental schools now require three years, and most dental students have a college degree. Predental work will include chemistry, English, biology, and physics.

Personal skills: A good visual memory, excellent judgment of space and shape, a delicate touch, and a high degree of manual dexterity are necessary for dentists.

How Many Women in the Field and Where Do They Work?

Of the total 126,000 dentists, 4.7 percent are women. Nine out of ten dentists are in private practice.

$ $ $ $ $

In 1980, the average income for dentists was about $55,000 a year. In 1981, first-year dentists started with the federal government at $22,500 a year.

What Is the Future for Women?

The outlook for dentists will be good through the 1980s. The more dental care taught in the public schools, the more dental care will be needed. Dentistry is the second highest paid profession, and it is a natural for women with an aptitude for science and an interest in dental care. It takes only six years beyond high school to become a dentist, the same number of years many women study for teaching certificates. In Finland, 80 percent of the dentists are women. Other than the fact that women think dentistry is for men, there is no reason why women shouldn't be in dentistry. It is a well-paid profession that you can have at home, where you can establish your own hours and size of practice according to your life situation. This is one of the few careers with excellent job opportunities.

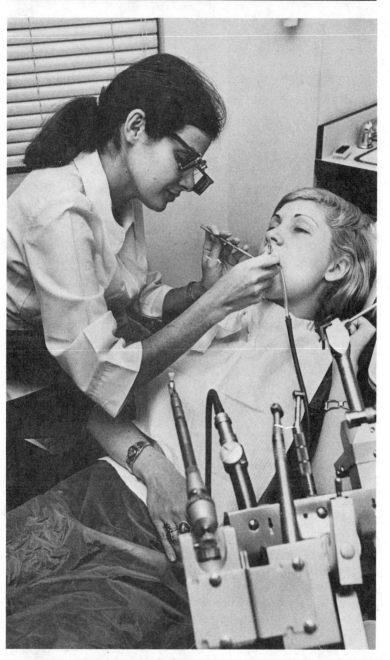

DENTIST

RELATED CAREERS
ophthalmologist
doctor
veterinarian

WHERE CAN I GET MORE INFORMATION?
Professional Groups
American Dental Association
Council on Education
211 East Chicago Avenue
Chicago, IL 60611

Association of American Women Dentists
435 North Michigan Avenue, 17th Floor
Chicago, IL 60611

Trade Journal
ADA News
ADA
211 East Chicago Avenue
Chicago, IL 60611

DOCTOR

Diagnoses diseases and treats people who are ill.
Works in research, in rehabilitation, and in
preventive medicine.

What It's Like to Be a Doctor?

"Very exciting, fatiguing, satisfying. It pays better than
most women's occupations; and remember, most women work
whether they are trained or not. The hours are long, but there is
a high degree of independence," says Dr. Mary Jane Gray, who
combines private practice, research, and teaching at Duke University's Medical Center in North Carolina. Dr. Gray describes
her day as follows: "Mornings begin with a lecture or conference, rounds and consultations in the hospital, and laboratory
work or operating all morning. Afternoons consist of office

hours once a week or research lab four days a week. Evenings include one or two professional meetings a week, a few hours of work at home, and deliveries of babies as they occur."

For the first time, women are going into every specialty in medicine. The fewest number of women are in urology. Dr. Mary Gannon from Iowa says about women in urology, "It's not the patients who give you a bad time, it's the other male doctors who want to become urologists, too. They think there's something weird about a young woman who wants to specialize in urology. The truth is we're just about as weird as the guys who want to specialize in obstetrics and gynecology."

What Education and Skills Will I Need?

High school: Preparation for college, with as much science and mathematics as offered. A strong B average in the sciences with top motivation for staying in a premed college program and in medical school are the main requirements. You don't have to be a genius to go into medicine, as many young women are led to believe.

College: Premedicine or biology are the usual majors to prepare for medical school. In addition to the physical sciences, the behavioral sciences and computer science are becoming more important in medical education. Changes in curriculum include a broader education in clinical work as well as in the classroom. After graduation from a four-year medical school, one year of internship in a hospital is required to be licensed to practice. Interns are paid by the hospital. Following the internship, they may do a paid year of residency or specializing in a field of medicine.

Personal skills: A strong interest and desire to serve the sick and injured are needed, as are persistence for continued study and ability to make fast decisions in emergencies.

How Many Women in the Field and Where Do They Work?

Only 13.8 percent of the 405,000 doctors are women. But in 1980, about 30 percent of the freshmen in 126 medical schools in the United States were women. Medical schools have traditionally had a quota against women in their admission policy, which is now being challenged and changed on the basis of antidiscrimination laws. In addition, medical faculties, like graduate faculties in law and theology schools, are very white-male oriented. The few women faculty in medical schools hold low-ranking, nontenured teaching and administrative positions. This environment prevents many female students from completing their programs, even though they are very well qualified to do the work. UCLA medical student Larrian Gillespie says that male chauvinism is rampant, particularly in specialties that men think are only for men. She says, "If a woman can do something in surgery as well as the men can, the general surgery residents get upset. They treated me so negatively that I was about to give up surgery and specialize in anesthesia, which apparently meets with male approval for women physicians." Sixty-five percent of women doctors choose the "three P's," which appear to cause the majority of them less anxiety: Women are supposed to like children (Pediatrics), are supposed to be mother figures (Psychiatry), and are supposed to earn very little money (Public Health).

$ $ $ $ $

In 1981, medical school graduates who had completed three years of residency started with the Veterans Administration hospitals at $38,500 a year. In addition, they received up to $13,000 in other cash benefits. Of doctors who worked full time, the average 1978 income of males after taxes was $67,450; the average 1978 income of females after taxes was $39,820. In 1980, physicians earned an average of $74,500.

What Is the Future for Women?

Dr. Marion Fay, past President and Dean of the Women's Medical College of Pennsylvania, says, "More women don't go into medicine because high school women are so often discouraged by counselors, parents, and teachers, who stress the difficulties of medicine and don't explain the rewards. Women are spending more time in graduate school now and can plan their families if they do marry. So if they are interested in science and a health career, they should take advantage of the tremendous rewards of being a doctor." With a surplus of 70,000 physicians predicted, the shortage of doctors is over. Despite the numbers, it is still hard to get doctors to fill inner city and rural jobs.

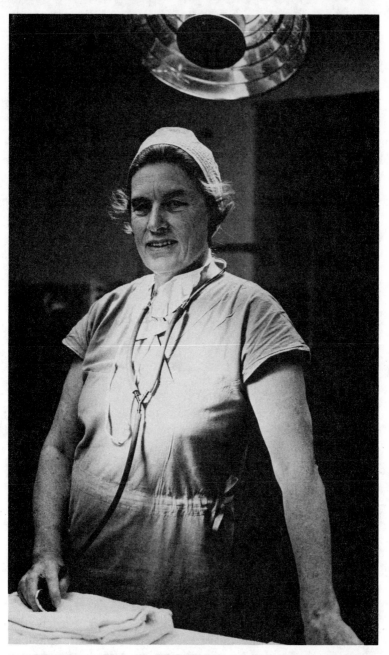

DOCTOR

RELATED CAREERS
   dentist
   optometrist
   audiologist
   veterinarian

WHERE CAN I GET MORE INFORMATION?
Professional Groups
American Medical Association
Council on Medical Education
535 North Dearborn Street
Chicago, IL 60610

American Medical Women's Association, Inc.
1740 Broadway
New York, NY 10019

Trade Journal
New England Journal of Medicine
Massachusetts Medical Society
10 Shattuck Street
Boston, MA 02115

NURSE

*Observes, assesses, and records symptoms,
reactions, and progress of patients; administers
medications; helps rehabilitate patients; instructs
patients and family members in proper health care;
and helps maintain a physical and emotional
environment that promotes recovery.*

What's It Like to Be a Nurse?

Nurses work with patients and families in a variety of settings. They provide direct care to patients in hospitals and
nursing homes by assessing the patients' needs and problems,
making nursing diagnoses, and planning and implementing

nursing actions that enhance the patients' recovery. They provide the medical care prescribed by the physician; teach patients about their illness; and teach them how to prevent complications and to promote good health practices. Within the hospital setting, there are areas of specialization, such as psychiatric nursing, coronary care, intensive care, pediatric nursing, intensive care nursing and obstetrics. Nurses who provide direct care to patients are called *staff nurses*, or *primary care nurses*. Administrators who provide indirect care to patients are *head nurses* and/or *coordinators, team leaders,* and *supervisors.* Nurses also provide care to clients and families in the community. *Public health nurses* and *visiting nurses* provide direct care to patients who have been discharged from the hospital. They also teach health and health practices, provide immunizations, and work with teachers, parents, and doctors in the community, home, and school. *Office nurses* help physicians care for patients in private practices or clinics. *Private duty nurses* work in patients' homes or in hospitals to take care of one patient who needs special and constant attention. After advanced training, *nurse practitioners* provide primary health care as independent decision makers. They often establish a joint practice with a physician or run their own clinics.

What Education and Skills Will I Need?

High school: Preparation for nursing education, with a college preparatory program and an emphasis in science.

Nursing education: By 1985, members of the nursing profession will be expected to have a minimum of a bachelor's degree in order to practice as a professional nurse. All others will be called technical nurses. There are three types of nursing education: a three-year diploma program conducted by a hospital, a bachelor's degree program in a college, or an associate degree program offered in a two-year junior or community college. Nurses who plan a career in teaching and research will be required to get a doctorate in nursing. There are many opportunities for specialization through a master's program, including a master's in public health for women interested in administration.

Personal skills: Ability to accept responsibility, initiative, good judgment, good mental and physical stamina, and ability to make reasoned decisions.

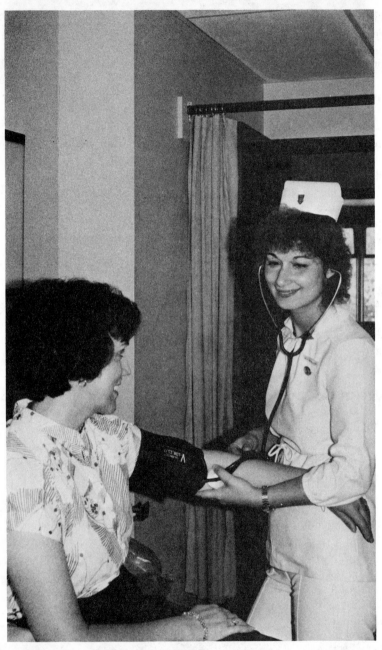

NURSE

How Many Women in the Field and Where Do They Work?

There are 1,050,000 registered professional nurses and 96.8 percent are women. Three-fourths of them work in hospitals or nursing homes, 40,000 are private duty nurses, 100,000 are office nurses, 120,000 are public health nurses, 20,000 are industrial nurses, and 40,000 are nurse educators. About one-third work part-time. Nursing care as a private business is a new trend. Nurse entrepreneur Jeanette Taylor Jones makes $42,000 a year in her Nursing Support Service in the St. Paul and Minneapolis areas.

$ $ $ $ $

In 1980, the average salary for staff and industrial nurses was $17,000 a year. Registered nurses working in nursing homes earned $14,500 a year; specialists earned $18,000 to $30,000; educators earned $20,000; and supervisors earned $40,000. The Veterans Administration offered inexperienced nurses with a college degree $15,933 as a starting salary.

What Is the Future for Women?

Nursing may be one of the most exciting, expansive, developing professions in the next decade. Salaries, advancement, and fringe benefits are increasing rapidly. Free cars, paid moving expenses, good work hours, and paid recruiters' fees are often part of the package. For nurses with degrees, opportunities will be excellent in administration, nursing schools, and clinics through the 1980s.

RELATED CAREERS
occupational therapist
physical therapist
physician's assistant

WHERE CAN I GET MORE INFORMATION?
Professional Groups
American Nurses' Association
2420 Pershing Road
Kansas City, MO 64108

National League for Nursing
10 Columbus Circle
New York, NY 10019

Trade Journal
RN Magazine
Litton Publications
Oradell, NJ 07649

OPTOMETRIST

Examines people's eyes for vision problems and disease, and tests eyes for depth, color, and focus perceptions.

What's It Like to Be an Optometrist?

Dr. Mary Jane McConnel, of Morresville, North Carolina, writes, "There is no more wonderful and challenging profession than optometry for a student interested in the field of health care. Being on the very front lines of prevention of blindness or helping a child who is having difficulty learning in school presents a challenge and a reward second to none. Most of my time is spent with children requiring refraction visual training, contact lenses, or care in developmental vision. Services for adults usually involve routine lens prescription for reading, aids for the partially sighted, or occupational lenses."

What Education and Skills Will I Need?

High school: Preparation for college, with emphasis in science.

College: Two or three years of college are required for admission to the four-year program of the College of Optometry to become a Doctor of Optometry (O.D.). Subjects required in college are English, mathematics, biology, physics, and chemistry. There are 13 schools of optometry in the United States.

Personal skills: Business ability (most optometrists are self-employed), self-discipline, and tact with patients are needed.

How Many Women in the Field and Where Do They Work?

There are 27,000 optometrists and only 3 percent are women. Most optometrists are self-employed, and half of them work in the following five states: California, Illinois, New York, Pennsylvania, and Ohio. To offset high costs of establishing a practice, there is a growing trend toward partnerships and group practice.

$ $ $ $ $

In 1980, beginning optometrists averaged $18,000 a year. Experienced optometrists averaged $45,000 a year.

What Is the Future for Women?

Employment opportunities will be favorable through the 1980s. Dr. McConnel feels that this profession is truly ideal for a woman since she can choose a work schedule that suits her lifestyle and family responsibilities. Dr. McConnell has three children in school and works three days a week in private practice; she plans to work a longer period when her children are a little older. She worked one day a week when they were infants, never having to give up her work completely. Very few careers pay as well, award a doctorate only six years after high school, and have as good part-time opportunities as does optometry.

RELATED CAREERS
  chiropractor   podiatrist
  dentist   veterinarian

WHERE CAN I GET MORE INFORMATION?
  Professional Group
  American Optometric Association
  243 Lindbergh Blvd.
  St. Louis, MO 63141

  Trade Journal
  Optometric Management
  20 Harlan Avenue
  White Plains, NY 10603

OSTEOPATHIC PHYSICIAN

*Diagnoses and treats diseases, with special
emphasis on the musculo-skeletal system — bones,
muscles, ligaments, and nerves.*

What's It Like to Be an Osteopathic Physician?

One of the basic treatments osteopathic physicians use is manipulation of the musculo-skeletal system with the hands. They also use surgery, drugs, and all other accepted methods of medical care. Most osteopathic physicians are "family doctors" who engage in general practice. These physicians usually see patients in their offices, make house calls, and treat patients in one of the 200 osteopathic hospitals.

What Education and Skills Will I Need?

High school: Preparation for college, with science and mathematics courses.

College: Most osteopathy students have a college degree, with biology, chemistry, physics, and English courses to qualify for a three-year or four-year program in one of the 14 schools of osteopathy.

Personal skills: A strong interest in osteopathic principles of healing, a keen sense of touch, and self-confidence are needed.

How Many Women in the Field and Where Do They Work?

There are 18,750 osteopathic physicians and 13 percent of them are women. Almost 85 percent are in private practice. They are located chiefly in states with osteopathic hospitals. Three-fifths of all osteopathic physicians practice in Florida, Michigan, Pennsylvania, New Jersey, Ohio, Texas, and Missouri.

$ $ $ $ $

In 1981, graduates of an osteopathic residency program started at $38,000 a year with the VA hospitals. In addition, they received up to $13,000 in other cash benefits.

What Is the Future for Women?
Chances for work will be very good through the 1980s, especially in states with osteopathic hospitals.

RELATED CAREERS
chiropractor   optometrist
dentist   veterinarian

WHERE CAN I GET MORE INFORMATION?
Professional Group
American Association of Colleges of Osteopathic Medicine
4720 Montgomery Lane
Bethesda, MD 20814

Trade Journal
The Osteopathic Physician
122 East 42 Street
New York, NY 10017

PODIATRIST
*Prevents, diagnoses, and treats foot disease
and injuries.*

What's It Like to Be a Podiatrist?
Podiatrists take X-rays and perform pathological tests to diagnose foot diseases. They perform surgery, fit corrective devices and proper shoes, and prescribe drugs and physical therapy. They treat corns, bunions, calluses, ingrown toe nails, skin and nail diseases, deformed toes, and arch disabilities. Most podiatrists are generalists and provide all types of foot care.

What Education and Skills Will I Need?
High school: Preparation for college, with strong emphasis in science and mathematics.

College: Most (90 percent) podiatric medicine students are college graduates and go on to one of the five podiatric schools for four years.

Personal skills: Manual dexterity, scientific interest, ability to do detailed work, and pleasant personality are all needed in podiatry.

How Many Women in the Field and Where Do They Work?

Most of the 12,000 podiatrists are in private practice in large cities. Only 6 percent are women.

$ $ $ $ $

In 1980, the VA hospitals offered $22,486 a year to new graduates. Established podiatrists earned over $50,000 a year.

What Is the Future for Women?

The chances for work are very good. The increase in sports medicine and in the numbers of joggers, the older populations, and the trend toward providing preventive foot care for children will increase the number of jobs. Like many traditionally male careers, podiatry has very few women. Podiatry pays well and is a good career for interested women.

RELATED CAREERS

chiropractor   dentist
doctor   veterinarian
osteopathic physician

WHERE CAN I GET MORE INFORMATION?

Professional Group
American Association for Women Podiatrists
20 Chevy Chase Circle, NW
Washington, D.C. 20015

Trade Journal
Journal of Podiatry Association
AACPM
20 Chevy Chase Circle, NW
Washington, D.C. 20015

VETERINARIAN

*Prevents, diagnoses, treats, and controls
diseases and injuries of animals.*

What's It Like to Be a Veterinarian?

Carlotta M. Fernandez, D.V.M., is a partner in a veterinarian business in suburban California. She starts her day at 8:00 A.M. and finishes at 6:00 to 9:00 P.M., depending on whether or not she covers evening office hours. Mornings are spent performing surgery, doing tests, and taking X-rays. Afternoons are spent in treatments and emergencies. "In general," says Dr. Fernandez, "practice is very physical, demanding, challenging work. There are not many quiet or dull moments, and I would say in an average 8-hour to 9-hour day, I'm probably off my feet a total of 45 minutes. A vet must really have an inquiring type of mind. So much of veterinary medicine, or any medicine, is a puzzle, and there is no book of treatments to cover all diseases or solve all problems." Specialties include research medicine, federal health services, teaching, or working for someone else's business on a part-time or regular basis.

What Education and Skills Will I Need?

High school: Preparation for college, with emphasis on biological sciences.

College: Two years of preveterinary medicine is required for admission into a four-year veterinary college.

Personal skills: Ability to communicate with animals is important for a vet, as is interest in food, health, and science. Since many animals are outside, a love of the outdoors is helpful.

How Many Women in the Field and Where Do They Work?

Only 3 percent of the 35,000 vets are women. But their number has nearly doubled in the U.S. and Canada since 1970.

$ $ $ $ $

In 1980, the average salary for experienced veterinarians working for the federal government was $34,100 a year. In 1981, the federal government started veterinarians at $21,065 a year. Private practice pays more, and self-employed vets start with less money but usually make much more than salaried vets.

What Is the Future for Women?

The number of graduates rose sharply in the 1970s to off-set the shortage of veterinarians. Women are still very under-represented after years of discrimination by veterinary medical colleges. If you decide to be a veterinarian, you will find employment opportunities because of the pet population explosion and the need for scientific methods of raising livestock.

RELATED CAREERS

chiropractor	doctor
dentist	podiatrist
optometrist	

WHERE CAN I GET MORE INFORMATION?

Professional Groups
American Veterinary Medical Association
930 N. Meacham Road
Schaumburg, IL 60196

Association for Women Veterinarians
c/o Judith H. Spurling, D.V.M.
2731 W. Belleview
Littleton, CO 80123

Trade Journal
Veterinary Economics
2728 Euclid Avenue
Cleveland, OH 44115

OCCUPATIONAL THERAPIST

*Plans and directs activities to help patients
return to work, and generally aids patients
to adjust to their disability.*

What's It Like to Be an Occupational Therapist?

The occupational therapist works as a member of a medical team with a doctor, physical therapist, vocational counselor, nurse, and social worker. She teaches commercial skills, use of power tools, and creative skills, such as weaving, clay modeling, and leather working. The therapist helps patients gain stability, combat boredom during long illnesses, and develop independence in routine daily living with skills such as eating, dressing, and writing. Jane Guyette, occupational therapist in a hospital psychiatric department, spends 4 hours a day with patients in groups; 2 hours with individual patients; and 2 hours in staff meetings, on rounds, and consulting with other staff members. Guyette strongly suggests that students interested in occupational therapy get a part-time job (paid or volunteer) in a hospital before they go into the career. She says there is a lot of misunderstanding of what the job is like. "It would be good to test your own responses to the occupational therapist's situation," says Ms. Guyette.

What Education and Skills Will I Need?

High school: Preparation for college, with emphasis on science and social science.

College: Fifty-three colleges and universities offer a degree in occupational therapy. Many college graduates go into occupational therapy after college from a variety of majors—often biology or physical education—and get a master's degree in one year.

Personal skills: An advocate's attitude toward the sick and disabled, manual skills, maturity, patience, and imagination are needed.

How Many Women in the Field and Where Do They Work?

Of the 19,000 occupational therapists, 8,400 are women. More than half work in hospitals; the remainder work in rehabilitation centers, home health agencies, nursing homes, schools, and special workshops for the disabled.

$ $ $ $ $

In 1981, the average salaries ranged from $19,000 to $23,000 a year, with directors earning more than $30,000. Beginners with the federal government started at $13,700 a year.

What Is the Future for Women?

Job opportunities are expected to be very good through the 1980s. The increase in community health centers, long-term care facilities, and home health care will add to the demand for therapists. Part-time workers will also find very good opportunities.

RELATED CAREERS
physical therapist
prosthetist
speech pathologist

WHERE CAN I GET MORE INFORMATION?
Professional Group
American Occupational Therapy Association
1383 Piccard Drive
Rockville, MD 20850

PHYSICAL THERAPIST
Uses exercise, massage, heat, water, and electricity to treat and rehabilitate people with disabilities.

What's It Like to Be a Physical Therapist?

"My everyday work goes like this," says physical therapist Donna Keefe. "Teach crutchwalking to a 55-year-old woman with a fractured ankle; talk with neurosurgeon on the phone concerning 15-year-old paraplegic patient; treat patient with severe burns with sterile Hubbard Tub for cleaning and maintaining joint movement; treat joints of 35-year-old mother of four for arthritis and instruct her in range of exercises; treat shoulder of 59-year-old man with bursitis. In addition, there are conferences with nurses, social workers, occupational therapists, and doctors regarding patients seen by one or several of us. I visit the hospital nursery to work on infants with birth injuries, and nursing homes to help elderly people with strokes, and at the end of the day I write reports on all cases."

What Education and Skills Will I Need?

High school: Preparation for college, with emphasis on science.

College: Most women interested in this career major in physical therapy in college and graduate with a degree in physical therapy. A one-year course is offered for college graduates, usually in connection with a hospital program. Many physical education majors and science majors go into this program. There are 51 schools of physical therapy in the United States.

Personal skills: Resourcefulness, patience, manual dexterity, physical stamina, and an ability to work with disabled people and their families are needed to be good in physical therapy.

How Many Women in the Field and Where Do They Work?

Three-fourths of the 34,000 licensed physical therapists are women. About half of them work in general hospitals; others work in nursing homes, rehabilitation centers, home health agencies, and clinics.

$ $ $ $ $

In 1981, beginning physical therapists earned $17,000 a year. Experienced therapists averaged from $21,600 to $27,000 a year.

What Is the Future for Women?

The opportunities will remain excellent through the 1980s. New graduates are in great demand, as there are not enough therapists for the growing number of jobs. Nursing homes will create many part-time jobs. One-fifth of all hospital therapists are part-time.

RELATED CAREERS
occupational therapist   prosthetist
speech therapist   respiratory therapist

SPEECH AND HEARING THERAPIST

*Diagnoses and treats people with inability to
speak or hear clearly.*

What's It Like to Be a Speech and Hearing Therapist?

"I do therapy with children or adults who have communications disorders (speech, hearing, language, learning). The therapy may be with one person or with small groups. Lessons vary from one-half hour to group classes of two hours. The work treats problems of stuttering, defective articulation, brain damage, mental retardation, or emotional disability," writes Nancy Wiggins of Elgin, Illinois. "Our responsibility at the clinic is to identify and evaluate the disorder, organize a program of therapy, and use and consult with the other specialists involved, such as physician, psychologist, social worker, or counselor."

Kay Hannah, mother of three school children, works for the Visiting Nurses Association in a hospital speech clinic. The program involves working with older people who have had strokes and with young people who have been in automobile accidents. "The most difficult part of the work is the patients' frustration in not being able to get their speech out. The work can be very slow, and evenings are spent writing reports to

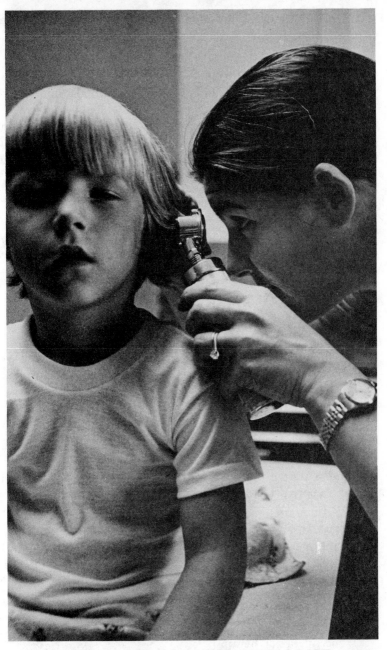

SPEECH AND HEARING THERAPIST

M.D.s and Medicare and Medicaid. Patients do improve bit by bit and then the work is very rewarding."

What Education and Skills Will I Need?

High school: Preparation for college, with a strong science program.

College: A master's degree from one of the 230 approved college programs is required for professional certification. To prepare for graduate school, major in speech and hearing or in any related field such as education, psychology, or education for the blind or deaf. Many scholarships and fellowships are available for graduate school through the U.S. Vocational Rehabilitation Administration.

Personal skills: Patience with slow progress, responsibility, objectivity, ability to work with detail, and concern for needs of others are important for therapists.

How Many Women in the Field and Where Do They Work?

Women represent three-fourths of the 35,000 persons in speech and hearing. About half work for the public school systems and clinical service centers. The rest work in hospitals, clinics, agencies, and private practice.

$ $ $ $ $

In 1981, the average salary of therapists working in hospitals and medical centers was $17,000 a year. The federal government started therapists with a master's degree at $18,600 a year. Experienced therapists averaged $21,300 a year.

What Is the Future for Women?

Job opportunities will be good through the 1980s. More emphasis on children's early grades and on learning disabilities will create jobs. The best chances for work will be for master's graduates outside of metropolitan areas.

RELATED CAREERS
occupational therapist
optometrist
physical therapist

WHERE CAN I GET MORE INFORMATION?
Professional Group
American Speech-Hearing Association
10801 Rockville Pike
Bethesda, MD 20852

Trade Journal
Audiology and Hearing Education
15300 Ventura Boulevard, Suite 301
Sherman Oaks, CA 91403

DIETITIAN

*Plans nutritious meals to help people maintain or
recover good health.*

What's It Like to Be a Dietitian?

Kathleen Curley, Yellow Springs, Ohio, explains that a hospital dietitian supervises tray service to patients, selects foods, and plans menus that meet nutritional requirements for health or for medical treatment. A dietitian plans modified meals and patterns for each day, teaches special diets to hospital patients and outpatients, and consults doctors and nurses about their patients' special needs in relation to prescribed drugs. Ms. Curley feels that the dietitian's primary responsibility is teaching other hospital professionals the value of nutrition for patients who are trying to recover good health. Clinical dietitian Joan Hamilton says, "There are a variety of jobs within the field. Some dietitians work with surgery patients, others do public health or public school work. Still others go into private practice where they work with an M.D. who refers patients to them." Because a hospital functions 24 hours a day, 365 days a year, a dietitian's schedule includes all hours and all days.

What Education and Skills Will I Need?

High school: Preparation for college, with an emphasis on science and computer science.

College: Preparation for a degree in the home economics department with a major in foods and nutrition, or in institutional management. To qualify for professional recognition, take one of the 68 approved one-year internships in a hospital. Most of the top jobs are offered to students who have completed the internship, which provides further education and on-the-job experience under supervision.

Personal skills: An aptitude for science, and organizational and administrative abilities are needed.

How Many Women in the Field and Where Do They Work?

There are 44,000 full-time dietitians and 90 percent of them are women. About half of them work in hospitals, including VA hospitals, and in the U.S. Public Health Service. Colleges, universities, and public schools employ almost all of the rest, except for the few who work in large business cafeterias and in the Armed Forces. Part-time opportunities are very good, with 15 percent of all dietitians working part-time.

$ $ $ $ $

In 1981, beginning salary for new graduates of an internship program was $15,800 a year. Experienced dietitians in hospitals earned as much as $25,872 a year.

What Is the Future for Women?

Both full-time and part-time job opportunities will be very good through the 1980s. The increase in all health institutions, in nursing homes, and in population will result in a demand for more dietitians. Small hospitals and small institutions often hire part-time dietitians.

RELATED CAREERS
  food technologist
  home economist
  food service manager

DIETITIAN

WHERE CAN I GET MORE INFORMATION?
Professional Group
The American Dietetic Association
430 North Michigan Avenue
Chicago, IL 60611

Trade Journal
Journal of Nutrition
9650 Rockville Pike
Bethesda, MD 20014

MEDICAL TECHNOLOGIST

Under the supervision of a pathologist, performs chemical, microscopic, and bacteriological tests to diagnose the causes and nature of disease.

What's It Like to Be a Medical Technologist?

Medical technologists perform several tests, including blood count, blood cholesterol level, and skin tests. They also microscopically examine body fluids and tissues for bacteria, fungus, or other organisms. In small hospitals, the medical technologists do all of the tests; in large hospitals, they specialize in an area, such as the study of blood cells or tissue preparation and examination. Medical technologists are usually assisted by medical technicians and laboratory assistants who perform simple, routine tests. Lynette LeBlanc says, "My morning begins at 7:00 A.M. when I walk into patients' rooms and convince them there is nothing they would rather do than let me use a needle to get a little bit of blood out of their arms and into test tubes. The rest of the morning is spent in the laboratory performing the various tests that doctors have ordered for the samples I've collected. This may involve anything from doing a simple screening, which takes approximately five minutes, to doing a test for vitamin B_{12}, which takes up to two days to complete. Since the laboratory is very automated, a good part of the morning is spent in starting up machines, setting them, and getting them ready for use during the day."

Supervisor of the blood bank in a university hospital, Sarah

L. Dopp says that medical technology is a challenging career for the person who is interested in science, curious about the medical field, can take responsibility for the work and tests she does, and wants a health career but not constant contact with patients.

What Education and Skills Will I Need?

High school: Preparation for college, with emphasis in science and mathematics.

College: A college degree program or one year of special training after three years of college is required. Chemistry, biology, mathematics, and computer science are the required courses in the program.

Personal skills: Manual dexterity and good eyesight are essential, as well as accuracy, dependability, and the ability to work under pressure.

How Many Women in the Field and Where Do They Work?

There are about 50,000 medical technologists and almost all of them are women. The majority work in hospitals, and some work in health agencies and research.

$ $ $ $ $

In 1980, new medical technologists started at $13,200 a year. Experienced technologists averaged $16,000 a year.

What Is the Future for Women?

General medical technology is not in demand because computer systems can do routine medical tests cheaper and more efficiently. The demands now are for those with advanced technological skills. The opportunities for specialists will be very good through the 1980s. Technologists with a degree and specialty will have the best chances for supervising other lab workers.

RELATED CAREERS
  chemistry technologist
  criminologist
  food tester

WHERE CAN I GET MORE INFORMATION?
  Professional Groups
  American Medical Technologists
  710 Higgins Road
  Park Ridge, IL 60068

  American Society for Medical Technology
  330 Meadowfern Drive
  Houston, TX 77067

  Registry of Medical Technologists of the American Society
    of Clinical Pathologists
  P.O. Box 12270
  Chicago, IL 60612

  Trade Journal
  Journal of Medical Technologists
  710 Higgins Road
  Park Ridge, IL 60068

PHARMACIST

*Selects, compounds, dispenses, and preserves drugs
and medicines to fill the prescriptions of
physicians and dentists.*

What's It Like to Be a Pharmacist?

"I dispense medication to hospital patients and staff, write up orders to pharmaceutical houses, compound and manufacture pharmaceuticals, and give drug information over the telephone to questioning nurses and physicians," says June Marie Jones, Assistant Director of Pharmacy in a university hospital. "In addition, I meet with nursing staff to discuss patient care and pharmacy, meet with physicians, and write the *Pharmacy Bulletin,* which informs doctors and nurses about the latest drug information." Yvette Matte, Manager and Chief Pharmacist in a university hospital pharmacy, says, "After gaining experience, I plan to go into business for myself. Most women in pharmacy work for others. I've decided I want to be the owner of a drugstore—where the money is."

What Education and Skills Will I Need?

High school: Preparation for college, with biology, chemistry, and computer science.

College: Pharmacy is a five-year college program leading to a degree. The program includes chemistry, physics, mathematics, computer science, zoology, and physiology. Each state requires its own licence to practice.

Personal skills: Business ability, an interest in medicine, orderliness, accuracy, and the ability to build customers' confidence are needed for success in pharmacy.

How Many Women in the Field and Where Do They Work?

Presently, 25 percent of the 141,000 pharmacists are women, and the numbers are increasing as the pharmacy programs enroll more women in college. Most women work in hospital pharmacies or laboratories, while most men are in the retail drug business, where the money is. About 25,000 pharmacists own their own drugstores.

$ $ $ $ $

Pharmacy pays better than most health-related careers that require the same level of education. In 1981, a first-year pharmacist earned $15,200 a year with the federal government, $21,300 a year in hospitals, and much more in the retail business. Experienced pharmacists in hospitals and medical centers averaged $27,200 a year.

What Is the Future for Women?

The best opportunities will be in hospitals and health facilities. Many localities will have many more pharmacists than jobs. The drug business, medical research, and government subsidies of medical bills will continue to rapidly increase the demand for pharmacists. Profits in pharmacy can be made by women as well as by men, if women would break the tradition and enter the drug-store business on their own.

RELATED CAREERS
pharmaceutical chemist
pharmaceutical sales representative
pharmacologist

WHERE CAN I GET MORE INFORMATION?
Professional Groups
American Pharmaceutical Association
2215 Constitution Avenue, NW
Washington, D.C. 20037

American Council on Pharmaceutical Education
One East Wacker Drive
Chicago, IL 60601

Trade Journal
American Druggist
Stanley Sieglman
224 West 57 Street
New York, NY 10019

SCIENCE
AND
TECHNOLOGY

Astronomer
Biologist
Chemist
Conservationist
Engineer
Environmental Scientist
Food Scientist
Mathematician
Physicist

About these careers   More than 3 million people, or nearly one-quarter of all professionals, are engineers, scientists, or other scientific and technical workers. The number of scientists and engineers has tripled in the past 25 years. This cluster includes careers for more than two million jobs.

A bachelor's degree is usually needed to enter scientific and engineering jobs. In mathematics and in physical and biological sciences, more emphasis is placed on advanced degrees. Some careers, such as astronomer, require a doctorate for full professional status. Undergraduate training for scientists and engineers includes courses in their major field, in related science areas, and in mathematics. Courses and skills in computer science are important for all scientists.

Students who want to specialize in a particular area of science should select their schools carefully. For example, those who plan to become biomedical engineers and biochemists should study at a university affiliated with a hospital. Those who want to be agricultural scientists can get the most practical training at state universities with agricultural experiment stations.

Scientific and technical careers, such as forester, range manager, engineer, geologist, and meteorologist, can involve considerable time away from home working outdoors in remote parts of the country. Foresters may work extra hours on emergency fire-fighting or search-and-rescue missions. Many engineers spend some time outdoors in mines or at construction sites. Others work under quiet conditions in modern offices and research laboratories. Exploration geologists often work overseas. They travel to remote sites by helicopter and jeep, and cover large areas by foot, often working in teams. Meteorologists in small weather stations generally work alone; in large stations, they work as part of a team.

New engineering graduates begin working under the close supervision of experienced engineers. To determine the specialities for which new engineers are best suited, many companies have programs to acquaint new engineers with industrial practices. Experienced engineers may advance to positions of greater responsibility; those with proven ability often become administrators and are promoted to top management jobs.

Women are under-represented in science and technical careers. Today, science and technology are where the jobs are. They are the careers of the computer age. If you want to be in on the money and the best opportunities, think seriously about science and technology.

ASTRONOMER

*Uses the principles of physics and mathematics
to study and determine the behavior of matter
and energy in outer space.*

What's It Like to Be an Astronomer?

"I enjoy the quietness and solitude of the observatory in the evening. I can read and study along with checking instruments. I spend a lot of time in the library trying to stay on top of current research projects. Days end usually at 1:00 or 2:00 A.M. and I still manage to have a very busy social life. Astronomy is for the woman who wants to be a part of the thrill and excitement of discovery in the space age," says Karen Hebb, an astronomer with the Harvard University Observatory. Astronomers collect and analyze data of the sun, moon, planets, and stars to determine the size, shape, temperature, composition and motion of these bodies. They compute the positions of the planets and make statistical studies of the stars. In addition to gathering information by telescope, astronomers use rockets and earth satellites that carry cameras and measuring devices.

Reta Beebe was one of the few female mission scientists on the Voyager I project that explored Saturn. "Saturn *is* astronomy to many people," says Beebe. But her job was the long and detailed process of relating data on Saturnian wind speeds and directions to observed phenomena. "It's the numbers and detail that make a science," explains the mission scientist.

What Education and Skills Will I Need?

High school: Preparation for a physical science major in college by taking as much mathematics, physical science, and computer science as high school offers.

College: Many astronomers major in mathematics or physics as undergraduates. A master's in astronomy is necessary for beginning jobs, but a Ph.D. is required for the top careers in astronomy.

How Many Women in the Field and Where Do They Work?

Seven percent are women in the small field of 3,000 professional astronomers. Over half of the astronomers teach and do research in colleges and universities. The percentage of first-year female graduate students in astronomy has increased to 14 percent.

$ $ $ $ $

In 1980, the average salary for astronomers was $26,000 a year. The average salary for space scientists in the federal government was $38,000 a year. Industries will pay more as their demand for astronomers increases.

What Is the Future for Women?

There are many more astronomers than jobs and federal money for research has been drastically cut. Expect keen competition through the 1980s for this work. Those who have had some part-time work experience will have the best chances for jobs.

RELATED CAREERS
    physicist
    other physical scientist
    mathematician

WHERE CAN I GET MORE INFORMATION?
    Professional Group
    The American Astronomical Society
    University of Delaware
    Newark, DE 19711

    Trade Journals
    Sky and Telescope
    Sky Publication Corp.
    49 Bay State Road
    Cambridge, MA 02138

    Weatherwise
    AMS
    45 Beacon Street
    Boston, MA 02108

BIOLOGIST

Studies the structure, evolution, behavior, and life processes of living organisms.

What's It Like to Be a Biologist?

Major industry is just beginning to find applications for the "new biology," that is, genetic engineering to manufacture living materials. For example, bacteria can be used to convert sunlight into electrochemical energy, or life forms may be bred to do the work of nuclear power plants. More traditional biologists are working to improve medicine, increase crop yields, and improve our natural environment. The biological sciences include many specialities, such as botanists who study all aspects of plant life, and zoologists who study animal life and usually specialize in birds, insects, or mammals. The bigger fields of biological specialization are genetics, horticulture, nutrition, and pharmacology. Biological scientists usually work in the field or in a laboratory with a team of scientists, write up their findings, and do some teaching. Sometimes called life scientists, they study all aspects of living organisms, emphasizing the relationship of animals and plants to their environment. Working to create entirely new foods and fibers by cheap and simple methods will be one of the biologists' jobs of the 1980s.

What Education and Skills Will I Need?

High school: Preparation for college and graduate school, with as much science, mathematics, and computer science as is offered in your school.

College: You can major in any biological science and should get as broad an understanding as possible of all sciences, including chemistry, physics, and computer science. Choose your graduate school by the particular biological program it offers. A Ph.D. is required for research jobs, university teaching, and a career in biological science.

Personal skills: Ability to work independently and with a team and good communication skills are necessary for the biologist.

How Many Women in the Field and Where Do They Work?

The biological sciences number 125,000 people, including 35,000 agriculturists. There are also 16,000 biochemists. Forty percent of these workers are women. Half of the biologists are employed in colleges, with many in medical schools and state agricultural colleges. Private industry, such as drug and food product companies, employs one-fourth of the biologists, and the Department of Agriculture employs the last fourth.

$ $ $ $ $

In 1981, private industry paid an average of $15,200 a year for biologists with bachelor's degrees. Biologists with master's degrees began at $15,193 or $18,585 a year for the federal government. Average salaries for all biologists in the federal government was $28,100 a year.

What Is the Future for Women?

From Toffler's *The Third Wave* comes the observation that biology will become increasingly more important in the next thirty years. Biologists will be involved with solving the energy problem; converting the oceans into food for the world; eliminating the need for oil in plastics, paint, and other manufactured products; and genetic engineering. In other words, biologists will be on the cutting-edge of the technical revolution, where future opportunities are just beginning to explode in many directions.

RELATED CAREERS
forester
soil conservationist
oceanographer

WHERE CAN I GET MORE INFORMATION?
Professional Groups
American Institute of Biological Sciences
1401 Wilson Boulevard
Arlington, VA 22209

American Society of Biological Chemists
9650 Rockville Pike
Bethesda, MD 20014

American Society for Horticultural Science
701 North Saint Asaph Street
Alexandria, VA 22314

Trade Journal
American Naturalist
University of Chicago Press
5801 Ellis Avenue
Chicago, IL 60637

CHEMIST

Studies the properties and composition of matter,
often relating study to performing chemical tests
on manufactured goods such as drugs, plastics,
dyes, paint, and petroleum products.

What's It Like to Be a Chemist?

Research chemists work in the laboratory looking for new knowledge about the nature of substances and for ways to use this information. Industries such as plastics and frozen foods, and artificial fibers such as nylon, were developed in the labs of chemists. Anne Briscoe, Ph.D., biochemist at Columbia University, and past President of the Association for Women in Science, finally got tenure after 20 years in academic life. About money and advancement for women in science, Briscoe makes the following observation in *Working Woman* (May 1981): "Because of the difficulty of getting grants, women tend to work for someone else, which makes them dependent. I know instances where a man and a woman collaborated on an idea for a project and, once he got grant money, he fired her. Abuses like this could be stopped if the National Institutes of Health, in Washington, and other funding organizations gave the grant in both names. Grants should be like property in a divorce — split down the middle. Many scientists claim that the peer review system helps women get grants, but from what I have observed as a member of such committees, it doesn't. The answer to this problem is for more women to get on the review committees and to make certain that women investigators get a fair hearing."

What Education and Skills Will I Need?

High school: Preparation for college, with as much science, mathematics, and computer science as possible.

College: Over 1,100 colleges offer a bachelor's degree in chemistry. Mathematics and physics are required of all chemists. You will need a Ph.D. with computer skills for the top jobs in research and/or university teaching.

Personal skills: Interest in studying math and science, ability to work with the hands for building scientific apparatus, and ability to concentrate on detail are essential to the chemist.

How Many Women in the Field and Where Do They Work?

Almost 21 percent of the 113,000 chemists are women. Sixty-six percent work in private industry, half of these for chemical manufacturing industries. Many chemists are employed by the food, petroleum, paper, and electrical equipment companies. Twenty percent of the chemists teach in colleges. The industrial states of New York, New Jersey, California, Pennsylvania, and Ohio employ half of all chemists.

$ $ $ $ $

In 1981, private industry started college graduates at $19,600 a year; master's degree graduates at $23,600 a year; and Ph.D.s at $29,800 a year. Experienced chemists averaged $30,000 with a master's degree and $35,000 with a Ph.D. As the salaries go up with experience and education, the gap between male and female salaries widens. "Women scientists," says Caroline Bird, author of *Born Female,* "are paid $2,500 to $3,000 less a year than men in the same positions."

What Is the Future for Women?

Work in college teaching will be limited, but chances for jobs in private industry to develop new products will be very good for chemists at all levels through the 1980s. Entry-level jobs with big companies are competitive, as there are more chemists graduating. A woman in research for private industry writes, "I am treated as an equal while on my job, but the company would rather not ask me to go on business trips."

RELATED CAREERS
biochemist
genetic engineer
food scientist

WHERE CAN I GET MORE INFORMATION?
Professional Group
American Chemical Society
1155 16th Street, NW
Washington, D.C. 20036

Trade Journal
Chemical Technology
American Chemical Society
1155 16th Street, NW
Washington, D.C. 20036

CONSERVATIONIST
*Manages, develops, and protects forests,
rangelands, wildlife, soil, and water resources.*

What's It Like to Be a Conservationist?

Foresters deal with one of our most important natural resources, which is becoming more valuable as wood is increasingly used for heat and energy. They often specialize in timber management, outdoor recreation, or forest economics. Range managers, sometimes called range conservationists, range scientists, or range ecologists, determine the number and kind of animals to be grazed, the grazing system to be used, and the best season for grazing in order to yield a high production in livestock. At the same time, they must conserve soil and vegetation for other uses, such as wildlife grazing, outdoor recreation, and timber production. Soil conservationists help farmers and ranchers conserve soil and water. They prepare maps with the soil, water, and vegetation plan of the farmer's land, recommend ways the land can best be used, and help estimate costs and returns on land use. Ann Fix, forester from Indiana, writes, "I supervise growth plots, Christmas tree plantations, and timber-stand improvement works. Since I have a family, I try to do many forestry related things with my children. I work in youth 4-H programs and have revised their forestry bulletins and publications for young people. I am a nature counselor for the Scouts; I have laid several nature trails for a variety of organizations; I have conducted nature hikes and talked to public school students, clubs, and Scouts."

What Education and Skills Will I Need?

High school: Preparation for college, with as much science as possible.

College: Major in one of the 43 approved forestry programs, or in range science at one of the 20 universities that offer this major. An advanced degree is necessary for the teaching and research jobs in a conservation career.

Personal skills: A love for the outdoors, physical hardiness, and a scientific curiosity for solving problems is needed to be happy in conservation.

How Many Women in the Field and Where Do They Work?

There are 30,000 professional foresters, 4,000 range managers, and 5,000 soil conservationists in the country. Only 500 professional foresters are women; however, the female enrollment in professional forestry schools went up from 6.7 percent in 1972 to 20 percent in 1980. One-fourth of the foresters are employed by the federal government in the Department of Agriculture, and one-third are in private industry, mainly in pulp, paper, and lumber companies. Most range managers and soil conservationists work for the government. The first woman park chief in the history of the National Park Service, Sherma E. Bierhaus, was appointed in March, 1982. There are 22 women unit managers among 333 areas of the park service, but Bierhaus was the first to run a national park.

CONSERVATIONIST

$ $ $ $ $

In private industry, starting foresters averaged $15,200 a year in 1980, and the overall average salary was $25,200 a year. In 1981, a forester with a master's degree started with the federal government at $15,193 a year. Experienced conservationists in state government averaged about $20,400 a year.

What Is the Future for Women?

Jobs are increasing in conservation, but the number of foresters and range managers is increasing faster. The job market will be competitive through the 1980s. Cuts in federal spending limit the growth of these jobs.

RELATED CAREERS

oceanographer   environmental scientist
biologist   food scientist

WHERE CAN I GET MORE INFORMATION?

Professional Groups
American Forestry Association
1319 18th Street, NW
Washington, D.C. 20036

Society for Range Management
2760 W. 5th Avenue
Denver, CO 80204

Soil Conservation Service
U.S. Department of Agriculture
P.O. Box 2890
Washington, D.C. 20013

Trade Journals
Forest Industries
500 Howard Street
San Francisco, CA 94105

National Wildlife
1412 16th Street, NW
Washington, D.C. 20036

ENGINEER

*Converts raw materials and power into useful
products at a reasonable cost in time and money.*

What's It Like to Be an Engineer?

An engineer's main job is to use scientific principles to solve practical problems of modern living. They do a great variety of work that includes developing electric power, water supply, and waste disposal systems; designing industrial machinery and equipment needed to manufacture goods; designing heating, air-conditioning, and ventilation equipment; developing scientific equipment for outer space and ocean exploration; and designing and supervising construction of buildings, highways, and transportation systems.

Anne Prowsky started out in general engineering, but she decided to combine her interest in engineering with medicine and specialize in biomedical engineering. She now works on the development of a cardiac pacemaker that regulates the heartbeat. Other engineers with whom she works are developing artificial hearts and kidneys and adapting computers to monitor patients using these devices. Mary Winston, a black activist, specialized in computer engineering. She is a data systems engineer for IBM computer systems. While working as a secretary for an engineering firm, Kathryn Anner learned that women can be engineers. She started night school, switched to full-time study, and is now a civil engineer. Anner has worked on all kinds of projects, including new designs for a whole tank in the New York Aquarium, a banking center in Kuwait, and Macy's in Connecticut. She says she is concerned with every phase of a job, "Not only are we supposed to make the building stand up, we also help the architect make the building as esthetically pleasing as possible and help the contractor build it as easily as possible."

What Education and Skills Will I Need?

High school: Preparation for college, with an emphasis on science, mathematics, and computer science.

College: Major in engineering in one of the 240 colleges and universities with a specialty in aerospace, agricultural, biomedical, ceramic, chemical, civil, electrical, industrial, mechanical, metallurgical, mining, nuclear, or petroleum engineering. Some specialities such as nuclear engineering are available only on the graduate level.

Personal skills: Ability to think analytically, a capacity for detail, and ability to work as a team member are necessary skills.

How Many Women in the Field and Where Do They Work?

Engineering is the largest profession for men, with 1.2 million engineers. At ten times the 1970 rate, only 3 percent are now women! The percentage of women by branch are: mechanical — 2.8; electrical — 3.8; industrial — 11.3; aeronautical — 1.2; and civil — 1.6. Half of the engineers are employed by manufacturing industries; one-fourth are in construction, public utilities, and building services; and the remainder are with the government and educational institutions.

$ $ $ $ $

In 1981, engineers with a bachelor's degree started at $22,900 a year. Graduates with a master's degree started at $25,500 a year, and experienced engineers doubled that salary. In 1980, average *starting* salaries for engineers by branch were:

Branch	Salary	Number Employed
Petroleum	$23,844	18,000
Chemical	$21,612	55,000
Mining	$20,808	6,000
Metallurgical	$20,712	15,000
Mechanical	$20,436	213,000
Electrical	$20,280	325,000
Industrial	$19,860	115,000
Aeronautical	$19,776	68,000
Civil	$18,648	165,000

What Is the Future for Women?

The opportunities in engineering will continue to be very good especially for women, who have been discriminated against for so long. Engineering students, who made up about 7 percent of college graduates in 1980, received 65 percent of the reported job offers. Engineering schools and firms are now actively recruiting for women. Purdue University, one of the most active recruiters for women, has one of the highest enrollments of women, up from 9 percent in 1975 to 20 percent in the fall of 1979. In 1974, Princeton University had 9 women in engineering and now has 150 out of 830 engineering students. In engineering schools, women now account for 15 to 25 percent of all entering classes. You must get the required mathematics and physics in high school to qualify for a major in engineering. Some universities, such as the University of Dayton, are now offering a fast-track, late-entry engineering program for women with a degree in mathematics, physics, or related sciences at *no tuition*. These programs are funded by the National Science Foundation. Engineering is one of the few professions that does not require a graduate degree. Young women should get in on the advantages of this high-paying profession that has increasing jobs for everyone who is qualified. Many jobs will be open in developing new sources of energy and in solving environmental pollution problems.

RELATED CAREERS

environmental scientist	mathematician
physical scientist	architect

WHERE CAN I GET MORE INFORMATION?

Professional Group
Society of Women Engineers
United Engineering Center
345 East 47 Street
New York, NY 10017

Trade Journals
Chemical Engineer
McGraw-Hill Publications
1221 Avenue of the Americas
New York, NY 10019

Civil Engineering
345 East 47 Street
New York, NY 10017

ENVIRONMENTAL SCIENTIST

*Geologists, geophysicists, meteorologists, and
oceanographers study the earth's land, water,
interior, and atmosphere, and the environment
in space. They preserve our natural resources
and control pollution.*

What's It Like to Be an Environmental Scientist?

Susan Russell-Robinson, geologist, was one of two women sent to Mount St. Helens to find out why it erupted in 1980. Working a 16-hour day in analyzing rocks, she will continue her study of other volcanoes for the U.S. Geological Survey. Russell-Robinson has been married to another geologist for two years. She says they have worked out an arrangement that allows them to get all the housework done without sacrificing their careers or hobbies. For example, when they are both home, she cooks one week and he cooks the next. The rest of the work they divide according to their likes and dislikes. Coming up with this system took a lot of discussion about what they wanted as a couple and as individuals. "When I'm in the field, my husband takes care of everything himself, just as he did when he was single!"

Geologists study the structure, composition, and history of the earth's crust. They spend a lot of time in the field studying rock cores and cuttings from deep holes drilled into the earth, and examining rocks, minerals, and fossils near the surface of the earth. They locate oil, coal, and other minerals crucial to our scarce energy supply. Geophysicists study the size and shape, interior, surface, and atmosphere of the earth, the land and bodies of water on its surface and underground, and the environment of the earth in space. They work mostly for oil and gas companies, often using satellites to conduct tests from outer space and computers to collect and analyze data. Meteorologists study the air that surrounds the earth, by understanding the motions, processes, and influences of the atmosphere's ingredients. Besides weather forecasting, they work to understand and solve air pollution problems. Oceanographers study the ocean, its characteristics, movements, and plant and animal life. Aquaculture is an industry for the 1980s, where oceanographers will be in high demand to get fish, food, and energy from a much needed resource.

What Education and Skills Will I Need?

High school: Preparation for college, with an emphasis on the physical sciences, mathematics, life sciences, and computer science.

College: A major in any environmental or related science will prepare you for graduate work, which is necessary for any job in the environmental sciences. A Ph.D. is required for a career in science, and a master's degree is needed for a beginning job in research or high school teaching.

Personal skills: Curiosity for new research, analytical thinking, and physical stamina for outdoor life are needed to be an environmental scientist.

How Many Women in the Field and Where Do They Work?

Of the 34,000 geologists, only 4 percent are women. Most environmental scientists work for private industry, oil and gas producers in the Southwest, the federal government, and in teaching. There are very few women in geophysics, a field of 12,000 professionals. Only 2 percent of the 4,000 meteorologists are women, and the weather bureau employs half of them. Almost none of the 2,800 oceanographers are women.

$ $ $ $ $

In 1980, beginners with a master's degree started at $24,600 a year in private industry. The average salary for experienced oceanographers in the federal government in 1980 was about $29,800 a year.

What Is the Future for Women?

Oceanography will be a major new industry in the 1980s. Opportunities will abound for the creative scientist to solve food problems, solve energy problems by "growing oil" in the sea, mine minerals, and be involved in new directions as yet undiscovered as the ocean becomes "settled." The physical sciences

ENVIRONMENTAL SCIENTIST

have been traditionally closed to women. While you are in high school take a strong mathematics and science curriculum, in order to qualify for the interesting careers that will now be open to you by law. Ms. Rita Sagalyn, geophysicist, makes an important point for any of you considering a physical science profession. She writes, "You will find this work more rewarding, challenging, and stimulating, and also will be in a better position to be selective, if your education is strong. While one realizes that the physical sciences do discriminate against women, the need for competent, well-trained individuals is so great that any women with the proper qualifications and motivation can find a very satisfying and creative professional career." Oceanography jobs will continue to be competitive through the 1980s, as the number of graduates exceeds the number of jobs. Meteorology will be fair, but geology and geophysics will have better chances for work because of the need to locate and recover oil and other minerals.

RELATED CAREERS
all environmental science and engineering careers

WHERE CAN I GET MORE INFORMATION?
Professional Groups
American Geological Institute
5205 Leesburg Pike
Falls Church, VA 22041

American Geophysical Union
2000 Florida Avenue, NW
Washington, D.C. 20009

American Meteorological Society
45 Beacon Street
Boston, MA 02108

Office of Sea Grant
National Oceanic and Atmospheric Administration
Rockville, MD 20852

Association of Women Geoscientists
Box 1005
Menlo Park, CA 94025

Trade Journals
Rocks and Minerals
Box 29
Peekskill, NY 10566

Sea Frontiers
10 Rickenbacker Causeway
Virginia Key, FL 33149

FOOD SCIENTIST

*Investigates the chemical, physical, and biological
nature of food for the processing industry.*

What's It Like to Be a Food Scientist?

Food scientists, sometimes called food technologists, study the structure and composition of food and its changes during processing or storage. They check raw ingredients to note freshness, maturity, and suitability for processing. Maria Martinez is a food scientist for a New Jersey frozen food company, and her job is to ensure that each new food product will retain its characteristics and nutritive value during processing or storage. Martinez must determine the various enzymes that are inactive after the product has been processed so that the food does not lose its flavor during storage.

What Education and Skills Will I Need?

High school: Preparation for college, with a strong program in mathematics, biology, chemistry, and computer science.

College: A bachelor's degree in food science, chemistry, or biology from one of the 40 approved colleges. A master's degree is required for management jobs in food science.

Personal skills: An analytical mind and an ability for and interest in detailed technical work are necessary.

FOOD SCIENTIST

How Many Women in the Field and Where Do They Work?

Almost 15 percent of the 7,500 food scientists are women. Food scientists are employed in all parts of the food industry and most of them work in California, Illinois, New York, Pennsylvania, Texas, Ohio, New Jersey, Wisconsin, Michigan, and Iowa.

$ $ $ $ $

In 1980, experienced food scientists earned an average salary of $29,500 a year. With 11 to 15 years of experience, they averaged $32,000 a year.

What Is the Future for Women?

Work opportunities will be slow through the 1980s because of the slow growth rate of food processing industries. Jobs will increase if the food industry responds to the need for a wholesome and economical food supply in the world. Research could produce new foods from modifications of rice and soybeans. For example, food scientists may create "meat" products, from vegetable proteins, that resemble beef, pork, and chicken.

RELATED CAREERS
chemist
environmental scientist
engineer

WHERE CAN I GET MORE INFORMATION?
Professional Group
The Institute of Food Technologists
221 North LaSalle Street, Suite 2120
Chicago, IL 60601

Trade Journal
Quick Frozen Foods
Cahner Publishing Co.
205 East 42 Street
New York, NY 10017

MATHEMATICIAN

Creates new mathematical theories and solves scientific, managerial, engineering, and social problems in mathematical terms.

What's It Like to Be a Mathematician?

Maureen Garofano, a statistician for General Electric, has been on the job for three years and loves her work solving financial forecast problems through mathematics. Garofano emphasizes doing the best you can in your subjects because you never know how you will be using them. "In high school, I had no intention of doing anything with math! I took the usual math courses for college, but not until my junior year in college did I plan to major in statistics." Large manufacturing firms such as GE, IBM, and Wang offer graduate courses at nearby universities in quantitative analysis, so employees can keep upgrading themselves in their careers.

Many young women think that math is a natural for men. "Not so," says GE mathematician Delbert O. Martin, married and the father of two elementary school children. He urges high school students to be persistent. Martin says, "Don't take the first failure seriously. I had to take elementary calculus three times before I passed it. I like being a mathematician because my work is exciting, challenging, and creative."

Cathleen Morawetz is an applied mathematician at New York University's Courant Institute. She is one of the few women to attain eminence in mathematics, a field in which many other women have become discouraged. Morawetz's major current interest is the mathematics of the scattering of waves. Scattering arises in all sorts of situations. When a wave—which can be electromagnetic, sound, or elastic—hits a barrier, it interacts with the barrier. The wave can be reflected, absorbed, or transmitted, depending on such things as the wave frequency and the properties of the barrier. The problem in scattering theory is to analyze how the interaction takes place and what can be observed from a distance. When her children were young, people often asked Morawetz whether she worried about them when she was at work. Her reply was, "No, I'm much more likely to worry about a theorem when I'm with my children."

What Education and Skills Will I Need?

High school: Preparation for college, with emphasis in mathematics and computer science. Many high school women give "female math anxiety" as the reason for not electing higher mathematics in high school. Be sure that you elect fourth-year and advanced-placement mathematics, because you want to try it and you need it. Forget that "girls don't need mathematics"! What you do need is to know how much mathematics you can do, and how well you can do it.

College: Major in mathematics, or in a related field with a minor in mathematics, to prepare for an advanced degree in mathematics, which is necessary for research and university teaching jobs.

Personal skills: Good reasoning ability, persistence, and ability to apply basic principles to new types of problems.

How Many Women in the Field and Where Do They Work?

About 20 percent of the 40,000 mathematicians are women. In addition, there are 26,500 statisticians, of whom one-third are women. Three-fourths of all mathematicians work in colleges and universities. Others are employed by private industry, such as electrical, aerospace, and manufacturing companies. Most statisticians work in private industry.

$ $ $ $ $

In 1980, college graduates started at $17,700 a year with private industries, and at $20,200 a year if they had a master's degree. Colleges and government paid slightly less. Average salaries for all mathematicians in the federal government was $30,100 a year in 1980.

What Is the Future for Women?

Mathematicians will find competition for academic careers, as the number of math majors increases and college jobs decrease. Related mathematics jobs are expected to increase. The growth in computer, engineering, and technical jobs will result in the use of many more mathematicians and statisticians. Applied rather than theoretical mathematicians will have the best chances for work.

RELATED CAREERS

computer programmer   actuary
systems analyst   statistician

WHERE CAN I GET MORE INFORMATION?

Professional Groups
American Mathematical Society
P.O. Box 6248
Providence, RI 02904

American Statistical Association
806 15th Street, NW
Washington, D.C. 20005

Association for Women in Mathematics
Department of Mathematics
Wellesley College
Wellesley, MA 02181

Trade Journal
Mathematics Magazine
MMA
1225 Connecticut Avenue, NW
Washington, D.C. 20036

PHYSICIST

Describes in mathematical terms the fundamental forces and laws of nature, and the interaction of matter and energy.

What's It Like to Be a Physicist?

Physicists develop theories that describe in mathematical terms the basic forces and laws of nature, such as gravity, electromagnetism, and nuclear interaction. Most work in research and development for private industry and the government, and they often specialize in areas such as nuclear energy, electronics, communications, aerospace, or medical instrumentation. Physicist Lindsay Schachinger, B.A. from Douglass College and Ph.D. from Rutgers University, works at the prestigious Fermi National Accelerator Laboratory near Chicago. She says that she has to work an eight-hour shift five to six days a week, sleep a few hours, work on the apparatus, and then work on the computer analysis of the data. "After five years of this, I've come to realize that I have to maintain some kind of personal life or I'll burn out. Nobody can be efficient 100 hours a week. It is hard for me to stop putting my personal life into neutral and do nothing but work, because, like many women, I am eager to prove myself and to combat the stereotype that women are not serious about their work. I'm starting to learn that I can have a personal life and still do good work."

What Education and Skills Will I Need?

High school: Preparation for college, with as much mathematics and computer science as possible.

College: Major in physics or mathematics in college to prepare for graduate school. A career physicist requires a Ph.D. and knowledge of computer science.

Personal skills: Mathematical ability, an inquisitive mind, and imagination plus the ability to think in abstract terms are needed to be a physicist.

How Many Women in the Field and Where Do They Work?

There are 37,000 physicists and 4 percent are women. Half of the physicists are employed by private industry primarily in electrical, aircraft and missile, and scientific instruments manufacturing companies. Of the other half, most are in colleges and universities, and some are with the government. More than one-third of all physicists work in three states—California, New York, and Massachusetts.

$ $ $ $ $

In 1980, beginning physicists in private industry with a master's degree started at $21,500 a year, and with a Ph.D. degree at $27,300 a year. Average salary for all physicists in the federal government in 1980 was $34,700 a year.

What Is the Future for Women?

Dr. Wood says, "If you think science is more fun than anything else you study in school, and if you're reasonably good at it (B grade or better), there is a good chance you can have a rewarding career as a physicist. Don't make the tragic mistake of training yourself for a job that isn't attractive to you because someone who isn't going to have to live your life told you that it was the thing to do." Employment opportunities for physicists are expected to be good through the 1980s. Even though many high school girls excel in physics and mathematics in high school, attitudes such as "Physics is for boys" or "Girls don't like physics" keeps them out of the career. A bachelor's degree will provide jobs in engineering and computer science.

RELATED CAREERS

astronomer	engineer
chemist	mathematician
zoologist	

WHERE CAN I GET MORE INFORMATION?

Professional Groups
American Institute of Physics
335 East 45 Street
New York, NY 10017

Association for Women in Science
1346 Connecticut Avenue, NW, Room 1122
Washington, D.C. 20036

Trade Journal
Physics Today
American Institute of Physics
335 East 45 Street
New York, NY 10017

SOCIAL SERVICE

Clergy
Extension Service Worker
Home Economist
Recreation Worker
Rehabilitation Counselor
Social Worker

About these careers Over 732,000 social service jobs are represented in the careers in this cluster. Like those in education, social service jobs require more education for less pay than other fields of work. If you are to be happy in this career, it will be because of your concern for people, not your desire for money. Patience, tact, sensitivity, and compassion are necessary personal qualities.

In social service careers, there are a great variety of settings and tasks. Depending on their specific occupation, workers advise consumers on how to get the most for their money; help people with disabilities to achieve satisfactory lifestyles; provide religious services; counsel people having problems in their jobs, home, school, or social relationships; or treat people with emotional problems.

Although social services are provided in many different settings, people in these careers require many of the same skills. In general, knowledge of the field is gained through a college degree. One to three years of graduate work in a professional school are required for many social service careers, such as counseling, clergy, and social work.

Beginning rehabilitation counselors and social workers who have limited experience are assigned the less difficult cases. As they gain experience, their caseloads are increased and they are assigned clients with more complex problems. After getting experience and more graduate education, rehabilitation counselors and social workers may advance to supervisory positions or to top administrative jobs.

After a few years of experience, recreation leaders may become supervisors. Although promotions to administrative jobs may be easier with graduate training, advancement is still possible through a combination of education and experience.

Social service jobs usually involve irregular hours, because the workers provide a wide range of services to people in many circumstances. For example, the clergy must go to people whenever they are in crisis, as well as visit regularly. Those in extension work frequently serve longer hours than they might in other jobs because they must be available for evening lectures and demonstrations. Recreation workers can expect night work and irregular hours, since they often have to work while others are enjoying leisure time.

Social service jobs often depend on government spending, because so many of the programs are tied to federal budgets. Right now, when money is tight and budgets are cut, the job situation is a very tough one.

CLERGY

Careers within the Jewish, Roman Catholic, and
Protestant religious institutions.

What's It Like to Be a Member
of the Clergy?

The traditional religious careers for women are in religious
education, nursing, teaching, missionary, and music work. Feminists are interested in religious careers that determine the religious institutions' policies, how the institutions spend their
money and time, and whether their language and concepts include women as equals. These careers are the clergy: rabbi,
priest, and ordained minister. The few ordained women who
have all of the necessary education and credentials are usually
given jobs as campus ministers, prison chaplains, assistant ministers, or jobs in inner cities where the vacancy cannot be filled
by men. Almost all religious institutions have a task force on the
status of women. These committees are making the clergy a very
exciting place to bring about change for the equality of women.
The Reverend Patricia Budd Kepler, Presbyterian Pastor in
Somerville, Massachusetts, urges women of all ages to stay in the
church and work together to bring women into positions of
religious leadership, as well as service.

What Education and Skills Will I Need?

High school: Preparation for a strong liberal arts college
program.

College: Major in religion, or theology, or any related
field to do with understanding people, in order to prepare for a
master's degree in divinity.

Personal skills: Religious careers require a deep conviction
in the religious and spiritual needs of people and the ability to
fill these needs through spiritual leadership of others.

How Many Women in the Field
and Where Do They Work?

Five percent of the 230,000 Protestant ordained ministers,
representing 80 different denominations, are women. On the
world level, 72 of the 168-member World Council of Churches

ordained women fully. The major communions not now ordaining women are the Roman Catholic Church, the Orthodox and Conservative Jews, and the Orthodox Churches. The Lutheran Church in America first ordained women priests in 1970. There are 3,000 rabbis and Sally Priesand became the first woman ordained to the rabbinate in this country in 1972. Other than one German, she was the first ordained in the history of Judaism. Eight years later, Rabbi Linda Holtzman was the only woman in the nation to be the presiding rabbi of a temple. In June 1973, Florence Dianna Pohlman became the first woman chaplain in the armed forces, and Rev. Lorraine Potter was the first woman chaplain in the Air Force soon after. In January 1974, Ms. Claire Randall was the first woman elected General Secretary of the National Council of Churches. In November 1974, 11 women were illegally ordained into the priesthood of the Episcopal Church in Philadelphia, and finally, in 1976, women were officially ordained into the Episcopal priesthood. There are 58,000 Catholic priests, and none are women. In late 1975, Roman Catholic leaders held an ordination conference in Detroit. The conference, "Women in Future Priesthood NOW," met in order to convene persons committed to ordaining women, to inform the church about women preparing for a full priesthood, and to develop strategies of action on women's ordination in the Catholic Church. The Rev. Jacqueline Means, first regularly ordained Episcopal priest, says, "It's difficult to understand the deep-seated reaction against women priests. About two-thirds of the 75 women who were ordained soon after me don't even have a job."

$ $ $ $ $

In 1980, the average annual income was about $15,000 a year for Protestant ministers, and $20,000 to $50,000 a year for rabbis. Catholic priests take a vow of poverty and are supported by their religious order.

What Is the Future for Women?

The decreasing number of church members and increasing number of theological students results in a very competitive job market for the Protestant and Orthodox Jewish clergy. Catholic priests are in demand because of a sharp drop in seminary enrollments. Opportunities for women in clergy careers will continue to change as women within the religious institutions work to eliminate sexism. Presently, there are Roman Catholic women in the seminary preparing for the priesthood, women in Protestant seminaries preparing for ordination, and many rabbinical students preparing to follow Rabbi Priesand in the synagogue. Children are taught that boys and men are just a little closer to God because only boys can grow up to hold the top religious jobs of minister, priest, or rabbi. When women have an equal chance for all religious jobs, their future career opportunities will be unlimited.

RELATED CAREERS

social worker   chaplain
counselor   missionary

WHERE CAN I GET MORE INFORMATION?

Professional Groups
Your local church or synagogue can offer you names and addresses of the headquarters of your religious group for career information.

B'Nai B'Rith Career and Counseling Services
1640 Rhode Island Avenue, NW
Washington, D.C. 20036 (Jewish)

National Sisters Vocation Conference
1307 South Wabash Avenue
Chicago, IL 60605 (Catholic)

Religious Formation Conference
1234 Massachusetts Avenue, NW
Washington, D.C. 20005 (Catholic)

National Council of Churches
475 Riverside Drive, Room 770
New York, NY 10027 (Protestant)

International Association of Women Ministers
c/o Rev. Carol S. Brown
143 Locust Street
Manchester, KY 40926 (Protestant)

Trade Journals
Christian Century
407 South Dearborn Street
Chicago, IL 60605 (Protestant)

Commentary
165 E. 56 Street
New York, NY 10022 (Jewish)

Commonweal
232 Madison Avenue
New York, NY 10016 (Catholic)

EXTENSION SERVICE WORKER

*Helps rural families solve their farm and home
problems and aids in community improvement.*

What's It Like to Be an Extension Service Worker?

County extension workers help farmers produce higher quality crops and livestock more efficiently. They help farm youth with recreational, health, leadership, and educational decisions. They work with homemakers on nutrition, enjoyment in the home, and family living. Mass media are used often for farm people, such as special newsletters, radio programs, and television programs. Extension service agent Louellen Watson finds the work more exciting and fun than she ever thought work could be. "The travel and variety in daily tasks are extremely challenging with never a routine week." Watson meets with community organizations such as day-care groups and Visiting Nurses program leaders. She teaches courses in nutrition, housing, child care, home furnishing, and bookkeeping. Most of her time is spent in the field with the farm people. "The only difficulty is that I need more help, especially in the fall at food preservation time," comments Watson. "Then the job leaves very little personal or family time." What she likes best is the opportunity to use everything she knows, from gardening to helping farm families with consumer fraud.

What Education and Skills Will I

High school: Preparation for college. A college degree is required.

College: Specialize in agriculture, family sociology, psychology, veterinary medicine, engineering, business, economics, or public administration.

Personal skills: Extension workers should have a specialty, an ability to work with people, and an interest in farm life.

How Many Women in the Field and Where Do They Work?

There are 14,000 extension workers. They manage the county programs and workers in all rural parts of the United States, as well as in the state capital of each state.

$ $ $ $ $

Extension workers earn the same as other college graduates in government jobs, averaging $20,000 a year in 1980.

What Is the Future for Women?

Job opportunities will be few through the 1980s. Cuts in federal spending and emphasis on the cities will slow job growth in rural areas.

RELATED CAREERS

dietitian   home economist
counselor   agricultural chemical salesperson

WHERE CAN I GET MORE INFORMATION?

Professional Group
County Extension Office
Personnel Division
U.S. Department of Agriculture
Hyattsville, MD 20782

Trade Journal
Extension Service Review
U.S. Department of Agriculture, Room 5044
South Building
Washington, D.C. 20250

HOME ECONOMIST

Concerned with improving products, services, and practices that affect the comfort and well-being of the family.

What's It Like to Be a Home Economist?

Half of the home economists are secondary school teachers. Eunice Marshall, home economics teacher from Titusville, Florida, says, "To be helpful to families in the world today, the teacher must be prepared to look at the family and all its relationships, including its consumer role; child-care responsibilities; household management of food and nutrition, clothing, and home furnishings; and the role of each family member outside the home." Other jobs in home economics include businesses who hire home economists to test products, prepare advertisements and booklets, and plan and present radio and television programs. They study consumer needs and help manufacturers find useful and saleable products. Clothing and textile majors work for textile and dress pattern companies, interior designers, and fabric manufacturers. Extension Service hires home economists for adult education programs and 4-H work.

The first woman lobbyist for a beer company was a home economics major. Flossie Robillard, State Affairs Representative for United States Brewers Association, Inc., mother of three, works closely with legislators, attends public hearings (usually at night), and works closely with alcohol education on the state level. Robillard urges young women to be much more flexible and open-ended in planning their career. "You never know where a major will lead you. Who would expect a home economics teacher to end up lobbying for beer?"

What Education and Skills Will I Need?

High school: Preparation for college, with emphasis on the sciences.

College: Major in home economics and specialize in any of the subject's areas that interest you: child development, family relations, clothing and textiles, foods and nutrition, or institution management.

Personal skills: Home economists should have an ability to

work with people from many incomes and cultural ba
the capacity for leadership, and an interest in the cha
within the family.

How Many Women in the Field and Where Do They Work?

There are 128,000 home economists, most of whom are women, in the following specialties: 75,000 teachers, 33,000 dietitians, 50,000 high school teachers, 7,000 college and university teachers, 5,800 extension workers, and 5,000 private industry workers. A growing number of men are entering this field, especially in college administration positions where the top money is.

$ $ $ $ $

In 1980, most beginning teachers in large secondary schools started at $11,500 a year. Extension work paid about the same, and private industry paid slightly more.

What Is the Future for Women?

Chances for work will be better in home economics than in most teaching jobs. Consumer education with computer skills will be in demand in business careers.

RELATED CAREERS
   dietitian
   food scientist
   hotel-restaurant manager

WHERE CAN I GET MORE INFORMATION?
   Professional Group
   American Home Economics Association
   2010 Massachusetts Avenue, NW
   Washington, D.C. 20036

   Trade Journal
   What's New in Home Economics
   Donnelley, Dun, and Bradstreet
   466 Lexington Avenue
   New York, NY 10017

RECREATION WORKER

*Helps people develop good physical and mental
health through recreation and group activity
within an organization.*

What's It Like to Be a Recreation Worker?

Recreation workers organize activities at community centers, churches, hospitals, camps, and playgrounds for all ages and interests. The major youth agencies are the Scouts, YWCA, Camp Fire Girls, 4-H Clubs, and American Youth Hostels. These organizations help people enjoy their leisure time and use it constructively in physical, social, and cultural programs. Recreation directors lead classes and discussions, teach skills, take charge of hikes and trips, and direct programs and camps. They operate recreational facilities and study recreation needs of individuals and communities. Nora Gilhooley from Dallas, Texas, says, "Watching people grow in recreation is one of the most hopeful occupations our country has. We in the YWCA work with schools, churches, and clubs to help each person develop her potential and enjoy living with new found skills." Increasingly, recreation work is including all age groups, rather than the traditional group of young people.

What Education and Skills Will I Need?

High school: Preparation for junior college or four-year college.

College: Half of the professional recreation workers are college graduates. The junior college graduate also has employment opportunities in recreation work. A major in physical education, recreation, or social science, and an interest in helping others through an organization and its ideals, are important in this field.

Personal skills: Skills in sports, music, crafts; creativity and enthusiasm about activities; and good judgment are necessary for success in recreation.

How Many Women in the Field and Where Do They Work?

One-half of the 135,000 full-time recreation workers are women. In addition, there are 100,000 part-time workers employed in the summer at parks, camps, and other outdoor recreation sites. The majority of the full-time recreation workers work for local government and volunteer agencies, religious organizations, national parks, correctional institutions, and the Armed Forces.

$ $ $ $ $

In 1980, beginners with a college degree made $11,500 a year. Community supervisors of recreation averaged $17,000 a year.

What Is the Future for Women?

Recreation jobs are competitive, and the best opportunities will be in therapeutic, private, and commercial recreation. Part-time opportunities are unlimited. Many new programs for retired people will create more jobs. The best chances will go to well-trained students with summer work experience.

RELATED CAREERS

club manager	camp director
town guide	physical therapist
physical education teacher	

WHERE CAN I GET MORE INFORMATION?

Professional Group
National Recreation and Park Association
3101 Park Center Drive
Alexandria, VA 22302

Trade Journal
Recreation Management
20 North Wacker Drive
Chicago, IL 60606

REHABILITATION COUNSELOR

*Helps disabled persons make a satisfactory
occupational adjustment, mainly through
counseling them.*

What's It Like to Be a Rehabilitation Counselor?

Norma McNall of Ardmore, Oklahoma, says, "I interview disabled persons to learn about their abilities, interests, and limitations. I work out a plan of rehabilitation after consulting with the person's social worker, medical doctor, and sometimes family. Most of my work is done with alcoholics, although some of my co-workers specialize with the mentally ill or retarded, and others help any person who can't adjust to working. I keep in contact with my patients' employers and look for more employers who will hire the disabled. The amount of direct counseling varies with each person, but we try to involve family and other agencies in helping the person as she or he tries to get back to work on a regular basis."

Married a short time, Vera Ryersbach is a rehabilitation counselor in a university teaching hospital. She works 50 to 60 hours a week at her job. She thinks the most important aspect for young people planning a career in rehab work is "not to be afraid to work with people who have disabilities. Learn to enjoy working with all people."

What Education and Skills Will I Need?

High school: Preparation for college, with emphasis on the social sciences.

College: Major in education, psychology, guidance, or sociology, in order to prepare for graduate school. A master's degree in psychology or in vocational or rehabilitation counseling is required.

Personal skills: Ability to accept responsibility, to work independently, and to motivate others are all necessary for good work in rehabilitation.

How Many Women in the Field and Where Do They Work?

Thirty-three percent of the 24,000 rehabilitation counselors are women. One-third of them are employed by state or local rehabilitation agencies. The rest work in hospitals, labor unions, insurance companies, and sheltered workshops.

$ $ $ $ $

In 1980, the average beginning salary in state agencies was $13,300 a year. Veterans Administration hospitals paid slightly more. Experienced counselors in the federal government averaged $23,400 a year.

What Is the Future for Women?

Counselors with master's degrees are expected to have fair job opportunities through the 1980s. Ms. Wendlin Myers, a newly married counselor, says, "In this job, I plan my own day. That's especially appealing to me. When I return to work after my 'expected children' are of school age, I think rehabilitation counseling will provide the challenge and flexibility I will need and want as a working woman with family responsibilities." There are 2,000 part-time counselors, and the opportunities will continue to be very good for part-time work. Federal cuts in social programs will limit the growth of job opportunities.

RELATED CAREERS
counselor
psychologist
social worker

WHERE CAN I GET MORE INFORMATION?
Professional Group
American Rehabilitation Counseling Association
Two Skyline Place
5203 Leesburg Pike, Suite 400
Falls Church, VA 22041

Trade Journal
Rehabilitation Record
Government Printing Office
Washington, D.C. 20402

SOCIAL WORKER

*Helps those individuals and families who cannot
provide for themselves or solve their problems
to use the government social services
available to them.*

What's It Like to Be a Social Worker?

Social workers interview people to identify their social problems, help them to understand what's wrong, and try to get them the service they need, such as financial assistance, foster care, or homemaker services. Social problems that concern agencies are poverty, broken homes, physical and emotional disabilities, antisocial behavior, racial tensions, inadequate housing and medical care, and lack of educational and recreational opportunities. Social workers plan and conduct activities for children, adolescents, and older people in settlement houses, hospitals, and correctional institutions. Family service workers help strengthen family life and improve its functioning. Child-welfare workers help improve the physical and emotional well-being of deprived and troubled children and youth. They advise parents on child care, and work with the school social workers and community leaders. Others work in hospitals and in schools. Psychiatric social workers work in mental health centers and clinics.

Helen M. Nienaltowski, social worker for a state agency, works two days on "intake" in the office and three days in the field seeing new referrals or her regular clients each week. "There is no typical day on my job. Each day, I set up my own schedule according to the priorities and needs of my clients. For example, I may spend half a day transporting a child to a new group home, or I may visit five families in one afternoon," says Nienaltowski. "Even with the magnitude of paper work and reports, social work is an exciting and rewarding profession as you see people become slowly but surely more independent."

What Education and Skills Will I Need?

High school: Preparation for college, with as broad an education as possible.

College: Major in one of the social sciences, in order to prepare for graduate school. A master's degree is required to be a professional member of the National Association of Social Workers. Some states hire college graduates without a master's degree and have in-service training programs.

Personal skills: To be happy in social work, you must be sensitive to others, as objective as possible, and have a basic concern for people and their problems.

How Many Women in the Field and Where Do They Work?

There are 345,000 social workers, and 64 percent of them are women. Two-thirds are employed by state, county, and city government agencies, and the others work in private agencies. The administrative jobs in social work are increasingly being held by men, even though most social workers are women.

$ $ $ $ $

In 1980, the starting salary for a caseworker averaged $12,000 a year. Social workers with a master's degree and one year of experience started at $16,300 a year in 1981. The federal government started social workers with a master's degree at $18,585 a year. The salaries are increasing as more men enter the field.

What Is the Future for Women?

Fair job opportunities for full-time, part-time, and temporary work will continue through the 1980s. The number of graduates is increasing, however, and in some parts of the country, the jobs are very competitive. Cuts in federal spending for social programs will severely limit job opportunities. Graduate schools are increasingly combining social work programs with business administration or public health, in order to increase the job opportunities for social workers.

RELATED CAREERS
    clergy
    psychologist
    counselor

WHERE CAN I GET MORE INFORMATION?
Professional Groups
National Association of Social Workers
1425 H Street, NW, Suite 600
Washington, D.C. 20005

Social Work Vocational Bureau
386 Park Avenue South
New York, NY 10016

Trade Journal
Social Work
NASW
1425 H Street, NW, Suite 600
Washington, D.C. 20005

SOCIAL SCIENCE

Anthropologist
Economist
Geographer
Historian
Political Scientist
Psychologist
Sociologist

About these careers *Social science is a career field
where a Ph.D. is needed for many entrance-level positions and for
almost all of the top jobs. Other than economists, most social scientists work in colleges and universities where the job market for
Ph.D.s has crashed. By 1985, there will be 40,000 more Ph.D.s in social
science than job openings.*

*There are 228,200 jobs in the basic social sciences described in
this book. Overlapping among basic social science fields — and the
sometimes hazy distinction between social science and related
fields such as business administration, foreign service work, and
high school teaching — makes it difficult to determine the exact size
of each profession. Economists, however, are the largest social
science group, and anthropologists the smallest.*

*The trend in some industries is to hire increasing numbers of
social science majors as trainees for administrative and executive
positions. Research councils and other nonprofit organizations
provide an important source of employment for economists, political
scientists, and sociologists.*

*Every liberal arts college in the country offers majors in most
of the social sciences. The choice of a graduate school is important
for people who want to become social scientists. Students interested
in research should select schools that emphasize training in
research, statistics, and computers. Opportunities to gain practical
experience in research work also may be available. Professors and
heads of social science departments often help in the placement of
graduates.*

*Working conditions in the social sciences are very good, because
most colleges provide sabbatical leaves of absence, life and health
insurance, and retirement plans. Working hours for professors are
generally flexible, with few teaching hours when a professor
actually must "be there." Professors with tenure have a low-stress job
with prestige. The biggest problem is finding employment. Clinical
and counseling psychologists often work in the evenings, since their
patients are sometimes unable to leave their jobs or school during
the day.*

*Social science has always attracted women, yet it's one of the
most overcrowded career clusters. If social science is where you want
to be, prepare for applied science by acquiring computer and
management skills.*

ANTHROPOLOGIST

*Studies people—their origins, physical
characteristics, customs, languages, traditions,
material possessions, structured social relationships,
and value systems.*

What's It Like to Be an Anthropologist?

Dr. Rhoda Metraux, an anthropologist working in a primitive village in New Guinea, writes, "Anthropologists are at work not only with the last primitive tribes living in faraway places, but also with people who are moving swiftly into the modern world, and with modern people, including Americans, all of whom need a better understanding of one another's ways of life. It is a science that draws on a person's different interests and talents. Are you a musician? Do you like to work with little children? Are you interested in photography? In tellers of tales? In the ways different people earn their livings? Are you fascinated by painting and carving? Or dancing? In working with languages? In finding out about the past, or in watching how people move into the future through change? Since anthropology has to do with every kind of human interest and activity, there is a place for every interest and talent an anthropologist may have. Anthropology is a human science, and it grows with the diversity of the people who choose it as a way of understanding human life."

What Education and Skills Will I Need?

High school: Strong college preparatory course to prepare for a competitive liberal arts college program.

College: Liberal arts degree to prepare for graduate work. Most anthropologists major in a social science, although you don't have to be an anthropology major as an undergraduate. A Ph.D. in anthropology is required for a professional career in a university or in research.

Personal skills: Reading, research, and writing skills are essential, as well as an interest in detail and an ability to work independently.

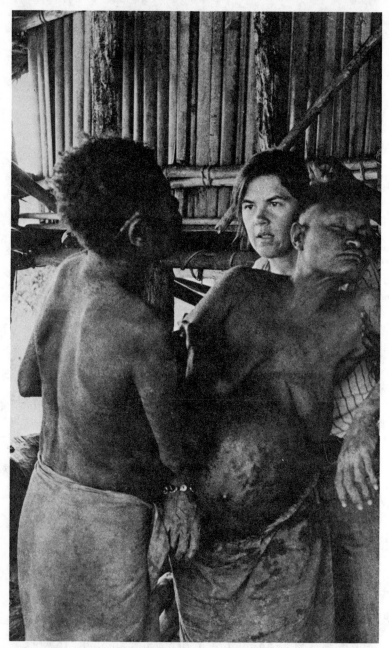

ANTHROPOLOGIST

How Many Women in the Field and Where Do They Work?

There are 7,200 anthropologists and about half are women. But even more important, the most prolific anthropologist in the world *was* a woman—Margaret Mead. Almost all anthropologists work in colleges and universities, although some are employed by the federal government, in museums, and in related social science jobs.

$ $ $ $ $

In 1980, starting salaries in college teaching for Ph.D. graduates were from $15,600 to $19,500 a year. Experienced anthropologists may earn up to twice that amount. Many anthropologists supplement their teaching salaries with grants for research in the summer, field trips for students, and summer-school teaching.

What Is the Future for Women?

As college enrollments decline, there will be little chance for a college teaching job through the 1980s. Very limited opportunities will be available in museums, research programs, and public health programs. There are many more Ph.D.s in anthropology than jobs.

RELATED CAREERS
sociologist   reporter
psychologist   community planner

WHERE CAN I GET MORE INFORMATION?
Professional Group
The American Anthropological Association
1703 New Hampshire Avenue, NW
Washington, D.C. 20009

Trade Journal
Anthropology Newsletter
The American Anthropological Association
1703 New Hampshire Avenue, NW
Washington, D.C. 20009

ECONOMIST

*Studies how goods and services are produced,
distributed, and consumed.*

What's It Like to Be an Economist?

Economists other than those in consumer protection deal with relations between supply and demand for goods and services, control of inflation, prevention of depression, and development of farm, wage, and tax policies. Others develop theories to explain causes of employment and unemployment, international trade influences, and world economic conditions. Barbara Annette Akins, who was the only black in her master's degree program in economics, is now a cost analyst for the Atchison, Topeka, and Santa Fe Railroad Company. She reviews contracts and cost statements for financial reports. Because women have not traditionally gone into fields related to mathematics, women in economics are very scarce. University teaching and business have the fewest numbers, but women are making some gains in government. Alice Mitchell Rivlin is the most visible economist since 1975, when she became the Director of the Congressional Budget Office. In 1978, economist Nancy Hays Teeters became the first woman member of the Federal Reserve Board. Teeters is an expert on budgets and unemployment patterns. One of the few female professors of top rank is Economics and Civil Engineering Professor Ann Friedlaender of M.I.T., who is head of the women's caucus of the American Economic Association. She has led the drive to get more women into tenured university positions. Two women who consider themselves "rarities" because they have top economic spots in business are Kathleen Cooper, who is with the Denver-based United Banks of Colorado, and Kathryn Eickhoff, Vice-president and Treasurer of Townsend-Greenspan, the economic consultants to many of the nation's largest corporations. These women are examples that "it can be done." Their very limited numbers mean that the advancement of women in economics has to be pushed if it is to continue.

What Education and Skills Will I Need?

High school: Preparation for a liberal arts program in college, with as strong a program as is offered in high school.

College: Major in economics or a related social science, or in mathematics with computer science and statistics, in order to prepare for an advanced degree in economics. A Ph.D. is required for the top college and research jobs in economics.

Personal skills: Ability to do detailed, accurate work and research. Most economists must be able to express themselves well in writing.

How Many Women in the Field and Where Do They Work?

Economics has fewer women than all the other social sciences. Sylvia Porter, daily newspaper columnist, is an exceptionally visible woman economist who shows you that it can be done. Only 10 percent of the 15,000 members of the American Economic Association are women. Even though women hold 10 percent of the Ph.D.s, they hold only 1 to 2 percent of the top teaching positions. Fewer women have top spots in business. The best opportunities for advancement are in government.

Three-quarters of the 44,000 economists work in private industry and research agencies, one-fifth teach in colleges, and one-sixth are employed by the government. The largest number of economists is employed in New York and Washington.

$ $ $ $ $

In 1980, the average salary of economists in the private sector was $38,000 a year. Starting salaries were from $12,300 to $19,300 a year.

What Is the Future for Women?

Jobs will be very competitive for economists through the 1980s. The best chances for work will be in business and consulting firms for those economists trained in econometrics and statistics.

RELATED CAREERS

financial analyst	accountant
bank officer	actuary

WHERE CAN I GET MORE INFORMATION?
Professional Group
American Economic Association
1313 21st Avenue South
Nashville, TN 37212

Trade Journal
Job Openings for Economists
American Economic Association
1313 21st Avenue South
Nashville, TN 37212

GEOGRAPHER

Studies the physical characteristics of the earth —
its terrain, minerals, soils, water, vegetation, and
its climate.

What's It Like to Be a Geographer?

Geographers teach in colleges; analyze maps and aerial photographs; and construct maps, graphs, and diagrams. They also analyze distribution and structure of political organizations, transportation systems, and marketing systems. Freda Wise, geographer with the federal government, supervises a food map of the world and says, "Looking at the world's population explosion, and the implications of that explosion for feeding the world, gives a perspective to living and working today that influences my whole life."

What Education and Skills Will I Need?

High school: Preparation for college, with emphasis on all social and biological sciences.

College: Graduate work is required for a career in geography. There are about 56 universities offering a Ph.D. in geography.

Personal skills: Reading, studying, computing, and research skills are needed, along with an interest in working independently.

How Many Women in the Field and Where Do They Work?

There are 15,000 geographers, and 15 percent of them are women. About two-fifths work in private industry for textbook and map publishers, travel agencies, manufacturing firms, insurance companies, and communications firms. Many geographers teach in colleges; the remainder are with the government, primarily in the Departments of Defense and Interior.

$ $ $ $ $

In 1980, graduates with a master's degree started with the federal government at $18,600 a year, and those with a Ph.D. started at $22,500 a year. Cartographers averaged $25,300 a year with the federal government.

What Is the Future for Women?

The outlook for work is better than for most Ph.D.s through the 1980s. Jobs for geographers with a bachelor's degree are expected to be competitive. Those with quantitative skills and training in cartography, satellite data interpretation, or planning should have the best prospects.

RELATED CAREERS
engineer
oceanographer
geologist

WHERE CAN I GET MORE INFORMATION?
Professional Groups
Association of American Geographers
1710 16th Street, NW
Washington, D.C. 20009

Society of Women Geographers
1619 New Hampshire Avenue, NW
Washington, D.C. 20009

Trade Journal
Annals
Association of American Geographers
1710 16th Street, NW
Washington, D.C. 20009

HISTORIAN
Studies the records of the past and analyzes events, institutions, ideas, and people.

What's It Like to Be a Historian?

"Bringing a sense of history to college students today, who are seeking new thoughts and concepts about Latin America and about women, both of which have been so neglected in our curriculum, is an exciting career for people concerned with understanding the world in which we live," says Dr. Martha Bennett, Associate Professor of History. Most history professors do some research and professional writing, as well as teaching. Many of them teach in interdepartmental areas, relating history to human behavior in terms of sociology and economics. History Professor Gerda Lerner of Sarah Lawrence College writes that women have been invisible in history. Their biographies can't be found in history books. Like Lerner, you have to find the history of women in their journals, their diaries, and their letters. According to Lerner, when men left their homes to fight the Indians, it was the efforts of women in the movement to the West that founded the churches and schools of the West. The institutional life of American communities got started only because of the persistence of women. After the schools and churches were established, men were hired from the East, and so the history record begins.

What Education and Skills Will I Need?

High school: Preparation for college, with a strong social science background.

College: Most historians major in history, with a minor in government, economics, sociology, or anthropology. A doctorate is necessary for a career in college teaching and for better government jobs.

Personal skills: An interest in reading, studying, and research, and the ability to write papers and reports are necessary for historians.

How Many Women in the Field and Where Do They Work?

Thirteen percent of the 20,000 historians are women. Seventy percent of all historians work in colleges and universities, with others employed by the federal government, archives, libraries, museums, and historical societies.

$ $ $ $ $

In 1980, the average annual salary for historians was $23,900 a year. They averaged $29,000 in the federal government and $28,300 as museum curators.

What Is the Future for Women?

Historians will have stiff competition for all employment opportunities through the 1980s. There will be thousands more Ph.D.s in history than jobs for them. People with computer skills are expected to have the best chance for a job in business and research. Many history majors do well in law and business administration.

RELATED CAREERS
   political scientist
   economist
   sociologist
   journalist

WHERE CAN I GET MORE INFORMATION?
   Professional Group
   American Historical Association
   400 A Street, SE
   Washington, D.C. 20003

   Trade Journal
   American Heritage
   551 Fifth Avenue
   New York, NY 10017

POLITICAL SCIENTIST

Studies how political power is amassed and used.

What's It Like to Be a Political Scientist?

Dorothy Jacobson, Assistant Secretary for International Affairs with the United States Department of Agriculture, meets with other agencies and with representatives of foreign governments concerned with agriculture. She studies and considers U.S. policy alternatives for various procedures, outlines speeches and makes reports on them, and gives talks to groups about the Department of Agriculture and how it works. Jacobson feels that professional-level jobs with the government involve too much time for a woman with the total responsibilities of a young family. She advises that a woman who is competing for these jobs plan to share family responsibilities with her husband, or have someone else take over the domestic work so that family demands are at a minimum. The question about work and family was put to a powerful politician, Representative Pat Schroeder (D-Colorado). When asked how she could be both Representative and mother, she was ready: "I have a brain and a uterus, and I use both."

What Education and Skills Will I Need?

High school: Preparation for college, with an emphasis on history, government, and the social sciences.

College: Major in political science or in a related field such as government, history, or economics, in order to prepare for graduate work. A master's degree is needed for beginning jobs in political science, and a Ph.D. is required for career-level jobs. A law degree is an alternative to a Ph.D.

Personal skills: Political scientists must be interested in detail, be objective in their thinking, and have good oral and writing skills.

How Many Women in the Field and Where Do They Work?

There are 15,000 political scientists and very few of them are women. About three-fourths are employed by colleges and universities, and others are employed by government agencies, political organizations, public interest groups, labor unions, and research institutes. For the first time, women are being elected as heads of major American cities. These mayors include Jane Byrne in Chicago, Dianne Feinstein in San Francisco, Margaret Hance in Phoenix, and Jean Whitmire in Houston.

$ $ $ $ $

Intelligence specialists with the federal government averaged $29,400 a year in 1980. In 1981, political scientists with a master's degree started with the federal government at $18,600 a year.

What Is the Future for Women?

Employment opportunities are very competitive in college teaching, business, and government. Well-qualified women with computer skills will find better chances for jobs in applied fields such as public administration and public policy, or in journalism and related fields.

RELATED CAREERS
    politician
    writer
    lawyer
    city manager

WHERE CAN I GET MORE INFORMATION?
    Professional Group
    American Political Science Association
    1527 New Hampshire Avenue, NW
    Washington, D.C. 20036

    Trade Journal
    Interplay
    Welkin Corporation
    200 West 57 Street
    New York, NY 10019

PSYCHOLOGIST

Studies the behavior of individuals and groups in order to understand and explain their actions.

What's It Like to Be a Psychologist?

A clinical psychologist working in a mental health clinic spends most of her time testing patients with individual psychological tests, scoring the tests, and meeting with the clinic team of social worker, psychiatrist, and educator to interpret the test scores and work out ways to help the patients. A psychologist often works with group therapy classes of young mothers, adolescents, children, or whatever group needs therapy in a particular community or agency. She has conferences with parents, community leaders, and educators about patients in the clinics, and tries to get all groups to coordinate their efforts toward helping troubled people.

What Education and Skills Will I Need?

High school: Preparation for college, with emphasis on science, computer science, and social science.

College: Most psychologists major in psychology. Some major in a related field such as sociology, anthropology, or education and prepare for graduate work in psychology. A master's degree is required for most practical work in psychology, including school psychologist, psychologist in a government agency, and mental health work. A Ph.D. is required for research and college teaching jobs.

Personal skills: Sensitivity to others and a genuine interest in people are important for counseling. Research jobs require an interest in detail, accuracy, and writing skills.

How Many Women in the Field and Where Do They Work?

Forty-eight percent of the 106,000 psychologists are women. Almost half teach in colleges and universities. Hospitals, clinics, and other health facilities employ the second largest group. In addition, government, public schools, and private industry employ psychologists.

$ $ $ $ $

In 1980, the average annual salary for a psychologist with a doctoral degree was $26,000. Self-employed psychologists who do consulting work and see patients privately earn more. Ph.D.s in business and industry average $36,700 a year.

What Is the Future for Women?

There is a great need for women to represent women on research teams studying human behavior. Traditionally, women's mental characteristics have been determined by men; consequently, women must adjust to what men tell us is our nature. Feminists look forward to the time when women will help define what "scientific fact" is. Recognition of women's sexual response occurred after a woman was finally on a research team studying sexual behavior. The research team was Masters and Johnson.

But the employment future is bleak, with 22,000 more Ph.D.s than jobs until 1985. Psychology, like education and English, are the majors where women flock. The best job opportunities are in school psychology. If you can take your psychology interests to sales or business, there may be more job opportunities.

RELATED CAREERS

psychiatrist	clergy
social worker	counselor

WHERE CAN I GET MORE INFORMATION?

Professional Groups

American Psychological Association
1200 17th Street, NW
Washington, D.C. 20036

Association for Women in Psychology
City University of New York
Graduate Center, Room 609
33 West 42 Street
New York, NY 10036

Trade Journal
Behavioral Science
Mental Health Research Institute
University of Michigan
Ann Arbor, MI 48104

SOCIOLOGIST

*Studies the behavior and interaction of people
in groups.*

What's It Like to Be a Sociologist?

Dr. Hope Jensen Leichter, Professor at Columbia University, creates new courses, teaches, and carries on several research projects. She says, "My interest in sociology is to provide the significant theory about how people are affected by their families, their schools, and their work, so that professionals in the helping careers such as social worker, educator, and nurse will have some idea of what makes people behave as they do." Leichter goes on to say that New York City has every kind of group one could hope for, and the possibilities for research are limited only by a lack of imagination. "Our graduate students are directed to do their research by collecting materials, preparing case studies, testing, and conducting statistical surveys and laboratory experiments. They may study the causes of social problems, such as crime and poverty; the normal pattern of family relations; or the different patterns of living in communities of varying types and sizes. The field is a fascinating one for anyone who wants to find out what makes people act as they do, and for anyone who wants to make a contribution to the social sciences by working to understand people through the groups they are a part of."

What Education and Skills Will I Need?

High school: Preparation for college, with a strong academic program and computer skills.

College: Major in any social science and prepare for graduate work in sociology. A Ph.D. is required for a career in sociology.

Personal skills: Study, research, and communication skills, especially in writing, are crucial for the sociologist.

How Many Women in the Field and Where Do They Work?

The majority of the 21,000 sociologists are men. Two-thirds are employed by colleges and universities, ten percent by government agencies, and the remainder by private industry and welfare agencies.

$ $ $ $ $

In 1980, the average annual salary for a social scientist with a doctorate was $26,000. Industry paid $33,600 a year, the federal government paid $34,400 a year, and education paid $25,600 a year.

What Is the Future for Women?

College jobs are very competitive, and there will be thousands of Ph.D.s in sociology without jobs through the 1980s.

RELATED CAREERS

anthropologist	political scientist
historian	community planner

WHERE CAN I GET MORE INFORMATION?

Professional Group
American Sociological Association
1772 N Street, NW
Washington, D.C. 20036

Trade Journal
Society
Box A
Rutgers, The State University
New Brunswick, NJ 08903

TRANSPORTATION

Airline Pilot
Air Traffic Controller
Flight Attendant
Merchant Marine Officer

About these careers There are 4.7 million workers in transportation and public utilities, and 7.4 percent, or 340,000, of them are college graduates. There are 184,000 transportation jobs represented by the careers described in this cluster.

Even though airline pilots are usually college graduates, most get their flight training in the military. Air traffic controllers come from many college backgrounds, flight attendants usually have two years of college, and merchant marine officers are trained at the United States Merchant Marine Academy at Kings Point, New York, or at one of six state merchant marine academies.

In transportation, jobs involve shift work around the clock. Air traffic controllers work a basic 40-hour week, but they are assigned to night shifts on a rotating basis. Air traffic controllers work under great stress. They must keep track of several planes at the same time and make certain all pilots receive correct instructions. Pilots usually fly 100 hours a month, but because their schedules are irregular, some fly 30 hours while others may fly 90 hours a month. Although flying does not involve much physical effort, the pilot often is subject to mental stress and must be constantly alert and prepared to make decisions quickly. Flight attendants have the opportunity to meet interesting people and to see new places. However, the work can be strenuous and tedious. Attendants stand during much of the flight and must remain pleasant and efficient, regardless of how tired from jet lag they may be. Merchant marine officers serve aboard ships. Their duties are hazardous, compared to other industries. At sea, there is always the possibility of injuries from falls, or the danger of fire, collision, or sinking.

Advancement in transportation is usually very clearly determined. In the airlines, opportunities usually depend on seniority established by union contracts. After 5 to 10 years, flight engineers advance on the basis of seniority to co-pilots; then, after 10 to 20 years, they advance to captains. In other airline jobs, co-pilots may advance to pilots and, in large companies, to chief pilots, who are in charge of aircraft scheduling and flight procedures. Advancement for all new pilots is generally limited to other flying jobs. Advancement opportunities for flight attendants are very limited. Advancement for deck and engine officers in the merchant marine is well-defined and depends primarily upon specific sea experience, passing a Coast Guard examination, and leadership ability.

Transportation offers a great range of opportunities for persons with a college education. Working conditions are generally good and the pay is fairly high. Many employees do a lot of traveling on the job and meet new and interesting people.

AIRLINE PILOT

*Flies planes to transport passengers and cargo,
to crop-dust, to inspect powerlines and other
situations, and to take aerial photographs.*

What's It Like to Be a Pilot?

Karen Kahn is a co-pilot for Continental Airlines. She is one of the few women pilots working for a U.S. scheduled airline. Currently, she is second in command, which means she assists the captain in air-to-ground communications, in monitoring flight and engine instruments, and in operating the controls of the plane. The pilot, called "captain" by the airlines, operates the controls and performs other necessary tasks for flying the plane, keeping it on course, and landing it safely. The flight engineer is third in line to advancement to pilot. The flight engineer monitors the operation of the different mechanical and electrical devices aboard the plane. She helps the pilot and co-pilot make preflight checks of instruments and equipment and watches these checks during the flight. Airlines are just beginning to hire women flight engineers. Many national airlines have no women hired, nor do they plan to hire them.

What Education and Skills Will I Need?

High school: Preparation for college, technical school, or the military.

College: Most pilots are college graduates and are trained through the United States military service, although they can be trained in private flying schools. But the required 1,500 to 2,000 hours of flying time necessary to get a job with a major airline costs more than most students can afford for private lessons. Most airlines hire licensed commercial pilots as flight engineers, who then work their way up to co-pilot and pilot. Pilots must be at least 23 years old and can continue to fly as long as they can pass the required physical examination.

Personal skills: Ability to make decisions and accurate judgments under pressure is a required skill for pilots.

AIRLINE PILOT

How Many Women in the Field and Where Do They Work?

There are 86,000 pilots and less than 1 percent are women. Purdue University has a pilot training program with 21 women out of 75 students.

$ $ $ $ $

Captains and co-pilots are among the highest paid wage earners in the country. In 1980, starting salaries for flight engineers averaged $14,400 a year. Scheduled airline pilots and co-pilots averaged $67,000 a year on domestic air transportation, and up to $110,000 a year on the biggest jets for international flights. In 1981, starting salaries for corporate Learjet pilots ranged from $18,000 to $24,000 a year.

What Is the Future for Women?

Nicole Radecki is Chief Pilot of a charter service, with more than 3,200 hours of flight time. She says, "Companies don't want women pilots. After sending out résumés to 55 corporations, I received five answers—all of them "No." Employment opportunities for all pilots will depend on the general economy through the 1980s. Because many qualified pilots have been put on "furlough" to be called when needed, there are more pilots than jobs. This means that women will continue to have a very bleak future in flying. Even worse is the fact that, until women have equal opportunity to learn to fly in the military, they won't be in a position to qualify for the flying jobs that do open. If you want to be an airline pilot, check with the Navy and the Air Force for opportunities for flight training.

RELATED CAREER
helicopter pilot

WHERE CAN I GET MORE INFORMATION?
Professional Groups
Airline Pilots Association
1625 Massachusetts Avenue, NW
Washington, D.C. 20036

Local Armed Forces Recruiters

Trade Journal
Flying
One Park Avenue
New York, NY 10016

AIR TRAFFIC CONTROLLER

*Keeps track of planes flying within an assigned
area, and gives pilots instructions that keep planes
on separate flight paths.*

What's It Like to Be an Air Traffic Controller?

Depending on the strike situation—chaotic! Air traffic controllers are federal civil service employees. The famous air strike of Summer 1981 was basically about whether or not federal employees should be able to strike, even though they take an oath promising not to. Air traffic controllers' immediate concern is safety, but they also must direct planes efficiently to minimize flight delays. They work in a tower near the airport runway to keep track of planes on the ground and in the air nearby. Some regulate airport traffic; others regulate flights between airports. Relying both on radar and visual observation, they closely monitor each plane and maintain a safe distance between all aircraft. They also guide pilots between the hangar or ramp and the end of the airport's airspace. Then they radio pilots to give them permission to taxi and take off, and notify enroute controllers to watch the planes after take off. They must keep track of many planes at once. Each enroute controller is responsible for a certain airspace, such as all planes that are 30 to 100 miles north of the airport and flying between 6,000 and 8,000 feet. All commercial planes are under the responsibility of an air traffic controller at all times.

What Education and Skills Will I Need?

High school: Preparation for technical or community or four-year college.

College: Most air traffic controllers have four years of college before taking the federal civil service exam required to be a controller. After they are hired, controllers are trained on the job. It takes two to three years to become fully qualified.

Personal skills: Speech skills must be perfect and vision must be perfect or corrected to 20-20. A yearly physical examination is necessary for this crucial job in air safety. A stable temperament and good judgment also are needed.

How Many Women in the Field and Where Do They Work?

There are 29,000 air traffic controllers and most work at the major airports or air-route traffic control centers near large cities. They are all hired by the Federal Aviation Administration (FAA). Very few are women because aviation traditionally has been a male-dominated field. As more women become pilots, more women will become aware of all the career possibilities in aviation.

$ $ $ $ $

In 1981, starting salaries for air traffic controllers were $12,300 or $15,200. Average salary for experienced controllers was $29,900.

What Is the Future for Women?

Very competitive. College graduates who have military or civilian experience as pilots, navigators, or controllers will have the best chance for work. Military-trained careers are difficult for women to get.

RELATED CAREERS
Airline radio operator
airplane dispatcher
flight service specialist

WHERE CAN I GET MORE INFORMATION?
Professional Group
Dial the toll-free number 1-800-555-1212 of the U.S. Civil
Service Commission Job Information and ask for the
number of the nearest Civil Service Job Information
Center, or check your local phone book.

Trade Journal
Journal of Air Traffic Control
525 School Street, SW
Washington, D.C. 20024

FLIGHT ATTENDANT

*Makes the airline passengers' flight safe,
comfortable, and enjoyable.*

What's It Like to Be a Flight Attendant?

Before each flight, Pat O'Neil, of USAir, checks supplies,
food, beverages, and emergency gear in the plane's cabin. She
greets the passengers, checks their tickets, and helps with coats
and luggage and with small children and babies. During the
flight, she gives safety instructions, sells and serves cocktails, and
serves precooked meals. Usually O'Neil flies 80 hours a month
and has 35 hours of ground work duties. She points out to new-
comers that all airline jobs with passenger contact have some
required shift work. Airlines run flights 365 days a year and 24
hours a day, requiring their personnel to take turns with this
schedule. Small planes carry 1 to 6 flight attendants; 747 jet-
liners carry as many as 16 attendants. What O'Neil likes least
about being a flight attendant are the 16-hour days when there
are 12 to 14 takeoffs and landings. "Physically and mentally it's
very wearing, and you really have to grin and bear it. We don't
have many of those days." What O'Neil enjoys most about her
job is meeting new people and the busy atmosphere. "The benefits are the best—travel and lots of vacations and time off!" She
reminds young women that flight attendants do more than serve
food and liquor and pass out magazines. "To routinely check the

emergency and safety equipment and have safety uppermost on our minds at all times are the reasons we are on board," says O'Neil.

What Education and Skills Will I Need?

High school: Preparation for community college, business college, or four-year college.

College: At least two years are required by major airlines. The ability to speak a foreign language fluently is essential for an international route.

Physical qualifications: You must be in excellent health, with good voice and vision. You must be at least nineteen years old. Even though airlines specify physical attractiveness, you don't have to be a beauty queen to be a flight attendant!

Personal skills: Poised, tactful, resourceful people are needed in this work to be helpful to the many customers who often are frightened by flying.

How Many Women in the Field and Where Do They Work?

There are 56,000 flight attendants and 80 percent of them work for domestic airlines. Most attendants are stationed in major cities at the airlines' main bases. College women also are in other airline jobs, including personnel, customer relations, and marketing departments of management and administration.

$ $ $ $ $

In 1980, the union contracts set the minimum salaries of flight attendants at $775 to $900 a month for domestic flights and 80 hours of flying time. The average salary for all flight attendants was $19,000 a year. Reduced air fare for attendants and their families is a benefit added to the salary.

What Is the Future for Women?

Jobs will be competitive through the 1980s. Women with two years of college and work experience with the public will have the best chance for jobs.

RELATED CAREERS
tour guide
airline ground host
social director

WHERE CAN I GET MORE INFORMATION?
Professional Group
Air Transport Association of America
1709 New York Avenue, NW
Washington, D.C. 20006

Trade Journal
Passenger and Inflight Service
665 LaVille Drive
Miami Springs, FL 33166

MERCHANT MARINE OFFICER

Represents the ship owners, directs the navigation and maintenance of the ship deck, and supervises the engine department on cargo ships and tankers.

What's It Like to Be a Merchant Marine Officer?

Deck department officers navigate the ship and direct the maintenance of the deck and hull. The chief mate, or first mate, is the captain's key assistant and plans and supervises the loading and unloading of cargo. The chief engineer is responsible for the efficient operation of the engines and other mechanical equipment. Chief engineers oversee the power plant and keep records of the fuel. The radio officer keeps contact with shore and with other vessels. The purser does the paper work required for entering and leaving port, assists the passengers, and prepares payrolls.

What Education and Skills Will I Need?

High school: Preparation for nautical science or marine engineering, with as much mathematics and science as possible.

College: A four-year program at the United States Merchant Marine Academy or one of the six state merchant marine academies.

Personal skills: Merchant marine officers should have a love of the sea and of ship life, which is based on a highly structured social system. They must be able to take orders and live in a small space with the same few people for months at a time.

How Many Women in the Field and Where Do They Work?

There are 13,000 officers, mostly men. About three-fifths of them are on freighters and the rest are aboard tankers. Very few are on passenger vessels. In 1974, eight women were admitted to the U.S. Merchant Marine Academy for the first time. The first woman graduated in the class of 1978.

$ $ $ $ $

Salaries depend on the rank of the officer and the size of the ship. For example, a second mate with a monthly base pay of $2,074 may regularly be increased to $3,110 a month with overtime and extra responsibilities. There are excellent pension and welfare benefits, and vacations range from 80 to 180 days a year.

What Is the Future for Women?

Chances for work are excellent for graduates of merchant marine academies. New jobs are being created on research vessels, on ships that carry supplies to offshore oil-drilling rigs, and on the dredges operated by the Army Corps of Engineers. Women have not yet entered the job market, but since legislation favors women being represented in all jobs, the chances will be excellent for the few female officers who graduate from the academies.

RELATED CAREERS
ship captain
ship master
pilot

WHERE CAN I GET MORE INFORMATION?

Professional Group
Office of Maritime Labor and Training
Maritime Administration
U.S. Department of Transportation
400 7th Street, SW
Washington, D.C. 20590

Trade Journal
Seaway Review
Harbor Island
Maple City, Postal Station, MI 49664

WOMEN'S COLLEGES AND UNIVERSITIES OF THE UNITED STATES

In a world where young men are brought up to be financially responsible for others and young women are brought up to be financially supported by someone else, where you as a woman are expected to find self-esteem through your family and your brother is expected to find his worth through his career, you may want to spend a few years away from the traditional world of men and women to evaluate your goals. In a woman's college, it may be easier to understand how you are systematically set up for certain choices. The more you become aware of that system, the more you will see a chance to vary it.

You may choose a woman's college because it encourages and promotes women to aspire to nonsex-typed majors and careers. For example, the percentage of women majoring in mathematics, chemistry, and biology at women's colleges is two to three times the national average for women. Historically, women's colleges have invested more money and resources in athletics and in career counseling. Many administrators of women's colleges understand that only energetic affirmative action can lead women achievers to nontraditional careers for women.

You may choose a woman's college because it can provide the best opportunity for leadership positions. For instance, in a college for women, all leadership roles are filled by women, as compared to only 5 percent of the leadership roles at coed institutions.

On the following page is a list of the women's colleges and universities in the United States. For more information about students at women's colleges, write to:

Women's College Coalition
1725 K Street, NW, Suite 1003
Washington, DC 20006

Alabama
Judson College
Marion, AL

California
Mills College
Oakland, CA

Mount St. Mary's
College
Los Angeles, CA

Scripps College
Claremont, CA

Connecticut
Albertus Magnus
College
New Haven, CT

Hartford College for
Women
Hartford, CT

Saint Joseph College
West Hartford, CT

District of Columbia
Mount Vernon College
Washington, DC

Trinity College
Washington, DC

Georgia
Agnes Scott College
Decatur, GA

Brenau College
Gainesville, GA

Spelman College
Atlanta, GA

Tift College
Forsyth, GA

Wesleyan College
Macon, GA

Illinois
Barat College
Lake Forest, IL

Felician College
Chicago, IL

Mallinckrodt College
Wilmette, IL

Mundelein College
Chicago, IL

Indiana
St. Mary-of-the-Woods
College
St. Mary-of-the-Woods,
IN

Saint Mary's College
Notre Dame, IN

Kansas
Saint Mary College
Leavenworth, KS

Kentucky
Midway College
Midway, KY

Louisiana
St. Mary's Dominican
College
New Orleans, LA

Newcomb College
Tulane University
New Orleans, LA

Maryland
College of Notre Dame
of Maryland
Baltimore, MD

Goucher College
Baltimore, MD

Hood College
Frederick, MD

Massachusetts
Aquinas Junior
College
Newton, MA

Aquinas Junior
College
Milton, MA

Bay Path Junior
College
Longmeadow, MA

College of Our Lady of
the Elms
Chicopee, MA

Emmanuel College
Boston, MA

Endicott College
Beverly, MA

Fisher Junior College
Boston, MA

Lasell Junior College
Newton, MA

Lesley College
Cambridge, MA

Mount Holyoke
College
South Hadley, MA

Pine Major College
Chestnut Hill, MA

Radcliffe College
Cambridge, MA

Regis College
Weston, MA

Simmons College
Boston, MA

Smith College
Northampton, MA

Wellesley College
Wellesley, MA

Wheaton College
Norton, MA

Minnesota
College of St. Benedict
St. Joseph, MN

College of St. Catherine
St. Paul, MN

College of Saint Teresa
Winona, MN

Mississippi
Blue Mountain College
Blue Mountain, MS

Mississippi University
for Women
Columbus, MS

Missouri
Cottey College
Nevada, MO

Stephens College
Columbia, MO

William Woods College
Fulton, MO

Nebraska
College of Saint Mary
Omaha, NE

New Hampshire
Colby-Sawyer College
New London, NH

Castle Junior College
Windham, NH

Notre Dame College
Manchester, NH

Rivier College
Nashua, NH

New Jersey
Caldwell College
Caldwell, NJ

Centenary College
Hackettstown, NJ

College of
Saint Elizabeth
Convent Station, NJ

Felician College
Lodi, NJ

Georgian Court
College
Lakewood, NJ

Douglass College
Rutgers State
University
New Brunswick, NJ

New York
Barnard College
New York, NY

Cazenovia College
Cazenovia, NY

College of
New Rochelle
School of Arts &
Sciences
New Rochelle, NY

William Smith College
Geneva, NY

Keuka College
Keuka Park, NY

Maria Regina College
Syracuse, NY

Marymount College
Tarrytown, NY

Marymount Manhattan
College
New York, NY

Molloy College
Rockville Centre, NY

Russell Sage College
Troy, NY

Wells College
Aurora, NY

North Carolina
Bennett College
Greensboro, NC

Meredith College
Raleigh, NC

Peace College
Raleigh, NC

Queens College
Charlotte, NC

Sacred Heart College
Belmont, NC

St. Mary's College
Raleigh, NC

Salem College
Winston-Salem, NC

Ohio
College of
Mount St. Joseph
Mount St. Joseph, OH

Lake Erie College
Painsville, OH

Lourdes College
Sylvania, OH

Notre Dame College of
Ohio
Cleveland, OH

Ursuline College
Cleveland, OH

Pennsylvania
Bryn Mawr College
Bryn Mawr, PA

Carlow College
Pittsburgh, PA

Cedar Crest College
Allentown, PA

Chatham College
Pittsburgh, PA

Chestnut Hill College
Philadelphia, PA

College Misericordia
Dallas, PA

Harcum Junior College
Bryn Mawr, PA

Immaculata College
Immaculata, PA

Manor Junior College
Jenkintown, PA

Marywood College
Scranton, PA

Moore College of Art
Philadelphia, PA

Rosemont College
Rosemont, PA

Seton Hill College
Greensburg, PA

Villa Maria College
Erie, PA

Wilson College
Chambersburg, PA

South Carolina
Columbia College
Columbia, SC

Converse College
Spartanburg, SC

Texas
Texas Woman's
  University
Denton, TX

Vermont
Trinity College
Burlington, VT

Virginia
Hollins College
Hollins College, VA

Mary Baldwin College
Staunton, VA

Marymount College
  of Virginia
Arlington, VA

Randolph-Macon
  Woman's College
Lynchburg, VA

Southern Seminar
  Junior College
Buena Vista, VA

Sweet Briar College
Sweet Briar, VA

Wisconsin
Alverno College
Milwaukee, WI

Mount Mary College
Milwaukee, WI

INDEX OF CAREERS

DESIGN CREDITS

Book design by Edward Smith Design, Inc.

Cover design by Terrence M. Fehr.

Composition in linofilm Baskerville and linofilm Spartan Extra Black Condensed and Spartan Black by Ruttle, Shaw & Wetherill, Philadelphia, PA. Printing and binding by R. R. Donnelley & Sons, Harrisonburg, VA.

PHOTO CREDITS

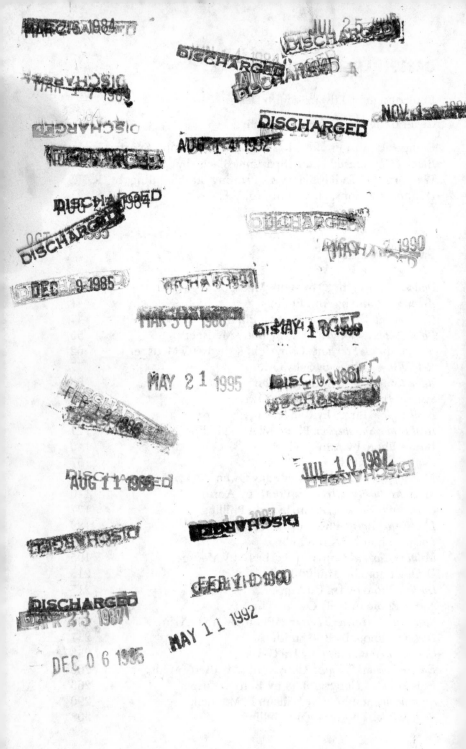